More Praise for *Autism Breakthrough*

"*Autism Breakthrough* provides enormous help to those who care for someone with autism. His chapter on helping people with Asperger Syndrome is a revelation."

—Lawrence P. Kaplan, Ph.D., founder of the US Autism & Asperger Association (USAAA) and author of *Diagnosis Autism: Now What?*

"*Autism Breakthrough* is remarkable. Raun K. Kaufman has done a stellar job weaving together sensibility, science, and the meticulous learning from his own life experiences as a boy with autism. He presents an approach that is accessible to all parents; a way of being that empowers them to become the "expert" for their child. Building on parents' innate desire and ability, he provides an easy-to-understand framework and practical exercises that help nurture and nourish children's minds and bodies—things you can do with your child in your own home. Raun shares the eye-opening perspective that turned his life around and that has helped countless children around the world."

—Julie Matthews, BS, NC, leading autism diet and nutrition specialist, cofounder of Nourishing Hope®, and author of *Nourishing Hope for Autism: Nutrition & Diet Guide for Healing Our Children*

"*Autism Breakthrough* is truly a unique, amazing book and absolutely essential for parents of and professionals working with children on the autism spectrum. Raun K. Kaufman provides a well-written, accessible (and humorous!) breakdown of The Son-Rise Program. The program, shown to improve communication and social skills in people with autism, uses a rich set of treatment procedures grounded in scientific principles, with current research attesting to its efficacy. Indeed, if I had a child with autism, I would definitely, with no question, select The Son-Rise Program to help him or her."

—Cynthia K. Thompson, Ph.D., distinguished professor of communication sciences and neurology at Northwestern University and world-renowned researcher in the brain and language processing

"With *Autism Breakthrough*, Raun K. Kaufman has done what few else in the field of autism treatment today would dream of doing. He has empowered parents to take charge again, given them real hope for positive change, and armed them with specific tools and techniques to make those hopes a reality for their children. My own son fully recovered from autism to become the president of his sixth-grade class today (in a regular, mainstream school) thanks to my family's adoption of the very principles of The Son-Rise Program that Raun explains in *Autism Breakthrough*."

—Wendy Edwards, M.D., pediatrician, B. Sc. N., F.R.C. P. (C)

"Raun K. Kaufman's book, *Autism Breakthrough*, is an amazing resource to help you right here and right now to make a huge difference in your child's progress. His super easy-to-digest guidance on using the techniques of The Son-Rise Program is a game changer. Given the program's record of success, the Autism Hope Alliance has funded families to take The Son-Rise Program courses at the Autism Treatment Center of America. My own son is the beneficiary of the principles explained in *Autism Breakthrough*. I gave birth to my son, but The Son-Rise Program gave him life."

—Kristin Selby Gonzalez, president, Autism Hope Alliance (AHA)

"Raun K. Kaufman has given humankind a roadmap for our journey to unravel the autism mystery. In my forty years in the field of disabilities, I have observed how well-intended behavior therapists, with their sophisticated behavior plans, have created more unwanted behaviors than benefits. *Autism Breakthrough* provides commonsense approaches on how to establish harmonious, humanistic relationships based on trust and unconditional allowance and acceptance. *Autism Breakthrough* is a successful guide to empower people on the autism spectrum to relate and thrive in our day-to-day world, and a significant contribution to the awakening of humanity to neurodiversity."

—Ken Routson, author of *The Gifts of Autism & Alzheimer's* and *Beliefology*

"*Autism Breakthrough* truly breaks through the 'autism is a lifelong condition' paradigm and shifts hopelessness to hope. As occupational therapists and international lecturers, we will be highly recommending this wonderful 'user-friendly' resource with all the principles, strategies, and techniques needed to support children and adults with social-relational challenges."

—MarySue Williams and Sherry Shellenberger, creators of the Alert Program® and authors of Alert Program® books, games, and trainings

"Insightful, personal, and accessible. A hopeful message, and one which only a person that has looked through the eyes of an autistic child could offer. *Autism Breakthrough* is a must-read for all parents of special children. Its depth will touch you and the practical advice will empower you to join your child on their journey toward achieving their unique and limitless potential."

—Alex Doman, coauthor of *Healing at the Speed of Sound* and founder and CEO of Advanced Brain Technologies, creators of The Listening Program®

"I highly recommend Raun Kaufman's new book *Autism Breakthrough* to all parents, to family members, and to practitioners of persons on the autism spectrum. It combines the scientifically validated therapies of The Son-Rise Program with an easy-to-read approach. I frequently refer our patients to The Son-Rise Program, and I have seen the objective improvements in my patients with my own eyes. It has also helped my own son and our family tremendously. *Autism Breakthrough* will help you make huge impact in the lives of persons of all ages with ASDs, and it will provide great benefit and comfort to the families and to practitioners."

—Phillip C. DeMio, M.D., executive director of the American Medical Autism Board and chief medical officer of the US Autism & Asperger Association

"In my practice of psychiatry in a teaching hospital over several decades, I have never been introduced to a set of clinical principles as powerful, elegant, and effective. The outcomes are truly stunning: children make concrete and sweeping progress, often far outstripping their original prognosis, and parents overcome feelings of devastation and learn to accept, enjoy, and meaningfully help their children. *Autism Breakthrough* not only provides the reader with clear techniques and documents amazing clinical outcomes, it is a testament to the impact of hope, love, and acceptance in our lives!"

—Ted McCarthy, M.D., former chief of psychiatry, Mercy Hospital, Portland, Maine

Autism Breakthrough

THE GROUNDBREAKING METHOD THAT HAS HELPED FAMILIES ALL OVER THE WORLD

Raun K. Kaufman

ST. MARTIN'S GRIFFIN
NEW YORK

 Printed in the United States of America. For information, address St. Martin's Press, 175 Fifth Avenue, New York, N.Y. 10010.

www.stmartins.com

Certain names and identifying characteristics have been changed and some individuals described are composites.

The Library of Congress has cataloged the hardcover edition as follows:

Kaufman, Raun Kahlil, author.
Autism breakthrough : the groundbreaking method that has helped families all over the world/ Raun K. Kaufman.—First Edition.
p. cm.
Includes bibliographical references and index.
ISBN 978-1-250-04111-1 (hardcover)
ISBN 978-1-4668-3726-3 (e-book)
1. Kaufman, Raun Kahlil—Mental health. 2. Autistic people—Biography. 3. Autism—Psychological aspects. I. Title.
RC553.A88K395 2014
616.85'882—dc23

2013033776

ISBN 978-1-250-06347-2 (trade paperback)

St. Martin's Griffin books may be purchased for educational, business, or promotional use. For information on bulk purchases, please contact the Macmillan Corporate and Premium Sales Department at 1-800-221-7945, extension 5442, or write to specialmarkets@macmillan.com.

First St. Martin's Griffin Edition: April 2015

10 9 8 7 6 5 4 3 2

To my magnificent parents.
You believed in me when no one else did.
You helped me when no one else could.
You've been there for me like no one else has.
"Thank you" doesn't even scratch the surface.

To the wonderful staff of the
Autism Treatment Center of America.
My colleagues, my partners, my dear friends.
You've given such love and caring to so many families.
It's been my joy and privilege to walk this path with you.

To all the parents out there with special children.
You possess a depth and intensity of love for your children
that nobody else in the world can touch.
I hope that, by the end of this book, you will see that you are
the best thing that ever happened to your children.

To all you special kids still waiting for the people
around you to see and appreciate your specialness.
You're perfect exactly as you are.
And there's nothing you can't accomplish.

CONTENTS

Autism Breakthrough

ONE

My Recovery from Autism and the Myth of False Hope

YOU LOVE YOUR child more than anything in the world.

In the early days of your child's life, long before any diagnosis was made, there may have been a hundred different hopes, dreams, and plans you had for your child. Maybe some were as simple as cuddling with your child or playing peek-a-boo. Perhaps some were as far-reaching as your child's high school graduation or wedding day.

But then your child was diagnosed with an autism spectrum disorder.

You may have felt that many doors were suddenly closed to the child you love because this diagnosis is often accompanied by a long list of dire predictions.

Your child will never talk.

Your child will never have friends.

Your child will never hold your hand.

Your child will never have a job or get married.

Perhaps even: your child will never love you.

You may have been told to discard many of those hopes and dreams and be "realistic" in the face of your child's diagnosis. Certainly, there are many, many parents who have heard the pronouncement: "Autism is a lifelong condition."

No one could fault you for feeling grief-stricken, scared, or even angry. You have just been told all of the things your child will never accomplish—as if it had been decided ahead of time. But before reading any further, it is crucial that you understand this: you don't have to accept the limits placed upon your child.

Your child has the capacity for learning and communicating, for experiencing real happiness, and developing warm, loving, and satisfying relationships. Your son or daughter can learn to enjoy affection, play a game, and laugh at something silly. He or she can learn to savor the experience of being hugged or held by you. That moment when your child spontaneously looks into your eyes with genuine joy and connection—that is something you can have, not just for a fleeting second but on a sustained basis. Do you ever imagine your child playing Little League, joining you on a bike ride, going on a skiing trip with you, playing with other kids at the park, or doing something in the future such as going to college? These events are possible. Children on the autism spectrum are capable of great change, including recovery.

Who am I to tell you this? I'm someone who's been there—not where *you* are, but where *your child* is.

I used to be autistic.

I know, I know. That one's a bit hard to digest. You don't often find "used to be" and "autistic" in the same sentence. This is truly unfortunate, because it points to the intense pessimism and utter hopelessness with which autism is viewed by the people doing the diagnosing. Do you know what my chances of recovery were, according the specialists assessing me?

Zero percent.

That's right: 0%.

Here's what happened.

MY STORY

When I was a young boy, my parents (authors and teachers Barry Neil Kaufman and Samahria Lyte Kaufman) saw that I was developing very differently from my two older sisters. I cried incessantly and inconsolably. When I was picked up, I let my arms dangle loosely at my sides.

Before my first birthday, I suffered a severe ear and throat infection, compounded by a violent allergic reaction to the antibiotics prescribed. My life briefly hung in the balance. After a battery of hearing tests, my parents were told that I appeared deaf. As months passed, I seemed increasingly cut off, spiraling ever deeper into my own world.

I stopped responding to my name.

I ceased making eye contact.

I appeared alternately repulsed by and oblivious to the sights and sounds around me.

I appeared deaf to a loud noise right next to me and then mesmerized by an almost inaudible whisper in the next room.

I lost all interest in other people, but I would remain transfixed by inanimate objects, staring at a pen, a mark on the wall, even my own hands, for long periods of time.

I didn't want to be touched or held.

I spoke not a word (nor did I cry, yell, point, or do anything to communicate my wishes), displaying a total muteness that stood in sharp contrast to my earlier crying marathons.

And then something startling: I became fascinated with the simplest of repetitive activities, spinning plates on their edges for hours on the floor, rocking back and forth, flapping my hands in front of my face.

As my condition worsened, my parents raced from specialist to specialist, trying to find out what was wrong. Tests. Tapping pencils. Shaking heads. More tests. (Keep in mind that, in 1973, the year I was born, autism was much less common than it is now, affecting one out of every five thousand children. The latest study from the Centers for Disease Control and Prevention (CDC) puts the incidence of autism at one out of every fifty children.) Soon I was diagnosed as severely autistic. My parents were informed that my IQ was less than 30.

What can feel like a devastating diagnosis is not really due to the autism diagnosis itself. The devastation comes primarily from the *prognosis*—all the things parents are told that their child will not do and cannot accomplish.

Like many parents today, my parents were told that the prognosis was certain. I would never speak or communicate in any meaningful way. I would never prefer people over objects. I would never emerge from my solitary world and be "normal." Moreover, I would never go to college, have a career, or play baseball. I would never fall in love, drive a car, or write a poem. I might, one day, be able to dress myself or eat with utensils, but that was the ceiling of my possibilities.

My parents, seeking solutions, were given only grim pronouncements. They searched for a light at the end of the tunnel and were given only dark predictions. Over and over again, it was drilled into my parents' heads: autism is a lifelong condition. The specialists explained that, when I got older, my parents would need to look into permanent institutionalization so that I could be properly looked after.

I am still astounded at what my mother and father chose to do in the face of such a damning verdict. They didn't believe what they were told. They didn't write me off. Instead, they turned their backs on all the dire prognoses. My parents looked at me and saw possibilities, not deficiencies. Instead of looking at me with fear, they viewed me with wonder.

And so they began an experiment. They began by seeking to create an environment where I felt truly safe. They didn't push me. They didn't try to change my behaviors. They sought first to understand me. Think about this for a moment. How often do we really do this—with *anyone*? People behave in ways we don't understand all the time. For most of us, our knee-jerk response is to try to get that person to change—whether that person is our partner, our friend, a store clerk, an employee, our parent, or, indeed, our child. When do we ever *begin* our response by truly seeking to understand without pushing, to provide the other person with an experience of safety and caring without trying to get him or her to change? How amazing that my parents began from this most kind and useful place.

Having heard thousands of parents tell me about their experiences with their children's diagnosis and treatment, how they were given a laundry list of things "wrong" with their child, this description from the opening page of my father's book *Son-Rise: The Miracle Continues* touches me deeply:

> His little hands hold the plate delicately as his eyes survey its smooth perimeter. His mouth curls in delight. He is setting the stage. This is his moment, as was the last and each before. This is the beginning of his entry into the solitude that has become his world. Slowly, with a masterful hand, he places the edge of the plate on the floor, sets his body in a comfortable and balanced position, and snaps his wrist with great expertise. The plate begins to spin with dazzling perfection. It revolves on itself as if set in motion by some exacting machine. And it was.
>
> This is not an isolated act, not a mere aspect of some childhood fantasy. It is a conscious and delicately skilled activity performed by a very little boy for a very great and expectant audience—himself.
>
> As the plate moves swiftly, spinning hypnotically on its edge, the little boy bends over it and stares squarely into its motion. Homage to himself, to the plate. For a moment, the boy's body betrays a just perceptible movement similar to the plate's. For a moment, the little boy and his spinning creation become one. His eyes sparkle. He swoons in the playland that is himself. Alive. Alive.
>
> Raun Kahlil—a little man occupying the edge of the universe.
>
> Before this time, this every moment, we had always been in awe of Raun, our notably special child. We sometimes referred to him as "brain-blessed." He had always seemed to be riding the high of his own happiness. Highly evolved. Seldom did he cry or utter tones of discomfort. In almost every way, his contentment and solitude seemed to suggest a profound inner peace. He was a

seventeen-month-old Buddha contemplating another dimension.

A little boy set adrift on the circulation of his own system. Encapsulated behind an invisible but seemingly impenetrable wall. Soon he would be labeled. A tragedy. Unreachable. Bizarre. Statistically, he would fall into a category reserved for all those we see as hopeless . . . unapproachable . . . irreversible. For us the question: could we kiss the ground that others had cursed?

Coming from this reverential vantage point, my parents asked themselves what they could do to understand me and my world. The answer began with something that my mother did. She wanted to understand me—and also to show me that she accepted me as I was. That I didn't have to change to be loved.

So she began to join me in my repetitive, supposedly autistic behaviors. I would sit on the floor and rock . . . and she would rock with me. I would spin a plate on its edge . . . and she would spin her own plate next to mine. I would flap my hands in front of my face . . . and she would flap with me.

My parents so respected me that they focused totally on what *my* experience was—not on whether I looked strange or different to other people.

Hour after hour . . . day after day . . . month after month, my mother waited. Patiently, my parents waited.

Every once in a while, and only while "joining," as my parents came to call this true participation in my interests and activities, I glanced at my mother. I smiled at her. I grazed her with the tips of my fingers.

And as my parents began to truly understand my world, as they communicated in a thousand different ways, over and over again, that I was safe, that I was loved, that I was accepted, something astonishing happened. A connection began to form. Slowly, carefully, I began to peek out from behind the veil of my special world. Tentatively, I began to join them in theirs.

As my mother spent hours upon hours on the floor working with me, she made herself my friend in my world. In so doing, a bond of trust evolved. She cherished and celebrated every look, every smile, every moment of connection for which my parents had waited so long. She cheered me on with every small step.

As my relationship with my parents and the world of people strengthened, my mom and dad continued to build an entire program of therapy around me. They helped me to increase my social connection to them and to others, encouraging me to play with them, to look at them, to laugh with them, to take their hands. They constructed interactive games based upon my burgeoning interests, such as animals and airplanes. At every turn, they accomplished this with a deep caring, encouragement, and support—never pushing, always inviting.

Can you imagine it? They embarked on this experimental journey after hearing nothing but hopeless predictions for me. They continued to reach out to me when I gave them nothing in return.

And they persevered in the face of consistent criticism. Learned professionals told my parents that their "joining" would reinforce and increase my "inappropriate autistic behaviors." These professionals chastised my parents for doing the opposite of the behavior modification techniques they recommended—and for having "false hope," for putting their time into an unproven (and just created) approach that "had no hope of succeeding." Family members expressed grave doubts and concerns that my parents were "doing their own thing" and not leaving my treatment in the hands of professionals who "knew best."

Remember, too, that, in those days, the world of autism treatment was a barren wasteland. There were no nightly news stories waxing on about the latest treatments or detailing the lives of families with children on the spectrum. There was no Autism Awareness Month.

My parents witnessed children being jolted with electric

shocks, tied to chairs, placed in dark prison-like rooms, held down—and were told that this was progress, the best modern medicine had to offer.

To help me, they had to walk in the opposite direction, alone. Without any support, they supported me. They worked and waited. They persisted and persevered. Not knowing what the future held, not requiring my reciprocation of their love, care, smiles, and cheers, they gave me every chance.

For three and a half years, they worked with me, painstakingly building a bridge from my world to theirs.

And it all paid off.

I recovered completely from my autism without any trace of my former condition. (Go to www.autismbreakthrough.com/chapter1 to see some childhood photos of me and my parents.) The years of work, the late nights, the persevering in the face of ongoing criticism, the love and dedication—it bore the kind of fruit it was never supposed to bear. It produced the outcome it was never supposed to produce. And I've lived the life I was never supposed to live.

THE CREATION OF THE AUTISM TREATMENT CENTER OF AMERICA

My parents developed this innovative, home-based, child-centered autism treatment program because of their very personal experiences entering my world. At the same time, the method they created was based upon what autism actually is—a difficulty connecting and bonding with others—rather than how autism is typically treated—as a problem of inappropriate behavior that must be extinguished, altered, and retrained.

They called their approach The Son-Rise Program.

There were several factors that made their approach unique. First, it was created by parents. That alone was a gigantic departure from the doctor/professional/lab-created norm. Second, my parents began with the premise that children on the autism spectrum are capable of limitless growth. Third, they started by joining me in my world rather than forcing me to conform to theirs. Fourth, they used motivation, rather than repetition, as the doorway to learning. Moreover, they focused on having a nonjudgmental and welcoming attitude with me, seeing that my responsiveness was largely dependent on the attitudes and emotions of the people working with me. And, finally, unlike every other treatment they saw, my parents prioritized human interaction over academics and tasks such as naming colors, adding numbers, and brushing teeth.

But until my recovery was complete, none of these concepts had spread beyond the walls of our house. Until my father wrote a book about it.

Shortly after my recovery in the late 1970s, my father wrote a best-selling book recounting our story entitled *Son-Rise*—now updated as *Son-Rise: The Miracle Continues*. (My father has written eleven other books as well.) Our story was then turned into an award-winning NBC television movie in 1979. As a result, people began to approach my parents for help.

In 1983, they founded the Autism Treatment Center of America (ATCA), part of a nonprofit, charitable organization. (As part of this not-for-profit organization, I've witnessed an incredible amount of generosity. So many sincerely giving people have donated money specifically to help families with children on the autism spectrum, allowing the ATCA to provide over $1.7 million in financial assistance last year alone.) The ATCA serves as the worldwide teaching center for The Son-Rise Program. It is situated on a gorgeous hundred-acre campus in Sheffield, Massachusetts. (I never appreciated how beautiful the campus was growing up. Only after living in Sweden, England, Ireland, Boston, southern California, and Portland, Oregon, did I realize the property's beauty.)

The Autism Treatment Center of America is a training facility for parents and professionals. (In the past, people have mistakenly concluded that the ATCA is a residential facility for children, which is not the case). It offers 5-day programs during which parents learn how to use the techniques of The Son-Rise Program with their own children.

The beginning program, called The Son-Rise Program Start-Up, is important to remember because I will be making reference to it in many of the case studies we will be discussing. Parents and professionals attend the Start-Up program *without* their children in order to learn the fundamentals of The Son-Rise Program techniques. The course focuses on areas such as language, eye contact, facilitating interaction, teaching new skills, dealing with challenging behaviors, constructing an appropriate learning and sensory environment, creatively challenging your child, training others to work with your child, and sustaining an attitude of hope and optimism about your child. The course is very interactive, with lots of activities, video examples, question-and-answer sessions, and breakout "high-functioning" sessions for parents of children with Asperger's syndrome and similar diagnoses. So when I reference the Start-Up in case studies during later chapters, you will know what I'm talking about.

LIFE AFTER AUTISM

After my recovery from autism, I went to regular schools, and my friends and teachers had no idea about my history unless I told them. That was nice, because I was a minor celebrity on the ATCA campus, and that wasn't something I really savored as a teenager.

I was a very social kid and I had a wide circle of friends. Academically, things also went quite well. I went to my local public school growing up, but I spent my last three years of high school at an academically rigorous prep school.

Throughout this period of my life, I really didn't think that much about my history of autism. Sometimes, though, it would hit me.

At my high school prom, a couple of my buddies and I put on our tuxedos, picked up our dates, and pooled the money we had saved to rent a white stretch limousine with a giant sunroof. We thought we were pretty cool rolling into school standing on the seats with our heads and the top half of our bodies poking out from the top of the limo.

As the night was beginning, I remember feeling so happy, so excited, but also a little wistful. This was the final night of high school. I had two close friends in the car, with dates we cared for and a seriously fun night ahead. And I knew that I was experiencing the waning light of my childhood, my old friends, my high school experience. In the fall, I would be beginning college.

As I was drinking in the emotion of the whole evening, I had the sudden realization that none of this would have happened were it not for what my parents did to help me—not my prom or all the years before it, not my friends or the matches I played on the tennis team, not my classes or the many Sundays I had spent on day trips with my family, not my first kiss or my last exam. I had to catch my breath at the enormity of it. For a moment, I stood captivated by a deep sense of amazement at how different my life could have been.

And then my friends called to me, and I left my thoughts behind and tumbled back into my life, enjoying my prom, like millions of typical kids in typical towns across the nation.

Four years later, I graduated with a degree in biomedical ethics from Brown University. I spent my third year of college participating in an exchange program at Stockholm University in Sweden, and, after graduation, I got a work visa that allowed me to spend a year in London, England, and Cork, Ireland.

In Cork, I linked up with a family who had a little boy with autism and volunteered in their Son-Rise Program for a time. This connection would prove to be especially important, as, seven years later, I was able to be of help to that little boy's mother when she was diagnosed with bone and lung cancer and given a

5 percent chance for survival. (That was ten years ago, and she's cancer-free and in excellent health—yet another example of how not buying into dire predictions can pay off.)

During my time at college and after graduating, I spent four summers working at, and then helping to manage, a summer program for teens on the campus of Wellesley College. Later on, I worked at an educational center for school-aged children in Boston and then opened and became the director of the same kind of educational center in southern California. These two jobs were seminal experiences for me, as I switched from a business focus to an education focus. I found the experience of working with kids to be so meaningful that it overwhelmed my interest in the business world, at least for a while.

I get asked by many parents about my love life. (And, yes, it can feel a bit strange to be asked for romantic details by someone you just met.) Though I don't think it's appropriate to go into detail about my former girlfriends, I will say that I feel very lucky in this regard. I have had the good fortune to be with some truly wonderful and caring women in my life. Although I am not yet married, I have found a very meaningful sense of intimacy and fulfillment in these relationships.

Because it is specifically relevant to this book—and because she specifically granted me her permission—I will, at various points, discuss one of my past girlfriends and her son (with names changed, of course). The reason for this is that she has a son with autism (we'll call him James), and while we were together, we co-ran her son's Son-Rise Program. I so loved and treasured my time with James, who was five and six during that time. I also had many different experiences with him that inform this book, over and above my professional experience working with parents and their children.

James's mom is an incredible woman on every level. She is an outstanding mother to James. She has a boundless energy and a sparkling intelligence that is so wonderful to be around. She's also pretty funny: when I asked her to choose the name that I would use for her in this book, she chose Charlotte because that is her favorite *Sex and the City* character. To me, she was a loving, tender, and devoted partner. Although our relationship did not ultimately work out, she remains one of my closest and dearest friends.

To answer a question I get asked a lot: no, I don't have any remnants of autism. I don't secretly crave a plate to spin, and I don't find social situations in any way difficult. I'm just a regular guy, living my life. Ironically, it is the interpersonal arenas that come most easily to me; I'm not so hot at the areas I should be good at, given my history—organization, routine, technical subjects. Go figure.

Since I get a lot of skeptical questions about autism recovery in general and mine in particular, let me go a bit further here. As a culture, we are still very much stuck in the "autism is a lifelong condition" paradigm. The problem here is that this mind-set cuts our children off at the knees and becomes a self-fulfilling prophecy.

I have spoken with parents who have been told—by people who have never met me—that I never recovered and am spending my life in an institution. On the rare occasions when I have met with people who made these claims and they see what a "typical guy" I am, they reverse their stance, instead saying that my autism was a misdiagnosis and that I must never have had autism in the first place.

Aside from the strangeness of them not noticing that they just switched positions, I find this claim interesting for the following reason. Remember the Son-Rise Program mom I was discussing earlier who recovered from cancer? (I know this seems like a left turn. Bear with me.) No one has ever approached her and said, "You know, since you don't have cancer now, you must never really have had it in the first place." Apparently we are willing to take one of the most deadly illnesses in the world and accept that people can recover, but when faced with a three-year-old child with autism, we are unable to accept anything other than a life sentence. This baffles me.

In the end, people can say what they will about my story because, although I may be the first, I am certainly not the last. For over a quarter of a century, parents from across the globe have been attending training programs at the Autism Treatment Center of America—putting in their time, energy, and love—and achieving remarkable results with their own children. Many children after me have made full recoveries. What are we going to do—say that *all* of them never had autism?

Of course, every child's journey is unique. I have seen so many children who, though they have not made full recoveries, have made astronomical progress. I've witnessed children with no language learn to speak. I've seen friendless children blossom into social kids with close friends. I watched as adults in their thirties left institutionalized environments to live on their own, with jobs, friends, and romantic partnerships. There are so many kinds of growth that our loved ones on the spectrum can achieve, and each one of these is a victory.

However, it is important that we acknowledge that recovery is possible so that each and every one of these children is given a chance. Though we can never predict where each child will end up, I know that my coworkers at the ATCA and I feel that the only ethical choice we have is to treat all of the children and adults that we work with as capable of recovery. That way, we aren't cutting children's chances off ahead of time, and we are ensuring that all children and adults get as far as they can go.

I can certainly tell you that, for me, working with all of these parents and seeing the depth of their love constantly renews my appreciation for my own parents' journey to help me. I am so grateful to have the opportunity, with the Autism Treatment Center of America's dedicated staff of over seventy, to enable parents to help their children in the same way.

THE EXPERIENCE BEHIND THE TECHNIQUES

I wrote this book so that you can use my experience for your child's benefit. It is packed with what we could call autism intel: the inside scoop on what is going on with your child and what you can do to address the core issues of your child's disorder. This information isn't limited to my personal story of recovery or my experience with James. It encompasses my experience working with children and families throughout my life, and professionally since 1998, and the vast know-how contained in the decades of work done by the staff of the Autism Treatment Center of America.

In my case, I have spent over a thousand hours working individually with over two hundred children on the autism spectrum, worked with over a thousand families in-depth, and addressed more than fifteen thousand people in lectures and seminars. And now, after serving as CEO of the Autism Treatment Center of America from 2005 until 2010, I am its Director of Global Education.

Many of the other senior staff at the ATCA have considerably more experience. My parents have been teaching The Son-Rise Program for thirty-five years, and several of the other senior teachers are approaching or exceeding twenty years. They have all worked with families from a vast assortment of cultures who have children with widely varying diagnoses spanning the entire age spectrum from toddlers to mature adults. It would not be an exaggeration to say that there is no type of situation that they have not seen. The knowledge and experience of all these devoted individuals stands behind every principle, strategy, and technique you will read in this book.

For these people, their work with families isn't a nine-to-five job. It's their life. For example, my older sister Bryn and her husband William have been working at the ATCA for more than twenty years. But autism has also touched them in a very personal way—and I don't mean because Bryn had an autistic brother. When their daughter Jade was two years old, she began to exhibit a wide range of autistic behaviors. She would cry for hours. She had very little language. Her eye contact was rare, and her interest in people was fleeting. She was very sensitive to any sensory input (sights, sounds) and would scream when any sound became overwhelming or when too many people would look at her. She did not want to be touched. She spent much of her days engaged in repetitive "stims," repeatedly lining up toys or shaking a box filled with marbles, using the exact same motion over and over again.

Bryn and William set up a full-time Son-Rise Program for their daughter. I left my job running that educational center in southern California and moved back to Massachusetts to be a part of Jade's program, and to help out at the ATCA for what I thought, at the time, would be one year.

For me, working with Jade was one of the high points of my life. I truly cannot do justice to this experience with words (though I will do my best!).

Two aspects of my time with Jade made it very meaningful to me. The first is that, even with all of my personal and professional experience, I didn't fully grasp what the experience of having a special child and running a Son-Rise Program over time was like until I participated in Jade's program year after year. As I witnessed the intensive work, effort, creativity, and love that Bryn and William put into working with Jade, I developed a deeper, more profound understanding of exactly what my parents did for me. I have always been enormously grateful to them, but I just didn't get it on a visceral level until I had my time in Jade's program. (And, certainly, I internalized this understanding on yet another level during my later experience with Charlotte and James.)

The second facet of my experience that so moved me was Jade herself. I had such an amazing time with her! She was so precious, and I felt continually honored to step into her world over and over again. I found that, when I was with her, I was able to bring forth the most loving, caring, and creative parts of myself. This emotional connection has affected every moment I have worked with children since.

This is what I wrote back in 1999 about a pair of Son-Rise Program sessions I had with her, which took place one and two years into her program, respectively.

> SEPTEMBER, 1998: The boat lists from side to side as it makes its way through the wavy ocean. Jostling around in my seat, barely able to keep myself from tumbling overboard, I look across the deck at Jade, who seems miraculously unaffected by the bounce and tip of the small, unstable boat. She sits in her self-constructed seat, staring intently at her stuffed animal (Ernie from *Sesame Street*), a small smile playing across her smooth, otherwise undisturbed features.
>
> To the untrained eye, our boat might appear to be a purple blanket laid out across a white carpet, with pillows arranged at one end in a makeshift chair and a single scarf perched on the other end. As far I am concerned, however, we are sitting on a real sailboat making its way haphazardly across a rough sea—with our friends Ernie and Cookie Monster.
>
> Earlier, Jade had made herself a plush chair with her pillows, and, when I asked her what I was to use for my chair, she casually deposited one of her scarves on my lap. And yet, despite the apparent disparity in the plushness of our chairs, I am incredibly excited. Not only am I greatly enjoying our time together, but I am now in the midst of a game that has gone on for almost 15 minutes! For Jade and I to be involved in a single interactive game for more than a few minutes is exceedingly rare, and I am savoring the experience.
>
> Jade is weaving in and out of her connection with me at this point, sometimes looking at me and speaking, other times staring at and playing with Ernie as if I'm not in the room with

her. Seeing that she is now playing with Ernie and less involved in our boat game, I take Cookie Monster and begin to look at and talk to it quietly but excitedly. Slowly, out of the corner of my eye, I notice Jade slowly raising her head. Her eyes lock onto me, and, for a moment, we both sit there, holding our stuffed animals and staring at one another. Then the (imaginary) boat rocks again, and I go tumbling overboard. Jade continues to eye me curiously, and so I reach up from where I'm lying on the carpet and ask her to help me climb back into the boat. She turns away from me and resumes her solitary play with Ernie.

August, 1999: The boat bounces around as it traverses the turbulent ocean. As I am being tossed from side to side by the motion of the boat, I glance across at Jade. She, too, is rocking around in the boat.

"This boat rocking around in water, Raun. Waves are coming in," Jade says.

"Here, Jadey, let's pull this sheet over us so that we don't get all wet." I say as I wipe some ocean water from my face.

She grabs her sheet and pulls it over her.

"You come in here, Raun. You come in close to me."

I scramble underneath the sheet next to her, and she slings an arm around me with great nonchalance.

"Thanks, Jade. You're a good friend," I say gratefully.

Jade smiles at me.

I can barely contain my excitement. Jade is being so sweet, so cuddly, so *interactive*. What's more, the two of us have been playing this particular game for over an hour!

Suddenly, another wave comes crashing into the boat, and I roll overboard.

"Hey, Jade! I'm in the water here. Can you help me out? Can you help me back into the boat?" I reach up from the carpet, and . . . *she grabs onto me with both hands and hauls me back onto the boat!*

"Thanks for helping me, Jade-alicious! Whew!"

Jade looks at me quizzically. "Why you say 'whew'?"

Such a simple question, but, on this particular day, it got me thinking.

Jade helped me climb into her boat . . .

. . . we're helping her climb into our boat . . .

. . . as my parents helped me climb into their boat so many years ago.

So much distance traveled.

So many people lining the path.

Such a journey for one little girl.

How could I *not* say "Whew"?

Jade progressed more slowly than I had, but progress she did. Five years later, her program was finished. Now a social young adult with lots of friends and a great sense of humor, you would never guess her unique and special past.

Now, upon hearing this story, you couldn't be blamed for thinking that maybe Jade was predisposed to autism because she was related to me and that, furthermore, maybe she had a better shot at recovery for the same reason. However, you could only think this because you are missing a crucial element of the story: *Bryn and William adopted Jade when she was eight weeks old.* It was not until two years later that she began to show symptoms of autism. Isn't that incredible? (View a documentary of Jade's journey at www.autismbreakthrough.com/chapter1.)

So no matter what you have been told, please know that there is hope for your child. Of course, people who don't know your child will see what your child *does not* do, and they will speak as if they know what your child *cannot* do.

But you are the parent. You have love, a lifelong commitment, and an everyday experience with your child that no one else can match. You may sometimes feel dismissed or brushed aside, but nothing can change the fact that you aren't *in* the way, you *are* the way.

The only reason I can write to you today is because my parents believed in me when no one else on earth did. So you keep believing in your child—without apology. You have every right to have hope for your child, to see the potential within your child, and to want more for your child.

I am continually flabbergasted at some people's sincere and strenuous concern about parents of children on the autism spectrum being given "false hope." I continue to be befuddled as to what they think hope will do that is so harmful to our children. Who decided that a life sentence was better than an open heart and an outstretched hand?

The bottom line is this: hope leads to action. Without action, none of our children can be helped.

I hear people complaining about false hope, but I never hear anyone worrying about false pessimism. There is broad agreement that we don't want anyone promising a particular outcome for a particular child ahead of time. Why, then, do we abide people making promises about what a child will *never* do? Why is it that telling a parent all of the things that will not happen for his or her four-year-old or ten-year-old or fifteen-year-old over the next six decades is perfectly sensible, but giving every one of these kids a chance is deemed false hope?

Any of you reading this book right now knows that if there is one problem that families with children on the autism spectrum are *not* facing in our society, it is an epidemic of too much hope for their children. Of course, no one can know in advance what your child will accomplish. But let's not decide in advance what your child will *not* achieve. Let's give your child every chance.

Together, we'll spend the rest of these pages doing just that.

TWO

Joining: Entering Your Child's World

OKAY.

So.

Where to start?

Well, if you are reading this book, I'm going to go ahead and assume that:

1. You have a child on the autism spectrum.
2. You love your child.
3. You want to help your child.

Pretty obvious, I know. But what might be less obvious is just how much power you have to impact your child's growth and development.

This book will give you some very simple and clear techniques you can use to help your child progress. In some cases, these strategies may sound like the exact opposite of what you have been told to do. This is no accident. Many of them *are* the exact opposite.

That's okay. Nothing to get nervous about. In fact, quite the opposite: this may be the best news you've heard in quite a while. Why? Because if what you were doing was working, then you wouldn't be reading this book, would you? And if this book was just going to reiterate what you've already heard or thought of, it wouldn't be useful to you.

So that means that the first order of business is to fully

acknowledge the following: the path you have been on thus far hasn't gotten your child where you want her to be.

Let's head down a brand-new path.

WHAT AUTISM IS, REALLY

Most of what parents are told about autism is not accurate or, unfortunately, helpful. Sure, whoever diagnosed your child may have told you the symptoms of autism and how your child's behaviors matched those symptoms, but I'm not talking about symptoms. I'm talking about the central aspect of what autism *is*.

First, let's talk about what autism is *not*. It is not a behavioral disorder. This is important because, 99 percent of the time, that's exactly how it's treated. The methodologies used on our children tend to focus on behavior change. Practitioners ask: how can we stamp out or eliminate *this* behavior and train the child to do *that* behavior?

The problem is, autism is not a behavioral disorder; it is a *social-relational disorder*. Do our kids behave differently? Sure. But those behaviors are symptoms, not causes. If you saw someone scratching his arm and then set as your goal the elimination of the scratching behavior, there are a number of approaches you might try. You might tell the person to stop scratching. You might threaten him with an unpleasant consequence if he continues scratching. You might try to distract him by putting something he wants (an ice-cream cone, for instance) in the hand he is using to scratch. You might even tie his arm to his body so that he couldn't scratch.

Or you could actually look for the *reason* for his scratching and discover that he has a mosquito bite. Then, you could put some anti-itch cream on the bite. Violà! No more scratching! And instead of not addressing the real issue while at the same time totally alienating the person, you solve the *cause* of the scratching—and the person is grateful!

This analogy illustrates the difference between trying to stamp out your child's symptoms and addressing your child's core challenge. Every autistic behavior your child exhibits is a symptom. Trying to extinguish these behaviors does not address the actual autism and only serves to seriously disrupt the trust and relationship between you and your child.

This trust and relationship is your most important asset in helping your child progress!

Why? Because autism is a social-relational disorder.

What does this mean, exactly? Well, the primary challenge that your child has is a difficulty bonding and forming relationships with others. (I say "child" regardless of your child's age because she is *your* child, even as an adult.) There are a few different reasons for this, which we will go over later, but, for now, know this: almost every other issue your child faces stems from this one challenge.

This is why, if you take a five-year-old nonverbal child labeled "severely autistic" and a sixteen-year-old adolescent with Asperger's syndrome, you won't, in most cases, find a single behavior in common. These two people will look and act very, very differently from one another. And yet, they are both on the autism spectrum. What do they have in common, then?

They both have difficulty communicating, making eye contact, reading nonverbal cues, dealing with people and social situations, coping with high levels of sensory stimulation, and being flexible with changing circumstances and with other people's wishes and agendas. Also, they both have powerful interests (labeled by some as "obsessions") that they can engage in for long periods of time, often seeming oblivious to the interests of others.

Isn't that interesting? No behaviors in common, yet a whole array of underlying challenges in common. So, regardless of where your child is on the spectrum, he or she has the same key deficits. This is actually a good thing. You may not see it as a good thing right this second. That's okay. But, really, it is. It means that by addressing this one area, you are also tackling almost every other challenge that your child faces. It also means that everything in this book is designed to enable you to help your child grow and learn while going *with* instead of *against* your child, bonding more with your child instead of doing battle with him.

This leads us to a most important, paradoxically logical idea: *overcoming autism is not about getting your child to change his behaviors.* Really.

A TOTAL REVERSAL

First, we want to change the question we ask ourselves when seeking to help our child. Instead of asking, "What do I need to do in order to change my child's behavior?" we want to ask, "What do I need to do in order to create a relationship with my child?" Once we ask this question, everything changes. Our whole approach shifts.

You want to begin to focus on doing your very best to *see through your child's eyes.* I'm not asking you to be psychic here. I'm talking about imagining, with every single interaction you have with your child, what this might feel like for your child. When you stop your child from stimming, how might that feel for her? When you take him to a noisy park and he's covering his ears, how do you think that is for him? When your child seems engrossed in tearing paper into tiny strips, what do you think that experience is like for her? When your child talks incessantly about windmills, what is it that he loves so much about them?

We want everything we do with our children from now on to be in service to bonding and relationship building. This means that you want to make being part of our world extremely appealing to your child. You want interacting with others to feel totally nonthreatening, fun, exciting, and satisfying for your child. In fact, you want to *sell* human interaction. I mean really sell it. If you went up to your child and said, "Dude, I've got the best deal to offer you! It's called being part of our world, and it's really awesome. You know what the best part is? When you join us in our world, you get to stop doing all the stuff you *love*, and start doing all the stuff you *hate*! Doesn't that sound fantastic?" Now, no child or adult on earth is going to take that deal. And yet, that's the deal we usually offer.

It's time for a total reversal. Instead of focusing on your child conforming to your world, you want to become a student of your child's world. *Let your child be the teacher.*

Of course, you have many, many things you want to teach your child. A number of the upcoming chapters will help you with exactly that. But if you ever want to get to a place where your child is actually interested in what you and others have to offer, you must first build trust and form a bond on your child's own terms. You've got to build a bridge to your *child's* world first. Only then can you take your child's hand and guide her back across that bridge to *your* world. That is why The Son-Rise Program is guided by the following principle:

> The children show us the way in, and then we show them the way out.

Okay, so how do we do that?

Everybody loves the second half of this sentence. *Yes, I want to show my child the way out! I want to get my child to look at me, communicate, learn new things, be more neurotypical!*

However, it is right here that the first and primary mistake is usually made. With children on the autism spectrum, you can't just yank them out of their world and into ours. You can't *force* them to learn or grow or change. And you certainly cannot *make* them want to interact with other people.

JOINING

So, if we want to show our children the way out, then we must begin by focusing on the *first* half of that sentence. This means that, rather than forcing these children to conform to a world they do not understand, we begin by joining them in their world. In this way, we establish a mutual connection and relationship, which is the platform for all education and growth.

And this leads us to our first key technique: joining. What is joining? Well, you know all of those stimming behaviors that everyone is trying to get your child to stop doing? Not only do we not stop these behaviors, but we *join in with* and *participate* in those very same behaviors.

When your child performs his or her repetitive autistic-looking behaviors, you are going to do them, too. When your child lines up blocks, you will get some blocks of your own and line them up, too. When your child shakes a pen while making an "eeeee" sound, you will do the same. When your child is stimming, you are going to stim with him. (And, yes, children and adults with Asperger's syndrome *do* stim. They just do it differently, as we'll discuss in Chapter 15.)

I've often heard the concern, from people who have not yet tried this technique, that joining will "reinforce the very behaviors that we want the child to stop." The idea is that joining will supposedly teach your child that her repetitive behaviors are appropriate, leading to more of these behaviors.

However, once you have joined your child the way that we do it in The Son-Rise Program (which we'll get into shortly), you will see firsthand that the last thing on earth it leads to is more stimming.

At the Autism Treatment Center of America, we have been joining children and adults for decades—kids from Great Britain and Nigeria, from Germany and Japan, from Argentina and across the United States, two-year-olds and thirty-two-year-olds, kids labeled "severe" and kids deemed "mild." We have never, ever seen it make anyone more autistic. We've never seen it lead to increased stimming.

In fact, we see the opposite: the more we join a child, the less that child stims. Time and time again, we join children and then watch as these children look at us more, pay more attention to us, smile at us more, participate with us more, and become steadily less interested in the stimming behavior by which they previously seemed so captivated.

When my mother began joining me, she was told that this was unwise and would lead to more stimming. She was told to say "no," take the plate away, and redirect my behavior whenever I put a plate on the floor and spun it on its edge for hours at a time. To my eternal gratitude, she didn't listen. She wanted so much to peek into my world. She wanted so fervently to show me that she loved me—to connect with me. She got her own plate and spun with me. That was when I began looking at her, smiling at her, and becoming more interested in her.

AN ANALOGY

To illustrate why joining works, let me give you an analogy. I want you to imagine that you've had a hard, busy week, and you are totally out of steam. (I'm sure that won't be difficult for you.) Finally, Saturday arrives. Lo and behold, you have the day to yourself—a day off. (Okay, that might be harder for you to imagine, but go with me here.) Your spouse (or someone else if that doesn't apply) is covering the kids, and you can do what you wish.

So, you go to a nice local park, and you take your favorite book by your favorite author to read. You sit down on one of the benches, get out your book, and begin reading. It's a beautiful day out, and you're totally comfortable. As you read, you finally begin to decompress from your trying week. You start to relax. You become absorbed in your book, tuning out all of the events of the week and the formidable list of things you have to do when you get back home. You're at ease.

Then I approach you. "Hey, what's up?" I ask in a loud voice, "How ya doing? Listen, I've been watching you read, and you've been at it for quite a while. Ya know, this isn't the best way to spend your day, being kind of antisocial and not really doing anything. I'll tell you what. Let's forget about the book and go see a movie. There's a great flick playing just down the road. My treat. How about it?"

You look up at me, a little annoyed. "Um, look, I've had a very intense week, and I finally got a day to myself. I just want to hang out here and read. Thanks for the offer, though."

I stare at you, a bit dumbfounded. I'm making a great offer, and movies are fun. Why aren't you putting your book down and going with me? Maybe I just haven't adequately gotten your attention yet. So I stand right in front of where you are sitting and squat down so that my face is at eye level with yours. I take my hand and push your book aside so you can see me.

"Hi," I say, "Can you look at me? Over here." I snap my fingers in the direction you are looking and bring my hand back to my face. "Hi. I'm over here. Listen, the movie is starting in fifteen minutes. Come on, stand up. Let's go. We're going to the movies."

Now you're getting pretty peeved with me. You stand up and face me. "Hey, look, buddy. Back off. I've had a tough week, and I just want to read my book in peace. If I wanted to use my one day off to see a movie, that's probably what I'd be doing, okay? So just leave me alone. I just want to read my book in peace."

Suddenly, I have a realization. What was I thinking? How could I have missed this? I know what the problem is! The problem is: your book. It's clearly very distracting to you. I mean, you keep staring and staring at it. You're kind of obsessed with it. So, if I just take the book away from you, problem solved.

I snatch the book out of your hands. You try to grab it back, but I pull it back out of your reach.

"Ah-ah-ah," I tell you, "You'll get the book back *after* you go to the movies with me."

Okay.

It doesn't take a rocket scientist to figure out what's going to happen next. The very *last* thing that's going to happen is you deciding to come to the movies with me. In fact, next Saturday, if you see me approaching, you're going to grab your book and run the other way.

YOUR CHILD'S EXPERIENCE

Now, the important thing to understand here is that this problematic situation is not occurring because I'm trying to make your life difficult. Quite the opposite. I'm trying to *help* you! My intentions are good. I genuinely believe that it's not healthy for you to sit by yourself all day, and I'm endeavoring to get you to do something I think will be better for you. I have the very best of intentions.

The problem is, you're not a mind reader, so you don't know my reasons and intentions. All you know about me is two things:

1. I'm right up in your face.
2. I keep giving you the same message over and over. And that message is: *stop doing what you want—do what I want.*

Now let's take a moment and step behind your child's eyes. If your child has an autism spectrum disorder, two big things are happening. (I'm not saying that these are the *only* things going on with your child, but they are two of the biggies.)

The first is that your child has difficulty processing and making sense of sensory input. This means that he sees, hears, smells, tastes, and feels things very differently than you or I do. When your child hears something, for instance, it sounds louder, softer, or just plain different than what you hear.

If you take a moment right now and just listen in silence to any background noise, you may notice a lot of little sounds—cars, wind, the heater or air conditioner, a TV or a conversation in another room, etc. You probably didn't notice all of these noises until just now. That's as it should be.

The human ear is bombarded by a continuous cacophony of sounds. One of the brain's chief tasks is to filter out irrelevant sounds and filter in the important sound, such as your spouse/boyfriend/girlfriend talking. (Well, at least we'd call that sound important *most* of the time!)

With your child, all of those noises are coming in at the same volume! (It doesn't work in *exactly* this way, but this is the closest approximation to your child's experience that we can get into right now.) So when you tell your child to pay attention and listen, what, exactly, should he listen to? Which of the twenty-five sounds is your child supposed to pay attention to?

This is your child's experience day in and day out. You know how you feel after you've spent the day at an airport (tired, overwhelmed, like you just want to veg out)? Well, your child wakes up, has breakfast, lunch, dinner, then goes to sleep—in the middle of a busy airport. Even if it's just your living room, it's an airport to your child. This is why making a big effort to see things through your child's eyes is so important.

You may have a child who likes to take his clothes off and run around naked. He may step into the house and tear all of his clothes off. You may ask yourself, *Why is my child misbehaving? He knows that he's supposed to keep his clothes on!* The thing is, your child is not "misbehaving." His clothes probably feel like sandpaper, and he is taking them off just to get some relief!

When I was little, I used to see and hear things very differently. I would test deaf on hearing tests, even though the tests were monitoring *involuntary* responses from my eyelids and skin. At the same time, I would mimic a song that was playing on a television show being watched in a distant room. I can remember things being visually different to me at times, and this continued to occur from time to time for a couple of years after my recovery. For instance, sometimes, when I looked at a person's face, it would seem like I was looking through the wrong end of a pair of binoculars. The person's face would look like it was far away and down a tunnel. Sound strange to you? Welcome to your child's world.

The second big issue that your child faces is that she has difficulty recognizing patterns. This means that everyday occurrences that seem predictable and understandable to you and me seem random and haphazard to your child. That's why your child is constantly seeking familiarity and routine!

If I walk up to you, say "Hi," and stick out my right hand, you know, without even thinking about it, that I am greeting you and trying to shake your hand. You know how this works and you know what to do.

If I did that with your child (in most cases), I'm just some guy thrusting his hand out. Your child doesn't necessarily know what this is or what to do. (What's worse is that everyone thinks that she *should* know what to do and is annoyed or upset when she doesn't.) Your child is living in an unpredictable, confounding, and tumultuous world.

Any of us facing just the latter challenge would endeavor to cope in ways similar (though less extreme) to how our children behave. We've all been in situations, such as being in a foreign country, where we have encountered small versions of these challenges. The people don't speak our language. They have cultural traditions that seem unfathomable—yet we're expected to follow them. Even flushing the (strangely arranged) toilet can seem like an exercise in code breaking. Why can't everything just be understandable?! And why won't people get off my back and stop expecting me to obey rules I don't understand?! Often, in these situations, we become less social. We seek to wall ourselves in. And we seek familiarity and control. The same is true for many of us when we start a new job, move to a new area, or marry into a family that's very different from ours.

This is *exactly* what your child does. In fact, your child is so brilliant and so creative that he has come up with a way to handle both challenges at once: the stim.

How does the stim do that? First, it enables your child to focus intently on one thing so that he can most effectively tune out the sensory bombardment that he is experiencing every moment of every day. (Interestingly, this is the same reason why some people meditate.)

Second, by doing the same exact thing over and over in a way that he can control, your child is, in essence, creating an island of predictability in an ocean of randomness. So, you see, your child is actually addressing both neurological issues with one behavior! He is doing the best, smartest thing that he can possibly do to address what is going on for him. In reality, your child is not behaving abnormally. Your child is behaving extremely normally in the face of the abnormal situation that he is facing.

Isn't that amazing?

BACK TO THE ANALOGY

Let's return to our analogy for a few moments. Now suppose you are sitting on your bench in the park, reading your favorite book by your favorite author, just like before. This time I approach, sit down on the same bench, and begin reading a book I've brought with me. I don't say anything to you; I'm busy reading my book.

After a while, you glance over at me. And then you notice something startling. Holy frijoles! You can't believe it, but it appears that I am reading the very same book that you are! You try to go back to reading your book, but you keep thinking of how unbelievable it is that I am reading not just the same book as you, but your *favorite* book.

After glancing over at me for the tenth time, you can't resist; you have to at least ask me about it. So you tap me on the shoulder and ask me why I'm reading this book, do I like it, do I read many books by this author, etc. I enthusiastically answer you, and we fall into a discussion of our favorite books and why we love them.

Then, it's time for me to go. I say good-bye and leave.

The next Saturday, you are sitting on the bench reading, and along I come again (with my book). We read a bit, chat a bit, and then part ways. The same process happens again the following Saturday and the one after that.

Then, after several Saturdays of this, we're sitting and talking on the bench, and I say, "Hey, check this out. Next weekend, the movie version of this book we've been reading is coming out. Isn't that awesome? Listen, how about, next Saturday, instead of reading here, we meet at the movie theater and watch that movie?"

Do you see what happened? Notice that, in both scenarios, I'm ultimately asking you to do *the exact same thing.* However, the *way* I got there is totally different. In the first scenario, it's all about *stop doing what you want—do what I want.* I have no interest in building a relationship with you, let alone trust. In the second scenario, I spend a lot of time building a meaningful relationship with you before I ask you for anything. What's more, we are building this relationship *around a common interest.*

This is important, because, although The Son-Rise Program

was unique in pioneering this idea with respect to autism, this is not at all new when it comes to how human beings relate to one another. Forming relationships based upon a common interest, combined with reciprocity (the two-way street of "I go your way, then you go mine"), has been the way human beings have been creating relationships for thousands of years.

What is incredible is not that we would use this model, but that it is still controversial to use it with children whose main challenge is creating relationships! It seems almost too obvious to state that, if a child has a social-relational disorder, we would want to use bonding and relationship-building techniques with that child rather than techniques that do the opposite.

Moreover, there is a growing body of research suggesting that, for our children, stimming has all sorts of positive effects on the nervous system—calming, regulating, and relaxing it. (See Appendix 1.)

And what do we do when our children finally find something to calm themselves, self-regulate, and effectively cope with their environment? *Quiet hands. Don't do that. Put that down. Do this instead.*

To be clear, we do this to help our children. We do this because we love our children. But, through their eyes, it's not helpful and it's not loving.

At the Autism Treatment Center of America, we had a little girl named Keri in our Son-Rise Program Intensive (a program where we work directly with the child, which you'll hear more about later) who would flap her hands by the outside edges of her eyes near her temples. (I've changed Keri's name and the names of all the kids in this book.) Her parents—who loved their daughter very much—were constantly trying to stop her from flapping. "Quiet hands, honey," they would say, and then they would gently take her wrists and push her hands down to her sides.

We taught Keri's parents to use joining to help her, but that's not why I'm telling you about her. I'm telling you this because, later on, Keri was examined by an ophthalmologist who told her parents that the rods in her retinas were defective. (You have rods and cones in your retinas. Cones see colors and straight ahead, rods see in black and white, peripheral vision, and are involved in depth perception.) This doctor went on to explain that when Keri flapped her hands at the outside edge of her vision, she was stimulating the rods in her retinas, thereby helping herself to see better as she navigated around a room, a sidewalk, etc. So, this little girl was just trying to see, and everyone around her, trying, of course, to help her, was saying "Quiet hands" and pulling her hands away from her eyes.

A boy named Vincent would get on the floor, put a ball or pillow underneath his stomach, and roll back and forth for hours. As with Keri, his parents, teachers, and therapists all tried to discourage him from doing this. Later, Vincent's parents were told by a physician that he had severe chronic indigestion that was probably causing a great deal of stomach pain. So Vincent was just trying to give himself some relief!

If your child is doing something for hours on end every day, surely there is a purpose to what she is doing. She is not stimming (or doing anything else, for that matter) for no reason. There is always a reason and a purpose—otherwise, she wouldn't be doing it over and over.

You see, it's hard to see the purpose and usefulness of our children's behaviors when we're trying to stamp out the behaviors. This, in fact, is another benefit of joining: it enables us, often for the first time, to get a window into our child's world. It gives us the opportunity to see the *reasons* for our child's behaviors. It allows us to begin to answer the question: Why is my child doing this? What is he or she getting out of it?

MIRROR NEURONS

Neurologists have increasingly been studying (and getting excited about) mirror neurons. (The book *Mirrors in the Brain* charts their discovery.) These are a special class of neurons present in every person's brain. Among other things, mirror neurons enable us to identify with, learn from, and connect with other people.

Mirror neurons fire in our brains when we see—or sometimes even hear about—someone else taking an action or having an experience. For instance, when we are watching a basketball game and someone shoots a basket, the same pattern of neurons fires in our own brain that would fire *if we were actually shooting the basket.* What you may think of as empathy is a mirror neuron phenomenon. Mirror neurons allow us to walk in someone else's shoes.

When you see someone on TV bang his knee, and you wince, that's your mirror neurons firing. When you watch someone throw a ball, and you imagine throwing it yourself, that's your mirror neurons. When someone shows you a dance move, and then you try it, you're using your mirror neurons. When you cry during a sad movie scene, it is your mirror neurons that allow you to imagine yourself in the place of the movie character.

There is evidence that children and adults on the autism spectrum have difficulty firing their mirror neurons. If a person's mirror neurons aren't firing, then he or she would have difficulty identifying with and being interested in others, being motivated by social things, looking in other people's eyes, knowing what to look for in social situations, imitating and learning from others, and so on. Sound familiar?

Guess what? One of the key ways that mirror neurons begin to fire in the developing brain is when children are joined. In fact, even babies immediately become more interested in those who do what they do. (The book *Mirroring People* explains this phenomenon well and discusses much about how mirror neurons operate.) So if we want to help our children's mirror neurons to fire, we need look no further than the very first principle of The Son-Rise Program. It turns out that the simple act of stepping across the bridge from our world to that of our children may help to stimulate the exact part of their brains that seems to be having such difficulty.

WHEN TO JOIN

It's very important to know when to join because we don't join with everything.

THE ISM

In fact, you only join when your child is doing one very specific type of behavior: isms. *Only* isms.

What is an ism? The simplest way to think of an ism is to think of it as a stim. Of course, you might justifiably ask why we don't just go ahead and call it a stim, as everyone else does.

It is much more helpful to our children if we use a word that is easily definable—free from a history of negative connotations or any other baggage that might cause confusion about what we mean. After all, if we are only joining with isms, and we clearly define isms, then we will be absolutely clear on exactly what to join with.

If your child is doing an ism, your child is performing a behavior that has two main characteristics:

1. It is *repetitive.*
2. It is *exclusive.*

I don't think that the word "repetitive" really needs further explanation, but the word "exclusive" does. When we say "exclusive," we are talking about a behavior whereby your child is *excluding* other people. Exclusive means that the behavior is a one-person show. Your child isn't looking at anyone else, interested in others watching, inviting anyone else to join in, or allowing anyone else to participate. By definition, your child is doing something where there is only room for her. In most cases (but not all), your child, when doing these types of behaviors, will not be responsive to what you say or ask. You can call her name or invite her to do something different, but you'll get no real response

Think of it like this: your child is a member of a tiny little club with only herself as a member. The solution isn't to try to destroy the club. Rather, the solution is to do whatever it takes to get in!

When your child is doing a behavior that is both repetitive and exclusive, we call that an ism. When your child is doing an ism, *we always join.*

HOW TO JOIN

Joining isn't complicated. The technical aspect of entering your child's world by joining in with his isms is quite simple. However, there is one essential piece that cannot be overlooked. The attitude you have while joining your child is absolutely critical.

The goal here isn't to prove you can copy, mimic, or mirror your child. Anyone can do that. A machine can do that.

You, however, have a special role in your child's life and world. You're not just anyone. You're not a machine. You *love* your child. You *care about* your child. You are *invested* in your child.

You may sometimes wonder if your child really understands that you love her—and just how *much* you love her. Joining is how you will express your love in a way that your child can see it and *feel* it. This means that *you* need to focus on feeling it. You want to put all of your focus on loving your child and honoring her world. Not only will this help to make your joining a deep bond with your child, but, when your child *does* pause in her ism to look at you, she will be able to see—right in front of her eyes—that you love her.

I cannot overstate how much this matters.

How many times do people untouched by autism ask you how your son or daughter is doing, and then, when you answer, you watch as their eyes glaze over, and they nod uncomfortably—and you see that they aren't truly interested in your answer? After enough instances like this, you stop telling people about your child.

Your child is exquisitely intelligent and perceptive. He knows the difference in a heartbeat between you begrudgingly "copying" him and really joining. And you know, too. So now it's time to make the real thing happen.

If you want your child to be inclined to share her world with you, you need to be genuinely curious and interested. As best you can, endeavor to be fascinated by what you are doing. Now, you may be thinking, *How can I be fascinated with repetitive hand-flapping* (or block-stacking, or listing all capital cities, or whatever)?

Here's the thing: as long as you're asking yourself that question, you can't be fascinated. You can't be fascinated or interested when you're looking down on the behavior. And you certainly can't be fascinated when you're thinking about ways to stamp out the behavior. So you have to let all of this go.

It's not that you have to let go of wanting your child to learn and grow. It's just that you need to let go of the idea that pushing your child to change what he is doing is the way to get there. Remember, your child is doing what he is doing because that is the best way he knows how to help himself. Focus on finding out what your child loves about that behavior. Become an enthusiastic student of your child's world. Imagine that you are working with someone from another country, and your job is to learn all about that person's culture.

If, for instance, your child is flapping her hands, sit down near her (or stand if your child is standing) and flap your hands like there's no tomorrow. Amazingly, the more interested you are in your *own* hand-flapping, the more interested your child will be in *you*.

If your child is doing something more complex than hand-flapping, such as making an intricate tower with blocks, circuiting from toy to toy, repeating phrases from movies, or playing with toy figures in an elaborate but repetitive way, then you are still going to join in the same way. Look at what your child is doing. Get fascinated. Then dive in, and do the same activity yourself as best you can.

A note: if your child glances at you while you are joining, you can feel free to smile at him, thank him briefly, but then go right back to joining.

WHAT NOT TO DO

1. **Don't stare at your child.**

   Once you begin, don't stare at your child or look at her every two seconds. Really get involved with what you are doing. Remember, you aren't trying to prove that you can mimic; you are getting involved with the activity that your child loves.

2. **Don't get in your child's face.**

   That's part of the reason that your child is isming in the first place—to tune out everyone who's in his face! You want to give your child some space. If your child is sitting down, then, by all means, sit down, but don't sit down an inch from where he's sitting. If your child is standing or pacing, then stand or pace, but not right up on top of him.

3. **Don't take your child's stuff.**
If your child is lining up small green cars, then, whatever you do, don't take her green cars and start lining them up. Yes, that's right, you've got to use the rejects. If your child likes to use the shiny green cars but shows no interest in the old, half-broken yellow cars, those yellow cars are all yours, baby! Use the same *type* of item that your child is using, but not the ones your child is actually using.

4. **Most important: Don't try to change your child's behavior in any way.**
This is the biggest mistake people make, and it's the mistake that is most detrimental to the whole point of joining. Your child is smart. If you try to use joining as a way to get your child to change, alter, or stop his behavior, your child will immediately see that, and you will have rendered the entire joining technique useless. This means no saying, "Hey, sweetie, look at me!" No trying to get your child to take his little car and race your little car. And no gimmicks to try to get his attention.

This last point deserves some more discussion. I could understand, for instance, if you were to ask, "I thought you said that joining will lead to my child becoming more interested in me and in others, my child looking and interacting more, and my child isming less. So why are you now saying *not* to use joining to try to change what he's doing?"

A totally fair question. The answer is that joining results in *child-initiated interaction* (which eventually replaces isming). A major characteristic of autism is the lack of social interaction *that is initiated and wanted by the child.*

One of the factors that makes The Son-Rise Program unique

is that it focuses on developing within each child the ability to *initiate* social interaction. We want to enter the child's world, wait for her to voluntarily initiate interaction, and then (and only then) use that interaction to invite her to stretch and communicate further.

We want our children on our side. The only way to achieve that is to join them in their world until they join us in ours. This simply cannot be forced.

Joining correctly means joining until your child stops isming of her own volition and looks at you or approaches you in some way. It does not mean that you set aside fifteen minutes for joining, after which your child must do as you say. *The length of the joining is determined by your child, not by you.* That is the key.

Interestingly, in the last several years, a number of autism treatment methods have sought to adopt aspects of The Son-Rise Program by doing what they *think* is joining as a way to create interaction. The problem is, these methodologies still end up missing the boat because they try to adopt joining without understanding it. (Ironically, they are trying to copy or mimic something without understanding it, which is the same mistake we make when we only seek to copy or mimic our kids.) I've seen programs where children are "joined" for a period of time—decided upon by the therapist. As the minutes progress, the therapist endeavors to guide the child into a more interactive activity. (By the way, this is the very best case scenario. With most treatment methods, no attempt is made at all to participate in the child's world.)

And this is where a true understanding of joining (and of autism) has real impact. Joining isn't a trick we use to sneak our child into a different activity or behavior. *Joining is the way we enable our child to form a bond with us.* We find that children become more interested in us, look at us more, and ism far less when we join. But these children do these things by choice—at their own initiation. *After* our children bond with us, trust us, and feel safe with us—which they show us by initiating interaction—then we can challenge them to do and learn new things, which is what the very next chapter addresses.

The Story of Reggie

Some time ago, a father came to our Start-Up program to help his son, Reggie. Now recall that the Start-Up course is a five-day introductory training course where parents and professionals learn the fundamentals of how to use The Son-Rise Program techniques with their children. Parents such as Reggie's dad attend without their children.

They learn strategies to increase language, eye contact, interaction, and new skill acquisition. They learn to handle—and then reduce—challenging behaviors. They are taught how to put together an appropriate learning and sensory environment, how to creatively challenge their children, how to train others to work with their children, and, of course, how to sustain an attitude of hope and optimism with regard to their children. The course is very interactive, with lots of activities, video examples, question-and-answer sessions, and breakout "high-functioning" sessions for parents of children with Asperger's syndrome and similar diagnoses.

One of the first things we do in the Start-Up course is to teach parents how to join. When we began this with Reggie's father, he was pretty skeptical. He explained that his son would play with LEGOs for hours and hours on end. But Reggie didn't play with LEGOs the way a neurotypical child would. Every day, Reggie would do the exact same thing. He would grab his box of LEGOs, take out the exact same pieces, and build the exact same thing—a simple L-shaped structure. Then he would build another one so that he had two. Then he would take these two structures, hold them close together so that it looked like he was making a square, and walk around the room holding the square up to lights and windows while quickly bringing the two LEGO structures together and apart, together and apart.

Reggie's father explained to us that he couldn't imagine joining his son in this activity. As teachers, we find that one of the best ways to help people is first to seek to understand where they are coming from. What we do *not* do is to start arguing with them when they are struggling with the idea of implementing one of The Son-Rise Program techniques. By endeavoring to understand them, we are best equipped to help them.

So we began by asking this dad some questions. Why couldn't he imagine joining his son with the LEGOs? He answered that he really couldn't stand watching his son do that behavior. Again, we asked him why. He replied, this time becoming quite emotional. Every time he saw his son playing with the LEGOs, Reggie's father would see how "autistic" his son looked. And this provided a constant reminder to him that his son was different. He didn't like that his son was different. Moreover, he wondered whether it was somehow his fault. He saw his son's autism as the enemy, and, by God, he was not going to make friends with the enemy.

We asked him what he meant when he said his son's autism was the enemy, and this led to a powerful and in-depth discussion for the whole class. One of the key realizations that Reggie's dad came to that day was that by making autism the enemy, he was making a part of who his son was the enemy. He concluded that he wanted to love and embrace *all* of who his son was, including the part that was autistic. One crucial way that he could do this was to join his son. (This particular transformation is a pivotal component of the journey that many Son-Rise Program parents experience.)

At the end of his week, Reggie's father went back home excited to see his son through new eyes. Understand that before this, whenever Reggie's dad saw him playing with his LEGOs, he would try to stop him. He would say no, he would take the LEGOs away, he would try to get his son to do something else.

Also understand this: Reggie would not look at or acknowledge his father in any way.

Reggie's father had never tried joining before, and he wasn't totally sure about it, but he had agreed to totally commit to joining his son for a few weeks and see what happened. The next morning, Reggie pulled the box of LEGOs out first thing, not acknowledging his father. With some LEGOs, Reggie built his two L-shaped figures. As he always had, he began walking around the room, holding the two figures up to the lights, moving them closer together and farther apart.

This time, however, his dad was different. He made his own L-shaped structures and began strolling around the room, moving the structures closer together and farther apart. Every so often, he'd look at his son and really study what he was doing so that he could understand it and get it right.

As he did this, he realized something. He had always thought that his son had been simply looking through the square shape he had created with the two L-shaped figures. He was wrong. In fact, Reggie was looking sideways at the surface of each structure. And when his dad did the same thing, he noticed that, when he held the figures up to the light, he could see a reflection of his own face on the LEGOs themselves. And when he moved the two figures farther apart and then close together, the reflection of his face would get fatter and skinnier, as if he was looking at himself in a carnival mirror.

Yes! He was ecstatic! He finally understood what his son was doing, and it was actually pretty cool! Whoo-hoo! He glanced back over at his son, and Reggie had dropped his LEGOs and was staring in abject amazement at his father. His dad, looking back at him, couldn't believe it. He smiled at his son, enjoying the moment. Reggie smiled back. Then, on an inspiration, he waved to his son. Reggie waved back!

These two people, father and son, shared this beautiful moment, looking at each other, smiling at each other, waving to one another. It was a moment unlike any they had shared before. It was the first time Reggie ever really acknowledged and showed interest in his father—but it wasn't the last.

Reggie's father began to enthusiastically join his son every day. Finally, he had a way he could be with his son!

Before that first day of joining, Reggie had been isming with his LEGOs for upwards of five hours a day. Several weeks later, Reggie's time isming with the LEGOs had dwindled to just under an hour a day. And, of course, much of that time was replaced by Reggie doing things that were far more interactive—with his father and with others.

This story illustrates so many different aspects of why joining works, from giving us a window into why our children do what they do to creating a bonded relationship. But it also highlights something else. When you join, you may make a most amazing discovery: almost inevitably, joining will change you, too. It is rare, indeed, to connect with your child in this deep, abiding, and honoring way without it altering the way you see your child and the beauty of his unique world.

When you join your child fully, you can feel a level of closeness beyond anything previous. It's very hard to judge or feel scared by your child's behavior once you've truly joined him. And you develop a real sense of camaraderie with your child. A deeper understanding of his experience. A delight in his world.

And no one will ever be able to take this experience away from you.

JAMES BEFORE BED

Remember James, the son of my former girlfriend Charlotte? Well, one night years ago, I saw tears in Charlotte's eyes as she left James's room after putting him to bed. I asked her what was wrong, and she said that nothing was wrong—quite the opposite. And then, crying, smiling, she told me an extraordinary story.

James had been very connected all day. So when Charlotte went to put him to bed, she had the idea of reading James a bedtime story. This was something that she had looked forward to as a mom—her reading him a story and him listening and enjoying it. But every time she had attempted this previously, James hadn't shown any interest. Because James had been so interactive that day, Charlotte felt that maybe this was the night.

When she entered his room, though, she saw that he was sitting on his bed with one of his books, tapping on it with his fingers. Charlotte knew that this was one of James's isms, but she really had her heart set on reading him a bedtime story. So she interrupted him and said, "Hey, James, I'm going to read you a bedtime story!"

He ignored her and kept tapping.

"Hey, kiddo, let's put that book down. It's time for a fun story!"

He ignored her and kept tapping.

Then it hit her ("like a frying pan hitting me in the head" she told me). She was making her plan to read her son a bedtime story more important than bonding with him by joining him in his ism. She had known to join him but had been so focused on reading him a story that she had ignored all of the signs he was giving her.

Upon realizing this, she immediately ceased trying to get her son to stop. She had just had a wonderful day with him. She loved him. She just wanted to convey that to him. She just wanted to show him that she accepted him exactly where he was.

So she got out a book of her own, sat down, and began tapping her own book.

After doing this for some time, she stood up and began quietly making her way out of James's room so he could go to sleep.

As she was leaving, he put his book down, looked up at her, and said, "I love you."

This was the first time he had ever said these words to her.

THE EXCEPTIONS TO JOINING

There are very few types of isms that you are not going to want to join in with. Most of them will be pretty obvious to you, and one of them may not.

First, if your child is doing anything that is dangerous or in any way putting his safety at risk (playing in traffic, opening a car door while moving, playing with a sharp object, standing on a high ledge), *stop your child immediately.* Safety always comes first. Don't join with anything dangerous.

Second, if your child is doing something such as touching her genitals or picking her nose, we are obviously not going to join with that, either. Importantly, this does not mean that you need to get uncomfortable and force your child to stop. This kind of behavior is very normal, it's just not something you would want to join in with. (As I said, very obvious points here.)

Third (not obvious), you don't want to join if your child is watching television (or a video). You can't really join in with watching TV. All you can do is just sit there, which is not joining with an activity, it's watching. So when it comes to television, either don't use that time to join or—better yet—turn off the TV and join whatever else your child does.

ACTIVITY TIME!

This is going to be super simple. Take a look at Table 1. All you are going to do is find five different behaviors—isms—that your child does that you haven't previously joined in with that you now will.

You don't have to fill out all five isms in one sitting. Take your time. You can fill out the first one or two that come to you, then come back to this table a day later, once you've noticed another ism.

The most important thing is to keep your eyes peeled for isms—and then to join your child in exactly the way we've discussed.

Ism	How you've been responding	What you will do now to join
1)		
2)		
3)		
4)		
5)		

Table 1

ONLINE RESOURCES

At the end of each chapter, the "Online Resources" section will point you to a special section of my Web site specifically oriented toward that chapter. There you will find a host of resources designed to help you more deeply understand and implement that chapter's principles and techniques, such as videos, webcasts, articles, and photos.

I want to very strongly encourage you to *use these resources.* They are completely free to you—to use as many times as you wish, as frequently as you wish.

For this chapter, please go to www.autismbreakthrough.com/chapter2. Enjoy!

STARTING POINT

When your child is isming, join him in what he is doing. Do it with delight! Get really involved in the activity. Remember to give your child some space and position yourself so that it is easy for him to glance at you.

THREE

Motivation: The Engine of Your Child's Growth

WANT TO LEARN the key to teaching your child new skills and facilitating learning?

I thought you might.

If joining is the right hand of The Son-Rise Program, motivation is the left hand. You need to join in order to get your child to a place where she is ready to learn and grow, and motivation is the lever you use to get the learning and growth to happen once she is ready.

Before we dive into the motivation principle and how to utilize it, it's important that we talk about the problems and pitfalls of the conventional way that children on the autism spectrum are taught.

THE TIMING PROBLEM

The biggest mistake we make is attempting to teach or challenge our kids when they are not in a state where they can take in new information. When your child is, for instance, isming, not giving you eye contact, not responding when you speak to him or call his name, he is giving you a red light. (We'll talk much more about red lights and green lights in Chapter 12.) When you try to teach, cajole, or enlist your child while he is giving you a red light, you are "running a red." When you're driving, and you run a red light, you might think you'll get to your destination more quickly, but, oftentimes, the result is quite different—maybe a fender bender, maybe sitting on the side of the road getting a ticket. Likewise, when you're with your child, you might run a red, thinking that you'll get where you want to go with him faster. However, the result here is also the opposite.

It is crucial to wait until your child is ready and available before doing any teaching or challenging. We call these windows of availability green lights. (Again, this will be reintroduced later.) If your child is not isming and is looking at you and responsive, you probably have a green light. That is the time for teaching or asking for something from him. (You'll get more of these windows of availability if you join consistently, by the way.)

When we challenge our children at the correct times, the speed of learning and quality of interaction is drastically accelerated. You really will not believe how much it will pay off to follow your child's learning schedule rather than yours or anyone else's.

THE MOTIVATION MISMATCH

Motivation is the engine of growth. It is the single largest factor in your child's learning and progress. When a child is following his or her own intrinsic interests and motivations, learning comes fast and furious. Fortunately, very few people will fight you on this idea; there is widespread agreement on the importance of each child's motivation. Unfortunately, the motivation principle is rarely, if ever, put into practice with any consistency—*especially* with children on the autism spectrum.

Ninety-nine percent of the time, our children are taught in a way that works "against the grain" and slows down their learning. They are taught according to the schedule, curriculum, and dictates of the adults who are teaching them.

At home, the adults usually decide what activities will occur (bathtime, learning, eating, playtime) and how they will transpire (with what toys, food, silverware, games, books). In a school classroom, this system of adults choosing the what and the how is even more prevalent. Even the best, most dedicated, most talented teachers cannot possibly customize their teaching to every child's individual motivation when they face a roomful of students, each of whom has sharply divergent interests.

To add to the mismatch, children on the autism spectrum tend to have unusual and esoteric interests in the first place. What neurotypical children find motivating rarely interests children on the spectrum. Therefore, traditional modes of teaching will hardly ever be motivating to these children.

The end result is that the manner in which our kids are taught is not matched to what they find motivating and interesting. A child is asked to sit down at a table and fill out a worksheet. But it turns out that she likes Star Wars themes—and could be easily engaged in an activity involving Darth Vader or the Millennium Falcon. A child is told to say two new words in a certain order (for no reason that he can fathom). And yet, he might love to be chased—and might be happy to say "chase me" or "run fast" in the context of a chasing game.

A little girl is asked to count to five by counting black circles on a piece of paper. But she loves dinosaurs. Wouldn't she learn to count faster if we played a game with dinosaurs where she had to count out five dinosaurs that she wanted?

When we talk about the principle of using each child's intrinsic motivations, what we mean is this: customize the presentation of the curriculum (i.e., anything you are helping your child to do or learn) to match your child's highest areas of interest.

The books *The Brain That Changes Itself* and *The Art of Changing the Brain* point out that if you really want to change the brain—put the brain in a maximum growth state and foster the most learning—the key is to find and capitalize on the interests and motivations that a person already has, not to force-feed someone information or try to "make" someone motivated. When a child or adult is excited and motivated, neurotransmitters are secreted that act to turn on the brain, priming it for growth, change, and learning.

You want to introduce every skill you want your child to learn, every educational goal you have, every new activity you want your child to try within games or activities that are built around what your child already finds motivating and interesting.

PITFALLS OF THE REWARD PRINCIPLE

It is usually at this point that schoolteachers or therapists will say to me, "We're already using this technique—have been for years. We find something that each child likes—say, m&m's or a favorite toy—and we use these things as rewards to get the children to do something that we are trying to help them do or learn."

To be clear, using rewards is the exact opposite of the motivation principle, but we'll get to that in a bit.

For now, it is important to understand that the reward principle is the single most widely used teaching technique in the entire world when it comes to children with autism. (I am using the term "reward principle" here for clarity and simplicity. It is not an academic or technical term.) I'm sure, without even meeting you, that your child has been worked with using the reward principle. And there is nothing remotely strange about this.

Everybody looooves the reward principle. Hey, it's awesome! It gets our kids to do stuff! Why wouldn't we love it?

Without question, there are definitely a sizable number of our kids who will do something we want them to do when we offer them the right rewards. However, doing this comes with some pretty huge side effects.

Detrimental Desserts

Look, if you offer me chocolate, my first reaction is *chocolate: me likey.* And I'm not exaggerating when I say that I *really* like chocolate. I like things covered in chocolate. Things with chocolate in them. Things made out of chocolate. Did I mention chocolate?

I tell you this to make a larger point (and to plant the seeds now, in case you're thinking of buying me a gift). If you stick a plate of broccoli in front of me, I'm not going to beat down any doors to get at it. Don't get me wrong. I have a healthy respect for broccoli, and I do eat it, but it's not my favorite thing in the world. Truth is, I eat it purely out of some twisted sense of biological obligation.

Now, if you tell me that if I finish that plate of broccoli in front of me, you'll give me a bowl of double chocolate ice cream with hot fudge and chocolate-covered peanuts, then we're in business. I will probably finish the broccoli.

But what happens when you don't have any chocolate to offer me?

Did offering me that dessert magically transform me into a vegetable-loving health nut? Will I now scarf down any plate of broccoli that crosses my path?

Heck no! Unless you cover every plate of broccoli from here to eternity in a pound of chocolate, good luck! But let's take a closer look at why this is, because it goes to the heart of how all human beings—including our kids—operate.

When we set up the reward system, we are basically saying this: "Listen, if you do this awful, terrible thing that you can't stand, I'll give you this wonderful reward! In fact, the only reason to do what I'm asking is for the reward."

(Interestingly, a growing body of research—explained in books such as *Drive*, *The Medici Effect*, and *The Upside of Irrationality*—shows that, in business, offering people financial rewards such as a monetary bonus ahead of time for doing a task that requires thought and learning actually causes a *decrease* in performance!)

Think about it. We are a nation of people that love fattening, sugar-laden treats. But most of us grew up with loving parents who coaxed (or compelled) us to eat our vegetables. What the heck happened? Well, we grew up with the reward principle—at least in the food category. We were told that if we ate our vegetables, we would get to eat our delicious dessert. Sure, we ate our veggies when we had to, but, in most cases, we came to see the healthy stuff as the gross, obligatory food that we had to "get through" in order to get to the "good stuff," which was the fatty, sugary poison we call dessert.

In fact, the very idea of dessert conjures up notions of the good-tasting sweet reward following the meal. Why do we need the reward? Why isn't the meal enough? If we saw the meal as delicious and truly satisfying in its own right, it *would* be enough.

This is the exact scenario that children on the spectrum are presented with, except they are presented with it for *everything*. Nothing is too big or small to warrant a reward. And the less our children seem to want to do something, the bigger the reward they get for doing it.

The net result of all of this arrangement is that they grow to hate doing the very things we are endeavoring to get them to do on their own. Sure, they'll do it (some of the time), but now they're doing it *only* for the reward.

This is especially problematic for our special group of children because we are, in essence, telling them: "Let's get through this stinky human interaction crud, and then you can get the good stuff." But the thing is, *we want the human interaction to be the good stuff!* That's our children's only ticket out!

If you are the parent of a neurotypical teenaged girl, you don't have to offer her a reward to get her to talk on the phone with her friends. (You may have to reward her to get her *off* the phone.) Why? Because for her, talking on the phone with her friends (human interaction, socialization, and interpersonal relating) *is* the reward. It *is* the good stuff. *That's where we want our special kids to be!*

Robotic Behavior

One of the most common complaints I hear from parents with respect to the reward principle is that, yes, their children do perform some useful behaviors, but that they do so in a way usually described as "robotic." Their children may put the puzzle together or ask, "How are you today?" or shake a person's hand when prompted, but they do so in a programmed manner without any apparent joy or spontaneity.

In fact, many of these parents have been told that robotic behavior is a key symptom of autism. And, indeed, many children on the spectrum do appear this way. However, in our experience, robotic behavior, devoid of joy or spontaneity, is not a symptom of *autism*. Rather, it is a symptom of *the way we teach children with autism*. It is a symptom of the widespread and excessive use of the reward principle.

James, though he is still on the autism spectrum, does *not* have robotic behaviors. When my niece, Jade, was autistic, she did not have robotic behaviors. When I had autism, I did not exhibit robotic behaviors. At the Autism Treatment Center of America, we have worked with many children who did not display robotic behavior. Robotic behavior is not ubiquitous in Son-Rise Program children. The motivation principle is not a magic cure-all, but one thing it does *not* do is produce robotic behaviors.

Compliance-Centric

I was once shown a video (as an example of success) in which a little boy was repeatedly told "coat on" and then given an m&m when he complied. As soon as he finished putting his coat on, a facilitator would take the coat off again, offer the little boy his coat again, and say "coat on" again. This method was seen as a success because, by the end, the little boy was reliably putting on his coat when asked. (I am not trying to paint every therapy with one brush, and I know that not all therapists do what I saw on the video. However, some version of this—the reward may change, the activity may be less repetitive, etc.—is still the norm in autism treatment.)

I highlight this video for a very specific reason. As I watched it, what struck me—in addition to my concern about what this experience might have felt like for this boy—was that, in reality, this boy had not learned the skill the facilitators were aiming for. At the end of the day, this little boy learned one thing: compliance. Now, I'm not saying that compliance is a bad thing. But it is very different than learning the actual skill that the therapists were claiming to teach. The actual skill of putting one's coat on (to use this very simple example), entails the following: I walk outside, I realize that it's chilly out, I step back inside, I put on my coat, I go back outside.

What the little boy in the video learned was to put his coat on when someone said "coat on." As I said, this is by no means a bad thing for him to learn, but it means that someone has to follow him around and tell him to put his coat on, take it off, put his shoes on, take his shoes off, etc.

To be independent—and to feel successful, and to interact socially in a meaningful way—this little boy has to learn the real skill. He needs to learn not only the real coat-donning skill, but also, much more importantly, real social interaction skills—being interested in others, communicating, enjoying an interactive game or activity, etc. (rather than having someone next to him telling him what to do and say every minute).

The ability of a child or adult to take something that he has learned and apply it in different circumstances (home, school, etc.) is called generalization. For our children, being able to generalize what they learn is absolutely critical.

Truly learning something, and then being able to generalize it, comes from *enjoying* it. It comes from being *interested* in it. And it comes from being internally *motivated* to do it.

While repetitive teaching with rewards is not bad for getting a child to follow instructions, this method is utterly incapable of manufacturing motivation. It cannot enable that child to sincerely learn, generalize, enjoy, and be interested in what she is being taught. This is even more the case when it comes to social skills, which are the very abilities our children could most use help acquiring.

In short, these are the three main side effects of the reward principle:

1. Robotic behavior.
2. Your child will learn to hate what he is being asked to do or learn.
3. Your child will not really learn the actual skill (only to follow instructions), and thus will have great difficulty generalizing the skill to other situations where there is not a prompt → behavior → reward system in place.

James used to love games that involved us running. To be precise, he especially enjoyed watching *me* run. He would say "Waun, wun fast!" (his version of "Raun, run fast!") and then break out into peals of laughter when I did so. (I'm not sure whether to take this as a compliment or an insult.) I could get him to do almost anything if it involved me running. Charlotte once called me to tell me that, *in his sleep*, James was giggling and saying "Waun, wun fast." (He was apparently dreaming.) Could you imagine this happening with the reward principle?

USING THE MOTIVATION PRINCIPLE

If the motivation principle is not the reward principle, how is it different? This is another one of those Son-Rise Program techniques that isn't just different; it's the exact opposite. To use this technique, we must flip everything.

A good place to start is to change your focus as you are trying to teach or challenge your child. First, the starting point is no longer identifying what you want your child to do. Instead, think about what your child's areas of interests (motivations) are. Does your child like Disney characters? Airplanes? Physical play? Science fiction themes? Chasing games? You're going to focus on these first, and *then* think about what you want your child to do or learn.

You will want to write down some of your child's interests and motivations. You may be wondering how you know what these interests are. All you need to do is to observe your child. What does your child do? What does she gravitate toward? Is there anything that she really enjoys watching you do? If your child is verbal, what does she talk about when an adult isn't dictating the conversation?

You will also want to write down a short list of some educational goals—or, more simply, things that you want your child to do. Specificity is very important here. It is very difficult to effectively pursue a broad goal with your child. For example, you may be helping your child with verbal communication, but a goal of "using words" is too general. Rather, you'd want a goal such as "using the word 'chase'" or "saying 'I want chase,'" depending on your child's language level. Goals are by no means limited to language. They can involve eye contact, length of time he is willing to stay involved in a game, taking turns, a specific activity like going to the dentist, even self-care skills included in daily living, such as toilet training, taking a bath, eating a particular food that isn't his favorite, getting dressed, or cleaning his room.

The Technique

At the core, it only takes three steps to implement the motivation principle:

1. Join your child until she is no longer isming, and she looks at you (more than just a one-second glance). Note: You can skip this step only if your child is already interacting with you and not isming at all.

2. Playfully invite your child to participate in an activity or game based upon something that she likes (as we've discussed).

3. **Beginner's version:** *If and only if* your child willingly gets involved in your game, keep that game going as long as possible. For example, if your child loves to be tickled or enjoys talking about the planets, simply participate in this activity (with great enthusiasm!) for as long as your child stays interested. Just having your child engage in that game for increasing amounts of time will stretch her interactive attention span—and thus her ability to interact with others.

   Advanced option: *If and only if* your child willingly gets involved in your game, add one thing. For example, if your child loves chase games, and you successfully get her to play chase with you, then try adding one thing, such as: you keep "running out of gas," and she has to keep saying "chase" to get you to chase her.

The Story of Pedro

Pedro's mother came to a Start-Up program exasperated and a bit desperate. She had been trying to toilet-train Pedro for six months. Not only was he not yet peeing in the toilet, but he had a greater aversion to anything toilet-related than he had six months prior. Pedro's mom brought this challenge up during one of the question-and-answer sessions of her Start-Up course, but she was not feeling optimistic about finding a solution.

We discussed the motivation principle, and we spent a few minutes coming up with an idea for her to use. First, we asked her what one of Pedro's motivations was. She hesitated, then said that her son loved stairs and anything (such as escalators or even stools) that had steps. She quickly added an apology, saying that she must not have chosen the right kind of motivation, since steps and stairs had nothing to do with peeing in the toilet.

We told her that this was exactly the right kind of motivation, as any of her son's interests would be. Sure, it was true that stairs and steps did not have anything intrinsically in common with using the toilet, but that was fine, as the whole principle is predicated on combining two things (a motivation and a goal) that don't necessarily relate together into one game or activity.

So, we helped her to come up with a game, and she returned home after the Start-Up, eager to try it with her son. Her first day back, she entered Pedro's room with a new three-step stool. Pedro walked over to it and climbed onto it, immediately interested. That first day, all Pedro's mom did was to play with him on this stool, in whatever way he liked.

The second day, she brought the stepping stool in again and invited Pedro to play on it once more. This time, however, the game involved her moving the stool to different locations around the room, and Pedro climbed on it only after his mom had moved it to its next "destination."

On the third day, they were playing this game again, and, at the height of Pedro's excitement and involvement, she pushed the stepping stool right up against the toilet and invited Pedro to walk up the three steps, stand on the stool, and pee into the toilet.

Pedro did it, and he did it happily and without a fight.

Now let's take a few minutes to uncover exactly why this worked. It would be reasonable for you to ask how it is possible that Pedro, a little boy who seemed unable to pee in the potty after six months of his mother trying, peed in the toilet for the first time in less than three days. (Furthermore, Pedro did not require rewards to continue to use the toilet. Over the next few days, his mom soon removed the stool, and Pedro was fine with using the toilet without it.) In fact, I used to be concerned that, when telling this story, the jump from six months to three days might seem too good to be true. But there is nothing mysterious about it. It's logic, not magic, that makes it work.

The motivation principle plays to your child's intelligence. It plays on the fact that your child has the intelligence to do many of the things that he isn't doing. Autism is not an intelligence problem. *Our job is not to make our children more intelligent; it is to unlock the intelligence that's already there.* Knowing this, we can say that Pedro's lack of toileting was not an intelligence problem; it was a motivation issue. Pedro did not lack the smarts to use the toilet. He lacked an interest, a trust, and a motivation.

And, in hindsight, this should not be at all surprising. First of all, he's getting his diaper changed every so often throughout the day. So, from his point of view, life is good—it's like living at a full-service gas station! He pees, he poops, and—poof!—someone swoops in, takes the smelly diaper away, cleans him up, and provides him with a fresh new diaper. Sounds good to me!

Do any of us really think that Pedro is lying in his bed at night thinking: *You know, this diaper situation is pretty cool, but it would be so much more socially appropriate for me to go directly into the toilet*? Of course not! It's *us* who want our kids to go in the toilet (and many other things). And that's fine. We certainly don't have to apologize for that. But what we do need to do is to realize that since *we* are the ones who want these things for our children, it is *our* job to find a way to get *them* as interested as *we* are.

Second, as Pedro's mother was endeavoring to toilet-train him for the first six months before seeing us, she was doing what almost all parents and teachers do. She was pushing Pedro to use the toilet, even when he didn't want to. She was offering him rewards, which immediately sent the message that the toilet was something unpleasant that he had to do to get the reward. And she conveyed the message, in countless subtle ways, that there was a right way and a wrong way to go on the toilet. (For instance, peeing and missing the toilet is the "wrong" way.)

Pedro's thinking *Hey, I liked this better when I was getting my diaper changed. No one was pressuring me, and I couldn't get it "wrong"!* And, really, I can't blame him.

What Pedro's mom did so brilliantly with the motivation principle was use an interest Pedro already had; she didn't break trust by pushing him, and she made the toilet something that was fun and motivating to Pedro in its own right.

Important: This case study illustrates an example of using the motivation principle for a basic skill. Please don't take this to mean that this principle is only useful for teaching these types of skills. In fact, this strategy is incredibly powerful with more complex skills, such as social and conversational skills. We will be discussing a case study on exactly this area in Chapter 15.

ACTIVITY TIME!

Take a look at Table 2. You'll notice that it has two columns. In the left-hand column, write down five motivations or areas of interests that your child has. (Don't worry about the order.) In the right-hand column, write down five specific, short-term educational goals. These are things that you are trying to get your child to do or learn.

Now, draw a line from one of the motivations to one of the goals. How will you decide which two items to connect with a line? Look over your table, and think about which motivation might most easily go together in a game or activity with which goal.

This does not mean the motivation and the goal have to be similar or naturally "go together." Remember the example from this chapter, when Pedro's mom combined a stepping stool with peeing in the toilet? Those two things aren't at all similar. Another mom worked on her son's eye contact using his interest in airplanes. A dad worked on his daughter's language using her interest in Disney characters. So you are just going to do your best. Once you've connected one motivation with one goal, draw a line connecting a second motivation with a second goal. Then continue drawing lines until each motivation has one goal connected to it.

This will be your beginning blueprint for coming up with games and activities to help your child gain skills and achieve goals. You can use this blueprint to begin generating an idea or two of what kinds of games and activities you can do with your child to help him progress.

Motivation / Area of Interest	Educational Goal
1)	1)
2)	2)
3)	3)
4)	4)
5)	5)

Table 2

ONLINE RESOURCES

For more in-depth help with the principles and techniques of this chapter, please go to www.autismbreakthrough.com/chapter3. Have fun!

STARTING POINT

Remember the three-step technique we talked about earlier:

1. Join your child until she is no longer isming, and she looks at you (more than just a one-second glance). Note: You can skip this step only if your child is already interacting with you and not isming at all.

2. Playfully invite your child to participate in an activity or game based upon something that she likes (as we've discussed).

3. **Beginner's version:** *If and only if* your child willingly gets involved in your game, keep that game going as long as possible. For example, if she loves to be tickled or enjoys talking about the planets, simply participate in this activity (with great enthusiasm!) for as long as your child stays interested. Just having your child engage in that game for increasing amounts of time will stretch your child's interactive attention span—and thus her ability to interact with others.

   Advanced option: *If and only if* your child willingly gets involved in your game, add one thing. For example, if your child loves chase games, and you successfully get her to play chase with you, then try adding one thing, such as: you keep "running out of gas," and she has to keep saying "chase" to get you to chase her.

FOUR

Creativity: How to Stay Fresh and Creative When Coming Up with Games and Activities for Your Child

One aspect of The Son-Rise Program that makes it unique and fulfilling—but also scary for some people—is that it utilizes the creativity of the people working with your child (including you!). For this reason, it is important to spend some time really focusing on how to be (and stay) creative. Once you have the tools provided in this chapter, you can be a never-ending generator of ideas.

WHY COMING UP WITH GAMES AND ACTIVITIES CAN FEEL STRESSFUL

Okay, so before we go any further, we need to address the elephant in the room. We can talk about motivation all day, but none of it will matter if you don't use it. And you're not going to use it if you're nervous and stressed about using it. If you are like every other parent I've ever worked with, you may be saying to yourself: *This strategy sounds great on paper, and it may* be *great for creative types, but I'm just not creative like that. I can't just come up with ideas. And, even when I come up with something good, I quickly run out of ideas after that.*

The very first thing you need to know is that *having these thoughts is completely normal.* It means absolutely nothing about you as a parent. It doesn't mean that you're not creative, and it doesn't mean that you can't do this—or even that it will be hard for you. All it means is that you have an inaccurate idea of what creativity is and how to tap into it.

If you sit down right now and try to push out ten great game ideas for your child based upon his or her motivations, it's going to be rough sailing. The first reason for this is your attitude about yourself. Having a perspective that you aren't creative enough—or "whatever" enough—may be normal (as in "usual"), but it isn't natural (as in "a necessary part of the human condition").

STOP STEPPING ON YOUR CREATIVITY

Every time you start thinking that you aren't creative, you need to pause. Remind yourself that you are just telling yourself this based on an inaccurate idea of what creativity is. You are absolutely, without question, creative. I'm not telling you this as some rah-rah motivational speech. I'm saying this because every person is creative. I have not worked with a single parent who isn't. The human mind is inherently creative. Saying you're not is like saying you don't have a brain, and since you're alive and reading this, I'm going to go out on a limb and say that you do, in fact, have a brain.

Now, you may have met people whom you feel are much more creative than you. What you need to know is that these people aren't more creative than you; they just don't step on their creativity.

We step on our creativity in three key ways.

1. **We tell ourselves that we aren't creative.**
This kills any chance at creativity that we may have. Contrary to the cultural stereotype of the depressed or angry creative artist, you need your brain to be loose, relaxed, and upbeat to have a free flow of ideas. So you need to make a promise to yourself that you will cease the self-condemnation.

2. We censor our ideas.

Most of us wait for (and write down) only the "good" ideas. This will stifle your ability to generate ideas. You have to vomit up ideas. I'm serious! Come up with as many as you can, as fast as you can. You're going for quantity.

Have your list of your child's interests matched with goals, and then come up with as many games as possible that contain one from each. If that seems hard, slow down. Begin by looking at a list of your child's motivations. For each one, come up with as many games or activities as you can.

If you catch yourself starting to judge an idea, you want to tell yourself that your goal is to come up with lots of "bad" ideas. "Bad" ideas are terrific! Many of my best ideas began as ideas I could have originally called "bad."

For instance, I love coming up with titles and names for things. I often do this with respect to the courses we offer at the Autism Treatment Center of America. Several of the titles and subtitles of our courses have come from my idea-generation sessions. All I do is sit at my desk, relax, get myself revved up about the task at hand, and then just type out as many titles as I can think of as fast as I can. I have tried, in the past, only typing out the "good" ones. An hour later, I have one or two titles, and they aren't even that good. When I just spit out ideas, actively welcoming potential "bad" ones, I have a gigantic list after half an hour.

Whatever you do, don't censor your ideas. If you have a copious list of ideas, go back through your list, working through each of your ideas one at a time to flesh them out and add some details of your game or activity. If, at that point, some of your ideas seem totally unworkable to you, feel free to ditch them. But don't discard any of your ideas until *after* you've come up with a long list.

3. We insist on perfection.

We tell ourselves that our ideas *have to* work with our kids. We hobble our ideas ahead of time by coming up with all of the reasons why they might not work, why our children might not go with them. In addition, we crush countless ideas after we try them because our children weren't immediately interested.

Unless you are a mind reader, there is no way on earth that you will come up with and attempt only ideas that work the first time or immediately catch your child's interest. Some of your ideas will work brilliantly the very first time, but a whole bunch of others won't. Do you know how many times I've come up with a game, introduced it to a child I was working with, and promptly saw that game flop? Many, many times. When this happens, I just say to myself: *Well, that certainly didn't work. I'll try something different next time, and maybe I'll fiddle with this game some more and try it again next time, next month, etc.*

Take the notion that your idea has to be perfect and has to work, and chuck it out the window. You will feel so liberated, and, more importantly, you won't hamstring your creativity. You'll need that creativity to be maximally helpful to your child.

CREATIVITY TECHNIQUE: ADD ONE THING

We've talked about what *not* to do when creating games and activities that capitalize on your child's motivation. So what do you do?

First, let's talk about a straightforward game-creation technique that I actually learned from my older sister Bryn (Executive Director of the Autism Treatment Center of America).

Bryn often teaches parents a technique that can be summed up in these three words: add one thing.

Imagine that you are endeavoring to come up with a language-building game that involves chasing, since you know your child likes to chase or be chased. Rather than trying to think of all the ways that you could possibly change or expand chasing to help generate more language from your child, you simply add one thing. It could be that he must say the word "chase" every so often to keep you running. It could be that you suddenly freeze every so often, and he has to tag you or say "go" to get you going again. It could be that you chase in slow motion—or only by hopping on one foot. If your child has more sophisticated language, it could be that you freeze every so often, and he has to answer a question to get you going again.

When you begin trying this technique, make sure that you stick to adding just *one* thing—not two or three. Start with the absolute *simplest* thing you can think of. You can:

- Speed things up
- Slow things down
- Skip a turn
- Do something silly
- Use only high voices
- Add one additional step
- Skip a step
- Change one of the game's rules
- Add one request or challenge

The Story of Charles

The "add one thing" technique also works with much more complex games. I recently worked with a nine-year-old boy in England named Charles who was very verbal. He loved history, especially imagining different times (the 1920s, the 1800s) and how things were different then. I was at Charles's house, doing something called an outreach, which is when a Son-Rise Program teacher or child facilitator spends a couple of days in a family's house helping them implement their program. If a family has an outreach with a teacher, as was the case when Charles's family had me, the teacher observes the parents working with their child and gives them pointers and feedback. The teacher also gives feedback to others who work with the child—and helps the parents to most effectively train them. Of course, the teacher will also answer any questions and deal with any issues that come up. We have a host of staff who perform these outreaches, though my own schedule doesn't allow me to do them very often anymore. What I do really enjoy about doing outreaches is the segment of time I get to spend working directly with the child.

In Charles's case, I had planned a game based on his interest in historical times. In our game, we would use a time machine. We would enter the time machine, I would bounce him around a lot as we traveled through time, and then we would step out and have a short adventure in whatever time we were in. I had planned this out in advance, but something happened that I wasn't prepared for.

This was my very first time with Charles, so I had planned the game with the goals of building trust with him and getting him to interact with me as long as I could. However, our game succeeded beyond even what I had planned for. Charles completely engaged in every aspect of the game, showing no signs whatsoever of tiring of our interaction together. So I realized that I had some room to challenge Charles more.

I knew that Charles had no deficits in language; his main challenges were being flexible in his games and allowing them to change based upon what another person wanted. Charles liked his games and activities to go a particular way, and he was not usually amenable to deviations instigated by others. This may sound trifling to those of you who have children just learning to speak, but this kind of difficulty with flexibility has far-reaching consequences for any child's ability to make friends or get through the school day successfully. (More on this in Chapter 9.)

I had only a few seconds to decide how I could challenge Charles in this way, since we were right in the midst of our game. I certainly did not have the time to sit down and come up with any kind of intricate plan. So I fell back onto the idea of changing one thing. Every time we reentered the time machine to go to a particular year, I would ask Charles one question. The question was: What is one activity that you like to do with your friends that we cannot do in the year we're going to? (You will understand in the next chapter why I chose a question about something he liked to do with others as opposed to simply having him answer a factual question about the year to which we were traveling.)

Keep in mind that I left everything else about the game the same—I only changed this one aspect. At first, even this one change proved challenging for Charles. He wanted to go to the next historical time immediately. Over time, as I stuck with this one change, he got better and better at it, becoming more patient and more flexible.

Later that day, when one of his facilitators arrived, he ran up to her, jumping up and down and saying excitedly, "Raun and I had a great time! We built a time machine and traveled to the past and the future!" And I probably had an even better time than he did.

CREATIVITY TECHNIQUE: ANYTHING CAN BE ANYTHING

The other creativity-boosting game or activity generation technique I find very helpful is this: anything can be anything. Sounds strange, but all it means is that any object in the room can be any object you want—any object that suits your purpose.

The BBC did a documentary following a family through The Son-Rise Program several years back. (Contact the Autism Treatment Center of America if you would like us to send you a DVD of this documentary. It is quite incredible and very moving.) There is one funny scene in which Bryn is working with the mom, helping her be more creative in coming up with games to play with her son. Bryn takes out a water bottle and says to the mom, "So, what could this be?" And the mom, with total sincerity says, "Something to drink out of?"

What makes this funny to watch is how this mom—at first—does what we are all trained to do, and that is to take the world exactly as it is. If someone tells you this is a water bottle, then, by gosh, that's what it is. But as the scene in the documentary continues, Bryn shows this mom how effortless it can be to think up scores of other objects that the bottle can be: a hairbrush, a trumpet, a rocket ship, an earring, a telescope, a telephone, etc. Soon this very sweet mom is creating with the best of them.

When you are coming up with a game or activity to do with your child, keep in mind the anything-can-be-anything idea. You may even want to practice with a few items ahead of time. For instance, take a water bottle, a pen, a ball, and a kitchen pot, and spend fifteen minutes thinking up ten other objects that each of these items could be.

One of the reasons that my parents were able to develop The Son-Rise Program and come up with ideas every day to help me was because they did nothing to hold themselves back from being creative and they did everything they could to foster their creativity. To this day, they remain among the most visibly creative people I know—not because they were born with creative brains, but rather because they have proactively chosen attitudes and perspectives that precipitate creativity. (We'll talk more about the importance of attitudes and perspectives in Chapter 17.)

In fact, they frequently practiced what most people might call "trial and error." When something didn't work, they didn't see it as a failure. Rather, they saw it as a fantastic opportunity to gather useful information about what did and did not work. So, really, it wasn't "trial and *error*." It was "trial and *info*."

ACTIVITY TIME!

Now is the perfect time to start flexing your creativity muscles—by using the anything-can-be-anything idea. Table 3 names four common household objects. Below each object, write down seven things that these objects might be in pretend play with your child. The only rule is that none of the seven things can relate to the original object. (For instance, you can't write down "canteen" under the object "water bottle" or "cooking utensil" under the object "frying pan.")

Frying Pan	Pillow	Ruler	Water Bottle
1)			
2)			
3)			
4)			
5)			
6)			
7)			

Table 3

ONLINE RESOURCES

For some assistance with the principles of this chapter, please go to www.autismbreakthrough.com/chapter4. Jump in, Dr. Creative!

STARTING POINT

Practice the anything-can-be-anything idea during an everyday activity with your child. Next time you are eating dinner with your child, take the spoon and make it an airplane. Take a frying pan and use it as a drum. Take your child's blanket, put it on the floor, and pretend it's a flying carpet.

Engaging in this practice will flex your creativity muscles and limber up your brain, which is crucial for developing effective motivation-based activities. On top of that, you will have more fun with your child!

FIVE

Socialization: The Son-Rise Program Developmental Model

MOST OF THE time, your child is being taught the *least* helpful things.

There is a national obsession (actually, it's worldwide) with teaching academic subjects to children on the autism spectrum. Teaching academics may sound like a good idea, but it really doesn't serve our children. Bear with me, and you'll see why.

The Story of Kwan

I sat in Kwan's house, observing his program. It was the first time I'd ever worked with his family, who had recently seen one of my lectures but had not yet been to the ATCA for a Start-Up course. They were running what would be considered by most to be an excellent in-home applied behavior analysis (ABA) program. (For those of you unfamiliar with ABA, see Appendix 2.)

Kwan was running back and forth in the kitchen when his lead ABA therapist arrived. Kwan ignored her and kept running back and forth. She stood in front of him (so that he had to stop momentarily) and put her hand a few inches in front of his face—and said "check schedule." In her hand was a Picture Exchange Communication System (PECS) card with a picture I couldn't make out.

Kwan immediately stopped running, walked over to his designated seat at his worktable, and sat down. His therapist sat down across from him and quickly pulled out some large flash cards. She turned to Kwan and said, "Show me you're ready."

He sat up and put his hands palms down on the table.

"Good boy," the therapist said approvingly.

She then flipped the cards over. Each card was a different color. There was a red, a green, and a blue card. "Kwan, point to the blue card."

He pointed to the blue card.

"Good boy, Kwan," she said, giving him a toy he liked. "Break time, Kwan. Two minutes."

Kwan played with his toy.

Two minutes later: "Okay, Kwan, show me you're ready."

Kwan sat up and put his hands palms down on the table.

The therapist showed Kwan three more cards, each with a different number. "Kwan, point to the number two."

Kwan pointed to the number two.

"Good boy, Kwan."

This continued for two hours.

This was among the most successful ABA sessions I had seen. I had, in the past, witnessed kids scream, hit, bite themselves, or completely tune out during these types of sessions. But Kwan had been completely trained into submission. And I could absolutely understand why these sessions—including their "successful" results—would be attractive to his parents and therapists. (At the same time, I knew his parents felt that something was missing; otherwise they wouldn't have attended my lecture, and they wouldn't have arranged for me to come to their home.)

Kwan was obedient, and he knew his numbers, colors, and the names of household objects.

Also:

Kwan had no friends.

Kwan could not play a game with another person.

Kwan displayed no interest in other people.

Kwan had very limited language.

Kwan had almost no eye contact.

Kwan did not engage in imaginative play.

Kwan did not laugh at jokes—or know what a joke was.

When left to his own devices, Kwan would ism for hours.

Kwan, like all children and adults with autism, had a social-relational disorder. His difficulties were social and interpersonal, not academic. And no matter how many colors he could name, no matter how far he progressed in math, with his current set of skills Kwan was not going to become social or interact successfully.

Is it bad that Kwan learned his colors and his numbers? Of course not. It's just beside the point.

Kwan's parents wanted more for him, and they set up a Son-Rise Program to help him in the areas where he most needed help. His journey, filled with many changes and successes, really inspired me, especially when I returned a couple of years later (I had been there a couple of times in the interim) and saw Kwan.

As I approached his house, I heard him open a window and call out to me, "Hi, Raun, did you come to play with me?"

When I shouted out a yes in reply, he waited for me at the door, took my hand, and escorted me into his playroom to play.

THE PROBLEM WITH MATH (AND OTHER ACADEMIC SUBJECTS)

If Chapter 3 focused on *how* to teach, this chapter zeroes in on *what* to teach.

There are reasons schools and therapists are preoccupied with teaching academics to children on the spectrum. First, academics are what schools are built to teach. Everything about a school is designed to teach math, reading, science, etc. This is by no means a criticism of schools. This is what schools are *supposed* to do.

Also, for both schools and therapists, academics are the low-hanging fruit. They are the easiest areas in which to generate (and measure) improvement. For a parent, being able to see (and easily explain to others) that their son or daughter with autism can name his or her colors, write his or her name, or count (or, on the other end, that their child with Asperger's syndrome can read Shakespeare or do calculus) provides a kind of tangible evidence that progress is being made.

So I truly, sincerely understand the appeal of teaching academics.

But teaching academic subjects to children on the spectrum just isn't going to affect what really matters. Not yet.

Autism isn't a math disorder. It isn't a color-naming disorder. And it isn't a reading disorder. It's a social, relational, interpersonal, interactional disorder. I know we've discussed this point at length, but it simply cannot be overemphasized.

When you are lying in bed awake at night, thinking and praying about your child's future, do you pray that one day your child will be at grade level in math? Do you fervently look forward to the day when your child will be able to recite the periodic table of elements?

Or do you wish and pray that one day your child will have a best friend? That your daughter will say "I love you" and really mean it? That your son will have a romantic partner? That your child will grow up to live a happy, independent, and fulfilling life? Or even that he will argue with you about using your car to go out with his or her friends? (I had one mom say that she dreamed that one day her son would complain to her about his taxes.)

We need to seriously think about what is going to make our children's lives fulfilling, satisfying, rich, and meaningful to them. Academics just aren't part of that equation. No matter how incredible your child gets at academic subjects, it will not give her the tools she needs to relate to people, laugh at a joke, make friends, and enjoy others.

Am I saying that academics are pointless or useless? Absolutely not. They are valuable. But they are only valuable to someone who can function in the world, and only social enjoyment, connection, and participation can make that happen. In fact, social-relational skills are essential even to succeed at the overall experience of school. Your child needs to be able to relate to the teacher and to other students and have the ability to cope with all of the activities, noises, room switches, and changes of the school day. Excelling at academic subjects is, ironically, not nearly as important.

To be totally clear, I am in no way against academics. My own academic life and attendance at an Ivy League university bears witness to the fact that I hugely value education and academics. But, with our children, focusing on academics first is utterly irrelevant to their success until they can connect with other people and the world at large. It is putting the cart before the horse.

In The Son-Rise Program, we have taught an enormous number of children how to read, write, and do math. But we have taught kids these subjects *after* we have gotten them to the point where they can interact and relate really well to people. When a child has crossed the bridge from his world to ours, then, by all means, let's work on academics.

Instead of seeing me as simply a skill-deficient, behaviorally challenged little boy, my parents saw what was *really* going on. They understood, way back in 1974, that I wasn't just a child missing skills; I was a child missing *social* skills. In seeing this, they were not only decades ahead of their time, but they were the *only* people at that time to really "get" autism. And so, for three and a half years, my parents focused single-mindedly on my social development.

And ever since my recovery from autism, the social, interpersonal arena has come the most easily to me. It is also the arena in which I get the most satisfaction and feel the most fulfilled. In high school, I did about equally well in all subjects, ranging from math to English, science to Spanish. So I could easily have chosen a profession in the sciences, mathematics, or computer sciences. I chose an extremely social and interpersonal profession because that is what I found most rewarding.

My parents, who founded and still teach extensively at the ATCA, are, to this day, very well-attuned to people's social and emotional states. People in our courses are often startled at the observations my parents make about them before they have even said anything.

You may wonder, if my parents worked so intensively with me on my social development, what happened academically when I entered school? Well, at first, in the very early days, I *was* missing academic skills. So my parents worked with me (post-autism) and caught me up. That was the easiest part of the process—the tutoring of a neurotypical child (me!) who was totally connected and completely integrated in their world.

If, years from now, your biggest complaint is that your child is now fully connected and social but is behind in math, what a great problem to have!

The Story of Callum

Callum was a little boy from Ireland with autism who was nonverbal and deeply enveloped in his own world. He would not relate to or interact with people for more than a few minutes at a time. Two and half years after implementing their Son-Rise Program, Callum was successfully attending a mainstream school. He was sweet and affectionate. After seeing Callum's swift and remarkable progress, the government-appointed specialist who had initially told Callum's parents not to do The Son-Rise Program became an enthusiastic proponent, telling other parents that The Son-Rise Program was the only thing she had seen that actually worked.

One day, well into Callum's program, he and his parents were walking in a local park with a pond. He was having a terrific time, laughing, feeding the ducks in the pond, enjoying himself. His parents, too, were having a magnificent time because Callum seemed so at ease, so much like the totally engaged child they had hoped for him one day to become.

Then Callum noticed a group of kids at the other end of the park. His parents watched with anticipation and some nervousness as their son casually approached them. *How would he do? Would he connect easily with the other kids. Would they notice anything different about him?* After all, this was what they had worked so hard for. This very moment.

Callum joined the group of kids and began talking to them. They responded. He became part of the group. A simple occurrence that a parent of a neurotypical child might not even notice. A "normal" event. But, for this mother and father, it was as if the heavens had opened up. They had been assured that nothing like this could ever occur for their little boy. They had worked tirelessly in their Son-Rise Program to put their son on a different trajectory, and now they were seeing the spectacular fruits of their labor and their love. It was a day they would never forget.

No amount of math, reading, or science would have led Callum to that day. Only social focus and human interaction can give your child a day like that.

OVERCOMING VERSUS COMPENSATING

Let's return to a point we touched on a few pages ago. Remember when I said that academic subjects were the low-hanging fruit? Why is this?

When we work with a child or adult on academic subjects, we are working on the nonautistic part of the brain—the part that is, essentially, working. (If it isn't working, that is often because the child is so enveloped in her world that her intelligence is not visible.)

The nonautistic part of the brain is also at work during tasks such as completing a puzzle, saying "thank you," learning the daily schedule, etc. All of these areas are attractive teaching opportunities for most parents and teachers because they are the easiest to teach, and they fulfill a basic goal that most of us have with our kids: compensation.

Compensation is the idea that since our children are so impaired in social and relational areas, we need to help them compensate for their deficits by teaching them to get really good at using the parts of their brains they *can* use. This is the same thinking, for instance, that goes into teaching someone who has lost an arm to get really good at using his one remaining arm. And, in the case of someone with one arm, this makes complete sense, since his arm will never grow back.

Unfortunately, this same thinking does *not* make sense with our kids, unless you are of the opinion (and many are) that our children have no possibility to ever grow and progress in the area of social and relational development. Focusing on helping our children to compensate causes us to miss the boat on the real key: overcoming.

Why not spend our time and energy helping our children to *overcome* their biggest deficits (socialization) instead of settling for helping them merely *compensate* by learning crutch skills? Why not shoot for the gold instead of forfeiting? This way, even if we fall far short of the gold, we have still helped our children to move forward in an area in which any progress at all will have immeasurable long-term benefits for them.

Helping our children to overcome their challenges will always yield more satisfying results than helping our kids to compensate for them.

THE IMPORTANCE OF WORKING THE WEAK MUSCLE

Suppose, for a moment, that I had been born with a condition that caused the weakening of the muscles in my legs, such that I could not walk. Suppose, also, that you had been hired as my physical therapist. How would you try to help me?

One strategy you could employ is to spend the next year working intensively with me on building my arm muscles. You could argue that, after all, my arms are perfectly healthy and capable of building muscle. You could point out all the benefits of having very strong arms—how it will help me get around, since I can't do much with my legs. Certainly, an argument can be made for this approach.

On the other hand, you might consider that, no matter how much time you spend building up my arms, no matter how strong you help my arms to get, I will never, ever walk. So you might choose a completely different approach, based upon this fact: the only way on earth that I will ever have a chance to walk is if you help me build up my leg muscles. There's simply no other way that walking is possible. No amount of arm strength will do it.

This analogy illustrates the principle of working the weak muscle. This strategy is a very powerful one, although it takes more work in the short term. In the long term, working the weak muscle pays off in a huge way. It is appealing to most people to work the strong muscle, and I understand why. We can already see what success looks like, and we can see immediate gain.

But when we work the strong muscle, we are always held back by the limits of the weak muscle. Strong arms will never lead to walking or running if our legs are weak.

When we work the *weak* muscles, it might feel challenging at first, but, in the long term, the sky is the limit. There is certainly no harm in working the strong muscles. But, until we work the weak muscle, its limitations will always constrain us.

How does this relate to your child? Your child's "weak muscle" is his socialization muscle. Your child's "strong muscles" (or potentially strong muscles) are his aptitude for memorizing movie lines, names of colors, how to introduce himself, words, daily schedules, directions, as well as possible talents in areas such as math, mechanics, or drawing. In simpler form, these "strong muscles" may manifest as stacking blocks perfectly, balancing objects with precision, or lining up toys in exactly the same order over and over.

It is wonderful that your child has these strong muscles, and there is nothing wrong with your child eventually having the opportunity to pursue these areas (or even in your using one of these areas in a game as a motivation). It's just that, first, you're going to want to help your child to work her weak muscle.

Working the weak muscle opens the door to a satisfying, independent, and emotionally fulfilling life for your child. Also, even if your child ends up wanting to be a mathematician, without making that weak muscle stronger, it's going to be extremely difficult to get there. Even day-to-day family events, such has having dinner together, going to the store or a park, playing a game, going to the doctor, or having an outing together all require basic socialization, coping, and flexibility. When it comes to our special and unique children, we never want to stop working the weak muscle.

SOCIAL GOALS *BEFORE* ACADEMIC GOALS

Not social goals *instead of* academic goals but social goals *before* academic goals. Waaaay before. Don't worry, I'm not going to argue this point again. What I *am* going to do is to give you some quick examples of what "social goals before academic goals" means in practice.

There are all sorts of times when you—or a teacher or

therapist—have opportunities to teach or work on something with your child. Sometimes it will be during a formal game or activity, and sometimes it will be during day-to-day events around the house. Most of us use these opportunities to challenge our children by, for instance, asking them questions such as:

- "How many are there?"
- "What's that called?"
- "What color is that?"
- "Tell him your name."
- "What do you say?"
- "Can you put that away for Mommy?"
- "What does that sign say?"
- "Can you tell her how old you are?"
- "What's the answer to that?"
- "Point to your nose."
- "Can you read that word for Daddy?"
- "What's that a picture of?"
- "What's his name?"
- "What animal is that?"
- "What sound does that animal make?"

None of these questions are bad or detrimental. They are just, as I mentioned before, beside the point. These aren't questions you need to avoid like the plague. But here is a list of questions or requests that are much more helpful to emphasize if you want your child to develop socially:

- "Which one do you want to show your friend Amy?"
- "Help me stand up so we can finish the fort!"
- "Grab the picture that shows all of your friends so we can write their names down for your birthday party."
- "What's your favorite . . . ?"
- "Which one does Daddy like?"
- "Who do you think . . . ?"
- "Which face should I make—serious or silly?"
- "When I make this face, do you think I feel happy or sad?"
- "I love when you look at me! Give me one more look, you silly goose!"
- "I love giving you this ride, but I'm so tired! Look at me so I can keep going!"

The above are all overtly social in nature. Instead of quizzing our kids on factual or academic questions, we can ask questions or make requests that challenge our children to think socially instead. All of the questions in the second list ask children to think about their friends (or therapists or family members), to look at you, to think about and help you, to think about other people's likes and desires, and to access their own personal opinions.

And thus we arrive at the perfect juncture to introduce a model for your child's development that is incredibly helpful and extraordinarily comprehensive.

THE SON-RISE PROGRAM DEVELOPMENTAL MODEL

There is no shortage in this world of developmental models upon which to measure your child. So we figured: *Well, there must be a simple social developmental model used in the area of autism that measures children's and adults' social functioning. We'll just use one of those models to measure our kids.*

We were wrong.

So we created our own. And it's pretty awesome.

This social developmental model was originally created by Bryn and William Hogan and then further developed by both of them plus Kate Wilde (Director of The Son-Rise Program), my parents, me, and, to some degree, our other staff members. It was developed over a period of years, based on decades of work with thousands of children and adults and the in-depth analysis of the development of people on the autism spectrum over long periods of time.

In the Start-Up program and our advanced courses, we delve into this model, discussing such areas as:

- How to pinpoint exactly what stage of development your child is at in four fundamental social areas
- How to track your child's social development over time
- Goal-setting
- What activities to use to reach these goals
- Perspectives to teach and model to your child
- The three to five components of each area of development
- How to tell whether a skill is not yet acquired, emerging, or acquired

It will seriously overload you if I even *try* to get into all of this here. If you really want to see the thirty-page layout of The Son-Rise Program Developmental Model, there is a link to it on this chapter's Web page. (but I still don't recommend downloading it yet).

Please, pretty please, believe me when I tell you: it will actually serve you and your child better if we start small and basic. Therefore, rather than laying out the entire model for you (which would really comprise a book in and of itself), I'm going to lay out just the vital areas for you to begin to focus on with your child.

THE FOUR FUNDAMENTALS OF SOCIALIZATION

There are four absolutely critical areas (each consisting of five stages of development) that you want to focus on if you are interested in your child's social development and progression through autism:

1. Eye contact and nonverbal communication
2. Verbal communication
3. Interactive attention span
4. Flexibility

Figure 1 shows where the four fundamentals fit into the overall blueprint of the model.

This diagram, and the ideas that underpin it, set up the framework of the next four chapters. We'll examine these fundamentals and explore techniques and strategies for helping your child move forward with each of them.

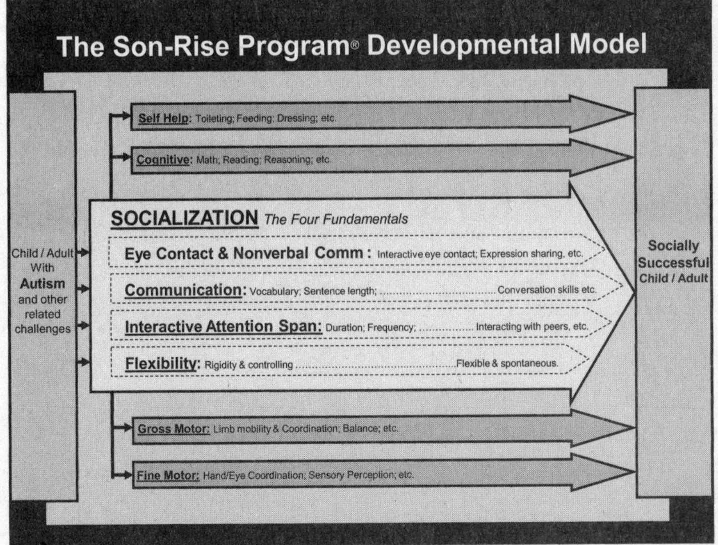

Figure 1

ONLINE RESOURCES

For more in-depth help with the principles and techniques of this chapter, please go to www.autismbreakthrough.com/chapter5. Enjoy delving into the model!

STARTING POINT

Guess what! There is no immediate action to take with your child from this chapter. Trust me: the next four chapters will keep you plenty busy! For now, just take a few moments and picture your child being more socially engaged and adept. What would that look like? What is one thing your child would be doing?

Now, let's make it happen.

SIX

Fundamental 1: Eye Contact and Nonverbal Communication

Eye contact is a very basic way that human beings connect with one another. It is also one of the most conspicuous traits missing in our children. Whether your child is a nonverbal three-year-old diagnosed with severe autism or a seventeen-year-old with Asperger's syndrome, eye contact is very likely something your son or daughter struggles with.

This makes total sense, given that autism is a social-relational disorder and eye contact is one of the most powerful ways to bond interpersonally. The largest concern with low eye contact is the correspondingly low social connection that goes with it. If you want your child to progress in the area of socialization, improving eye contact is a must.

However, the limited number of behavioral programs that work on eye contact tend to do so, not surprisingly, in a behavioral way. These approaches usually train children to give eye contact as a behavior. For example, "Look at me. Look at me. Look at me if you want to be allowed to play with the toy." Since the main point of eye contact is human connection, we want our children to look because they *want* to. This entails making eye contact fun, easy, and very celebrated.

"THE MORE THEY LOOK, THE MORE THEY LEARN"

This is a saying that I picked up from my sister Bryn. What it articulates is the direct correlation between how much our children look and how much they learn, take in, and develop. Looking helps our children to speak because they are looking at people's faces as they are speaking. It enables them to take in information because they are looking at the people talking to them. It improves their interactive attention span because they are looking at what we are doing and are thus "plugged in." It helps them to develop facial expression because they are looking at our faces. And it paves the way for learning to read others' facial and nonverbal expressions—one of the most socially limiting deficits our children face.

NONVERBAL COMMUNICATION IN GENERAL

While the first of the four fundamentals notes eye contact as a major priority, it also includes all other types of nonverbal communication: making gestures, reading the gestures of others, being more expressive facially, reading others' expressions, prosody—having inflection in one's voice and reading the voice inflections of others.

Nonverbal communication rarely gets sustained focus. Verbal communication tends to get the lion's share of attention. And while verbal communication is extremely important (it is, after all, the second fundamental), the vast majority of interpersonal communication takes place nonverbally.

Admittedly, nonverbal communication can be a bit more complex to notice and to work on with your child. The Son-Rise

Program Developmental Model tracks and measures nonverbal communication and includes goals and activities to develop this area. For now, though, it will be best for you to simply model nonverbal communication by exaggerating all of your own facial expressions, gestures, and voice inflections—while focusing your teaching efforts and goals around eye contact.

STRATEGIES

You want to take every opportunity to request eye contact. There are several strategies to do this.

1. **Ask for it directly**. Examples: "I love when you look at me! Give me one more look, you silly goose!" or "I love giving you this ride, but I'm so tired! Look at me so I can keep going!"
2. **Ask for it indirectly**. For instance, "Who are you talking to, sweetie? I'm not sure because you're not looking at me." Or, simply point to your eyes.
3. **Position for eye contact.** You want to make it as easy as possible for your child to look at you with the least amount of effort. This entails keeping your face at his eye level as much as possible (without being in his face). If your child is playing on the floor, you want to get down on the floor and sit or lie with your face as low as possible so he doesn't have to twist his head all the way up to look at you. You want him to be able to easily flick you a glance. If your child is staring at something off to his left, you can get your face down low next to what he is staring at. Again, you don't want to be right in your child's face. In fact, distance can often be more helpful

here. If you create a bit of physical distance between you and your child, it will actually be *easier* for him to look at you because he will have to move his head and eyes less.

4. When you offer something to your child that she wants, **hold it up next to your eyes.** This can apply to food, a toy, a ball, a bracelet—whatever. As you are doing this you can ask, "Is this what you want?" Or you can simply say, "Here's your ball!" You can even say nothing and simply hold the item up by your eyes with an excited expression on your face.
5. **Celebrate eye contact** whenever you get it from your child. This might feel funny at first, but it is very important. Every single time you get eye contact, thank your child or cheer for your child. (Of course, you will want to make this celebration appropriate to your child's age and maturity level, and you will want to be aware of not shouting if your child has sensitive hearing.) We will talk more about celebration overall in Chapter 11.

ACTIVITY TIME!

Pick a fifteen-minute block of time during the day or evening when you have one-on-one time with your child. This can be when you give her a bath, when you put her to bed, when you read her a story, during a meal, or simply when you are playing or hanging out with her.

Before you begin your session, note down in Table 4 how many times you think your child will look at you—right at your eyes or face—during this fifteen-minute period. *It does not matter in the least if you are right—or even if you are remotely close.* This is just so you can begin to see the difference between your guess and reality.

Just before you begin, make sure you have a pen and paper. During the fifteen-minute time, you are going to make a tick mark on your paper every time your child looks at your face or eyes. You don't have to be perfect. Don't stress about it. You are just trying to get a ballpark figure.

After the fifteen minutes are over, count up your tick marks, and write that number in the appropriate box in Table 4.

You can use this table as often as you like. It is designed to get you started so that you can begin to pay attention to roughly how much eye contact you're getting. (You may be surprised by how much less eye contact you are getting than you originally guessed.)

The good news: following the principles in this book can lead to exceptional gains in this area.

	Your Guess in Advance	The Actual Number
Number of Looks		

Table 4

ONLINE RESOURCES

For more in-depth help with the principles and techniques of this chapter, please go to www.autismbreakthrough.com/chapter6. Happy exploring!

STARTING POINT

Cheer and celebrate any eye contact that you get. This is the most important beginning principle for increasing voluntary eye contact. Have fun!

SEVEN

Fundamental 2: Verbal Communication

UNLESS YOUR CHILD is highly verbal, you are probably very aware of your child's speech deficits—and very motivated to help your child overcome them. Before we get into specific language-building strategies, though, it is vital to discuss the necessary precursor to all speech in children with autism.

BELIEVING THAT YOUR CHILD CAN SPEAK

I want to talk for a moment to those of you who have a child who has not spoken at all yet. A common trap that people fall into is to start believing—either because they've been told or because they've been waiting a long time to hear their child speak—that their child *can't* speak.

Your child's current lack of speech tells you absolutely *nothing* about his future speech. It tells you nothing about his potential to speak. It only tells you what is happening right *now.*

The perspective you want to hold is not: *My child can't speak.* Rather it is: *My child hasn't spoken yet.* And, furthermore: *My child can do this!*

As I said about creativity earlier, I'm not making these statements as part of some rah-rah motivational speech. Believing that your child can (or cannot) speak has a practical impact on two things: whether your child speaks and whether you hear your child speak when he does.

Let's discuss that last bit for a moment. We have a course

called The Son-Rise Program Intensive where parents come to the ATCA with their child. The family stays in their own private apartment, which includes a state-of-the-art autism-friendly playroom; there our child facilitators work one-on-one with each child for five days. At the same time, our teachers work one-on-one with the parents in an individualized program that is customized around each family's needs and concerns.

I'm telling you all of this because of something fascinating that we've seen multiple times in the Intensive program. We've had numerous instances where a child will speak for the very first time during this program. One of the walls of the child's playroom is made of one-way glass, on the other side of which is an observation room where parents can sit and observe what we are doing with their child whenever they like. (As a side note, I would counsel that you beware of any program or school where they don't permit you, as the parent, to observe what is happening with your child.)

Not surprisingly, when parents witness their child speak for the first time, they often have a huge emotional reaction. Some cry, some clap, some stand up and cheer, some turn around and hug one of us on staff if we are in the observation room with them. Participating in such an experience is indescribably beautiful.

However, in some cases, we see no reaction at all. This might sound strange to you. If your child has not yet spoken, you're probably thinking that you would sprout wings and fly if you heard your child speak, right? So why would any parent not react?

The answer is simple. Every parent reacts with joy, excitement, gratitude, and great emotion the first time their child speaks. *Unless they don't hear it.* You read that right. We have had parents with no hearing problems whatsoever who are sitting in the observation room watching their child speak for the very first time—and they neither see nor hear it.

When this occurs, it is because these parents have been told many, many times that their child cannot speak, and, eventually, they believed it. We have had scenarios where we have had to play back video footage of a child speaking seven or eight times before the parents watching could hear their child speaking.

Think about this: if you cannot hear when your child speaks, you cannot react to it and build upon it.

On top of that, we find that parents, therapists, and teachers don't persevere in endeavoring to get speech when they don't believe that the child is capable of speaking. And yet, it is precisely this perseverance that is necessary for many of our children to develop language!

It is of monumental importance that you believe that your child has the capability to speak—no matter what you've been told. Just remember: my parents were given a long list of items—including speech—that they were told I would never be capable of. Instead of believing in the predictions, they believed in me.

GIVING LANGUAGE MEANING

Sometimes, in our singular effort to get our child speaking, we can become overly focused on getting our child merely to repeat words. I see parents fall into this trap in one of two ways. The first is to point to an object, name it, and then try to get the child to repeat the word just spoken. The second is to say a sentence, leave the final word blank, and attempt to get the child to say the missing word. For example, a parent might say, "It's time to go to ________," then endeavor to get his or her child to say the word "sleep."

The problem with these strategies is that, even when you are successful at getting your child to say the word, there is no real communication being taught. Your child does not know what the word means and *has no independent interest in the word being taught.*

Many parents come to the Start-Up program seeking help

with their children's language. Indeed, we have specific parts of the course devoted to verbal communication. (During those segments, parents of highly verbal children are in a separate class more appropriate for their children.) Before Charlotte attended the Start-Up program, her son James was totally nonverbal. During the week following the conclusion of that course, he said his first three words: "Dipsy" (his favorite Teletubby), "red ball" (his favorite bouncy ball), and "Tiger" (his favorite stuffed animal).

I tell you this to highlight a particular point. All three of James's first words had intrinsic meaning to him. He didn't say them because Charlotte felt that they were the most important words for her son to learn first. He said them because they referred to items that were important to *him*.

When helping your child to use language, you always want to challenge her to use words that have meaning to her. You want the words to be linked to things that she already wants or cares about. If your child likes squash (as James does), you can begin with the word "squash"—but only when you have squash handy. Then you can take a piece of squash out, get excited about it, offer it to your child, and say "squash" right as your child takes it. Next, you can offer another piece, this time inviting your child to say "squash" for you to hand it to her. I have to tell you, when James would say, "I want quash please" (he wasn't big on the *s* sound yet), I felt like I was going to keel over from cuteness overdose. (As a side note, Charlotte and I never focused on teaching James to say "please"—we had bigger fish to fry. He simply picked it up from hearing his polite mom.)

Many children like having their feet squeezed. Here, you could do the same thing as with the squash. You might enthusiastically place your hands right above your child's feet and say "squeeze." Then you give his feet a big squeeze. Next, you could offer the squeeze again, this time inviting him to say the word—and immediately responding with a huge squeeze if he does. (When James would say this, he would drop the initial *s* and say

"Queeze my feet, please," which would lead me to yet another near-death cuteness overdose.)

The point is that you want your child to be learning words that are relevant to him, not just words for words' sake.

WORDS: MAKING THEM WORTH YOUR CHILD'S WHILE

It is crucial that your child see using words as worth her while. How you respond to your child's language or attempts at language will be the chief factor in making this happen. Since you might have a child who must work extra hard (for now) to produce language, your child needs to see an immediate and powerful connection between using words and getting what she wants.

Here are five key strategies to make using language far more appetizing for your child:

1. **Move fast.** When your child uses a word, such as "ball," *run* and get it. Don't stroll. Don't walk briskly. *Run.* If you are getting something on a shelf, get it *fast*—and with great excitement. Oftentimes, we meander over to get our children what they want when they use language. Other times, we are busy and tell them "later." From now on, unless something is on fire, you want to stop the presses and move heaven and earth to get your child what he wants when he uses words. Don't worry about "spoiling" your child. Right now we want language. (If your child is crying, pulling, or tantruming to get what he wants, that's a different story. We'll go over these types of situations in Chapter 14.)
2. **Celebrate any language you get.** We will talk more about celebration overall in Chapter 11, but we don't

want to forget about its importance here. It's easy to leave this out, especially as your child speaks more. Always, always celebrate language. Celebrate words. Celebrate parts of words. Celebrate sentences. Say something like, "Thank you so much for using your words! Here you go!" (Then hand your child what she is asking for.) You can vary this so that you are celebrating in a host of different manners.

3. **Request language.** This might seem obvious, but I watch many parents give their children items when their child points, pushes, cries, etc. Since you know your child so well, you may be able to discern what he wants with these kinds of signals, as opposed to actual words. I can totally understand if you feel tempted to read and respond to all of these nonverbal signals. Next time, when you get one of these signals, pause and ask for a word. ("Oh, I know you want something. Use your words, and I'll run and get it!" or "Say 'ball,' and I'll get it right down for you!") Note: only request language when your child clearly wants something. That's when you have his engagement—and, thus, leverage.

4. **Choose useful words.** When choosing which words to ask for, pick words that are either items your child wants (nouns such as "ball," "block," "food," "tiger," "drink," etc.) or actions *you* can do that are fun (verbs such as "squeeze," "tickle," "rub," "bounce," "ride," etc.). You want to choose words that are specific for objects you can immediately give or actions you can immediately do. (Don't choose items you can't or don't want to provide or do, such as "ice cream" or "drive.")

5. **Get progressively more clueless.** As your child improves her language, you want to keep shifting what you under-

stand so she has to expand the length of her sentences in order to be understood. If your child already says single words ("ball"), start to understand only two-word phrases ("want ball" or "red ball"). If she already uses two-word phrases, work on three-word phrases, and so on. ATCA's Programs Director, William Hogan, developed the concept of the Communication Ladder to outline this process.

THE COMMUNICATION LADDER

The steps of the Communication Ladder are:

1. From crying, screaming, tantruming, pushing, etc. to partial word sounds (i.e., "ba" for "ball").
2. From partial word sounds to single words.
3. From single words to multiple-word phrases.
4. From multiple-word phrases to sentences.
5. From sentences to single exchanges. (We call these "loops." One loop would be when you make a statement or ask a question, and your child responds—or vice versa.)
6. From single loops to multiple loops.
7. From multiple loops to conversations.

Let's look at the first three steps a little more closely for those of you whose child has little or no language. The first order of business is to make your home an environment where your child cannot simply get everything for himself. Most children that we work with live in homes where most of what they want is directly accessible to them. They can open the refrigerator and get food. They can retrieve any toy that they want to play with. The problem with this situation is that there is no reason for a child who has huge difficulties with language to try to produce words when he can simply get what he wants himself. You can ask for language all day, but if your child needs only to reach for what he wants, you have an uphill journey ahead of you.

If your child has little or no language, you must be the getter of all things. Everything must be out of reach so that your child has the chance to see that if he says something, you are going to get it for him. Language has force. Language has power. Language is useful. And *you* must be the vehicle to show this to your child.

Second, make sure that, in the early stages of your child speaking, you are very responsive to parts of words, such as "ba" or "ga." Do your absolute best to discern what these sounds mean, and respond according to the steps above. Let your child get used to seeing that these partial words work to communicate. Once he is using these sounds regularly, *then* you can move to the next step in the Communication Ladder by getting more "clueless" and asking for or responding to whole words.

Third, in these early stages of language development, you will have the most leverage to challenge your child to speak when he wants something. So make sure you use every one of these instances to ask for, respond to, and wildly celebrate language. At first, you may find that your child becomes a "wanting machine," using language mainly to ask for things and give people orders. That's okay. In fact, that's wonderful! He is learning the key fundamentals of verbal communication!

When your child gets proficient and consistent at asking for (or demanding) things that he wants, then we move to the next stage.

BEYOND "I WANT"

Verbal communication is not just about using words or about vocabulary size, although these things are certainly important.

Computers can use language. But they don't have friends. So, although vocabulary size is one of the aspects of communication that is tracked in The Son-Rise Program Developmental Model, it is not, by itself, the be-all and end-all of language.

Because most people tend to focus only on numbers of words in a child's vocabulary, one of the items that gets missed is what a child is using her words *for*. In The Son-Rise Program Developmental Model, we call this the *function* of verbal communication. This area is particularly relevant to children on the autism spectrum.

The first function—or purpose—of using language is to get needs and wants met. *I want food. I want my toy. I don't want a bath.* Indeed, helping your child to clearly see that using words is the most powerful way to get what she wants is essential. The good thing about this stage is that there is a very clear connection between talking and getting an immediate want met.

We don't want to stop here, though. Once your child can reliably articulate what she wants (or doesn't want), we want to build up to more overtly social kinds of language, such as:

- Speaking to start or continue an interaction or game
- Explaining or talking about a particular aspect of an interaction or game
- Sharing a story
- Telling someone how you feel or what you like
- Finding out more about someone (what they want to do next, what they like, how they feel, etc.)
- Eventually, discussing points of view, interests, hopes, and dreams

These are the functions of language that give verbal communication its richness. We can begin to build these parts of language by making them into goals. Some sample goals:

- Saying a word to indicate what is happening, such as exclaiming "running" when he or someone else is running
- Articulating her enjoyment of something, such as saying "feels good" when you are squeezing her feet.
- Saying one feeling he has
- Explaining simple instructions of a game to you
- Sharing something that she likes to do before bed
- Telling a story of something that happened that day
- Asking you one question about yourself
- Asking you what you want

NOT TEACHING VERBAL COMMUNICATION IN A VACUUM

Often, parents, teachers, and therapists get verbal communication tunnel vision. They know the value of language, so it becomes the overriding priority. Without question, speech is very important. But, remember: autism is a social-relational disorder. Language is part of a much larger issue. If it weren't, you would have a child who looks at people, loves people, plays interactive games with people, is flexible, laughs at jokes, makes friends, and gestures emphatically and understandably to express his thoughts. In other words, you would have a nonautistic child who simply has a speech deficit.

When we teach verbal communication in a vacuum, it means that we don't teach it in the context of other types of communication. For instance, I've met children and adults on the spectrum who can speak fluently but have no eye contact, no voice inflection, no facial expression, no friends, and little interest in other people. It is not that this is bad or a failure in any way. It is wonderful that these people have come as far as they have. But they could be helped so much more if, in addition to language, someone were helping them with all of the components that go *with* language.

DON'T FORGET CLARITY

One area of language that is especially easy to overlook is clarity. Because you really know your child, you have a heightened ability to understand her. In many ways, this is a testament to your love and caring.

However, you might not realize if your child is not making herself understood to others. Being able to speak so that nonfamily members understand her is an important part of progressing through the five stages of verbal communication.

As you begin to address this challenge, I have two recommendations. The first one is to have one or two people come to your house (not at the same time) and see if they can understand what your child is saying. This will help give you a more objective picture.

The second recommendation is to "play dumb." If your child says something to you in a mumbling way, you can say something like, "Thank you, sweetie, for telling me what you want! I want to get it for you, but I couldn't understand you. Can you say it again slowly?" Then pause exactly where you are, and wait for her to try again.

There are additional ways to improve clarity, but for now the idea is to become much more aware of how clearly your child speaks (if your child speaks) and to keep encouraging more clarity.

We've talked a lot about what to do with regard to developing language. Let's highlight some very important things not to do.

TALKING TOO MUCH

One of the most common mistakes I see is for people to constantly narrate what is happening when they are with their child. "There you go bouncing the ball." "Wow, that's a big castle you're building." "I'm giving my doll a special hairdo." "Oh, look, there's a picture of two rabbits running across a field." "And there we go. I give one to you and take one for myself." There's nothing inherently wrong with any of these sentences by themselves. But I often hear parents and therapists conducting a nonstop string of these sentences. Sometimes I feel like I'm watching a narrated play.

What's the problem with narrating? When you do this, *you take up all of the verbal space.* When you take up the verbal space, *there is no room for your child to speak.*

Unless you have a fluently verbal child, it takes a lot of effort for your child to produce speech. And it takes a lot of time. You need to give your child that time. The more space (that is, silence) you give, the more opportunities your child will have to speak.

Along similar lines, don't constantly pepper your child with questions. This can also take up a lot of verbal space. In addition, it creates what your child will often perceive as pressure around language, which he may push against. (I'm not saying not to ask questions; I'm just saying not to produce a constant stream of questions.)

Fifteen years ago, when I began working with my niece Jade, I was Mr. Talkative. I asked her lots of questions. I made lots of statements. I threw out lots of suggestions.

And Jade didn't say a word.

Bryn and William observed my first session, and they told me that I was taking up all of the verbal space with my own speaking. I took in what they said, but I was secretly thinking to myself, *Aw, I'm sure I didn't talk that much.* Then they played me back a video of my session. I was flabbergasted by the sheer quantity of my talking! I cringed as I watched, wanting to shout at myself, *Just shut up for a minute!*

The next time I worked with Jade, I focused on *listening* to her. It wasn't that I never ever spoke in that session, but since I was deeply focused on being attentive to her and to anything she might say, I found that I had a lot less to say.

In that session, Jade, who was in the early stages of speech, blurted out a word every few minutes. The difference in her quantity of speech in the two sessions was astounding.

So, make sure that you leave plenty of room for your child to speak. You can do this not by trying to stifle yourself but, rather, by having a strong and ongoing intention to *listen to your child*.

USING DIFFERENT TERMS FOR THE SAME THING AT DIFFERENT TIMES

Sometimes, when offering your child food, you might say "eat." Other times, you might say "food." When offering your child a Thomas the Tank Engine toy, you might call it "Thomas" one time and "train" the next. This can make things very confusing for your child.

It is very helpful to be totally consistent with the words you use. It doesn't matter what you decide to call the big purple ball with the pictures of Shrek on it, but whatever you decide, *call it the exact same thing every time*.

This does not apply, of course, to fluent, highly verbal children where language is not their challenge. With these children, you actually want to encourage more variation. But for children just learning to speak, using the same word for the same thing every time is key.

TEACHING "MORE" AND "AGAIN"

This one's a biggie. "More" and "again" are two easy words to teach, and your child will love to use them. Why? Because, once your child learns these two magic words, she doesn't need to learn much else! Your child can get 90 percent of what she wants with these two words (or with the sign language versions of them).

You know how we talked about it being worth your child's while to speak? Well, you don't want to create a situation where your child has no earthly reason to learn and use new words. You want to teach your child to use specific words for specific things. You want her to say "ride" (not "again") when she wants another ride on your back. You want her to say "grapefruit" (not "more") when she wants another grapefruit. This is how language is built.

USING COMMUNICATION AIDS

This one might be hard to hear. You've probably been extensively schooled in using either Picture Exchange Communication System (PECS), sign language, or some variation of both. You may have put a lot of time into these aids. And maybe your child has gotten quite good at communicating with them.

The thing is, what you really want is verbal communication. The only route to verbal communication is through spoken language. If you give your child a way to communicate and get all of his needs and wants met without speaking, why is he going to put in all of the hard work it requires to speak well? After all, your child now has a way around that.

I'm not saying that it is impossible for your child to speak when you use these communication aids. But there is a dramatically reduced necessity for him to do so. And there is certainly no rush. Remember: we want verbal communication to be worth your child's while.

In the short term, ditching these aids will make it harder for your child. The only way to effectively communicate will be to use words, and, if your child was using communication aids, then, by definition, using words is difficult for him. But if he gets better at verbal communication, and does so faster, then this will be a gigantic boon to him. Only a tiny population understands PECS or sign language. But *everyone* understands the spoken word! So, every time your child gets even a little better at speaking, an entire world opens up to him.

You might be thinking: *But what about those children who are truly unable to speak? Wouldn't we want to at least give those children some way to communicate?* That is a legitimate question. In fact, we have had a few children over the years (not many) who have severe bio-physiological obstacles that seem to prevent them from speaking. In those cases, yes, we *do* use PECS or sign language.

But the real issue is who we are going to put into that category. We require a very, very large amount of convincing before we are willing to say, "Let's forget speech for now and focus on these other ways of communicating." We need to have attempted to get speech, full-throttle, using Son-Rise Program principles, for *at least* a year before we will even consider going down this other road.

A VERY SPECIAL THANKSGIVING

It was Charlotte and James's first Thanksgiving with my family. My parents, my brothers and sisters and their families, and a couple of long-time family friends were all gathered at my parents' house for the day.

Throughout the day, members of my family took turns doing one-hour, one-on-one Son-Rise Program sessions with James in a bedroom set aside for this purpose. I have had many experiences of being thankful for my family, but few could compete with the emotional gratitude I felt at this incredibly sweet and meaningful expression of love.

I had my session early in the day, and Charlotte had hers last. At the end of Charlotte's session (it was early evening at this point), she came downstairs with her son. James was at a stage where he was very sensitive to environmental noise and commotion, and all of us, who had been engaged in an animated discussion in the living room, immediately hushed as Charlotte and James entered.

Charlotte was holding her son in her arms, and he was staring at us with a very serious expression on his face. My mother said hello to James sweetly. James paused for a moment, then said "Tan ups." At that time, he had trouble with the *s* sound if it was followed by a consonant, so he would drop it and move the *s* to the end of the word or phrase. So "tan ups" really meant "stand up." Often, if someone who was working with James would sit down, he would tell them to stand up. (I guess he wasn't a fan of idleness!)

In this case, the moment he told us to stand up, every single person in the room (there were a lot of us!), without any consultation with one another, wordlessly stood.

James stared, transfixed. It was as if he were thinking, *I said one little thing, and it got immediate and perfect results! I speak and the world moves!*

We waited silently, smiling at him.

"Sit down," he said.

Without a word, everyone sat.

James could not take his eyes off us.

"Tan ups," he said, asking us to stand again.

We all stood.

"Sit down," he said.

We all sat.

I looked at Charlotte, who had tears in her eyes. Never had she—or her son—been in a responsive, loving, and James-friendly environment!

Moreover, James, at that point in his life, would never speak—certainly not unsolicited—in the presence of a group. He might say those phrases in a one-on-one situation, but not with a host of people around, including many whom he barely knew.

James continued to order us to stand, then sit, then stand again for fifteen minutes. Then his mom took him to bed.

Brief though it was, Charlotte and I would never forget that event.

ACTIVITY TIME!

Table 5 is designed just to get you paying more attention to your child's language—and how you react to it. Spend fifteen minutes alone with your child, focusing on verbal communication. Your goal will be to remember one to three words or phrases that she said to you during your fifteen minutes. If your child isn't saying words yet, you will mark down speech-like sounds, such as "ba" or "ak."

Very important: For each word, phrase, or sound, you will write down *how you responded*. Did you clap? Did you cheer? Did you run and get your child something? Did you do nothing?

As with Table 4 in the previous chapter, keep the session to no longer than fifteen minutes for now. Getting an accurate reading of what your child is saying and how you responded is the most important thing at this stage.

Verbal Communication		
Word or Phrase	How You Responded	Did You Over-Talk or Narrate? (Yes/No)

Table 5

ONLINE RESOURCES

For more in-depth help with the principles and techniques of this chapter, please go to www.autismbreakthrough.com/chapter7. Cheering you on!

STARTING POINT

The next time your child wants something, enthusiastically request that he use words (one word, one sound, or multiple words, depending on where his language is right now). Resist the urge to act upon your child's other signals—reaching, moving your hand, looking at what he wants—and be persistent in your request for language. Believe in your child's ability to speak (or speak more)! Then, *make sure you pause and leave space for him to speak.*

Also, make sure that your child's immediate environment is arranged so that he cannot simply retrieve everything that he wants on his own. Remember, it has to be worth your child's while to speak!

EIGHT

Fundamental 3: Interactive Attention Span

LET'S ACKNOWLEDGE ONE thing: your child probably has an awesomely long attention span. After all, if your child isms for hours, that's some quality attention span! So, attention span is not the issue. *Interactive* attention span is.

What's the difference?

Ladies (those of you who have a male significant other), I'm sure many of you have noticed how your man seems to have a perfectly healthy attention span when he takes some reading on a bathroom excursion or when he's watching a game on TV, but when you want to tell him about your day, his attention span suddenly shrinks to about sixty seconds. You see how very different those two types of attention span feel to you?

Attention span simply measures how long your child can stay involved in an activity. *Interactive* attention span refers to how long your child can stay involved in an *interactive* activity with *another person* (before your child disconnects, isms, etc.). Your child's interactive attention span may be thirty seconds, two minutes, fifteen minutes, or possibly even an hour.

Here's the thing: if your child's interactive attention span is low (especially in the thirty seconds or two minutes category), she can never learn to participate in a bona fide social interaction. You can't have a real conversation or play a game in thirty seconds. But interactive attention span is a highly malleable skill. And as your child's interactive attention span increases, it will create a positive feedback loop whereby longer periods of participation lead to increased interest in what other people are doing, which, in turn, builds a longer and longer interactive attention span. Isn't that terrific?

You will want to become very aware of your child's interactive attention span. Start to keep track of how long your child spends engaged with you in any activity. Keep in mind that if your child is isming, he's not engaged. If your child is not responsive to you, he's not engaged. Your child must be interacting with you or someone else (playing, talking, chasing, looking) for it to count as "engaged time."

Suppose your child is isming and you are joining. Suddenly, your child interacts with you for a minute. Then, he goes right back to isming. You join again. Then he interacts with you for another minute. Then he resumes his ism.

That's an interactive attention span of one minute, not two. If a minute is the longest you get before the isming resumes, then that is what you are starting with. I want to emphasize that this is only what you are *starting* with; it tells us *nothing* about how much your child can improve or how much longer it will be in six months.

If your child's interactive attention span is low right now, then you can actually see that as a good thing. It means that your child's abilities and deficits only reflect what he is capable of *given his current interactive attention span*. Think of how much more is possible once we lengthen it!

STRATEGIES

Once again, the joining and motivation principles provide the building blocks here. The more you join, the shorter the isming periods and the longer the interactive periods. And when you focus the interactive activities around your child's areas of strong motivation and interest, you will always get longer periods of engagement than you will without utilizing your child's motivations. Here are some other key ways to begin increasing your child's interactive attention span:

1. **Include plenty of "the good stuff."**
   Find the part of the game or conversation that your child likes, and include lots of it. If your child likes the part of the chase game where you catch and tickle her, do more of that. If your child enjoys watching you fall down, drop to the floor more often. If your child loves it when you swing her, swing her more. If your child likes the part of the "taking a trip" game where the (pretend) plane takes off, make that happen more often. If your child loves talking about Star Wars, ask her a Star Wars question when her interest in the conversation starts to wane.

2. **Keep coming back to your game or activity.**
   Many parents are afraid of their child losing interest in an interactive game or activity once they've gotten their child's attention and interest. Maybe you feel this way. Check in with yourself. Have you ever seen your child disconnect and begin isming in the middle of a game or activity? (I bet you have!) Hopefully, you then joined him, right? (Right? Right? Say yes!) And then, possibly, he reconnected. So here's the key question: Have you ever, in this situation, decided not to attempt to engage your child in the previous game or activity because he appeared to "lose interest" last time? (If you have, don't sweat it—most parents have done exactly the same thing!) It is very beneficial to your child for you to endeavor to *continue the same activity where you left off.* When you have your child's willing attention again (after you've joined), you can say something like, "Hey, you know what? We still haven't finished our game! It's your turn!" or "I'm so glad you're back! We're almost up the mountain!" or "I'm so excited to hear your answer to the question I asked you before—what *is* your favorite animal?"

3. **Invite your child to come back to the game or activity—*once.***

Just as important as being willing to reintroduce an activity is being willing to let it go. Have you ever found yourself so excited to have your child engaged with you in a particular activity that when your child disconnects, you miss your child's signals—and keep trying to get your child to stay with the activity? (If so, I promise you that I have yet to work with a parent who has not done this, so you're in good company!) In practice, though, this type of pushing breaks down the rapport and trust that you have painstakingly built. So, when you are in the middle of an activity with your child, and you see her beginning to disconnect, invite her to continue. *Once.* Make sure you do this in a fun and easy way, such as saying, "Oh! Oh! It's your turn! Let's finish your turn!" or "You silly goose, you can't drive the truck from over there! Come over here and take the wheel," or "Wait! Wait! Stay for two more minutes so we can finish the game! I'm having so much fun, and we're almost done!" Of paramount importance, though, is that you only do this once. *If your child is not responsive, it is important to stop asking.* At this point, bond with her by joining, being super user-friendly, nondemanding, etc.

ACTIVITY TIME!

Table 6 tracks interactive attention span. Spend fifteen minutes with your child. Do your best to spend that fifteen minutes playing some sort of interactive game. I would suggest keeping it very simple. Pick something basic that you know he likes. Often, it's easiest to pick a physical game, such as a chase game or wrestling. Remember, too, that you don't want to go in and deliberately pick a toy, object, or activity that your child does a lot of isming with. (We're tracking *interactive* attention span, not regular attention span.)

You're going to use Table 6 to begin to keep track of the types of interactive games or activities that your child sticks with the longest (and the shortest). In the first column, write down a few words that sum up what the activity was, such as "chase game," "building a fort," or "checkers." In the second column, write down how long the activity went. In other words, how long did your child stay involved before he disengaged, started to ism, left to do something else, etc.?

Remember, you are not trying to be perfect by doing only games that will be wildly successful at engaging your child. The whole point here is to be a detective, try several different things, and start to notice what does and does not engage your child.

If your child does happen to remain engaged for the whole time, yippee! Next time, you can try for longer.

Interactive Attention Span	
Game/Activity	**Length of Time**

Table 6

ONLINE RESOURCES

For more in-depth help with the principles and techniques of this chapter, please go to www.autismbreakthrough.com/chapter8. Enjoy!

STARTING POINT

Pick one game or activity from Table 6 and introduce it once a day for a week. See if there is any change in whether your child engages and for how long.

Remember to introduce the activity in a fun but totally non-pushy way. If your child engages more with the activity by the end of the week, wonderful. If she doesn't, that's also great; now, through "trial and info," you know that this activity is not engaging yet for her. You can still try again in a month or two!

NINE

Fundamental 4: Flexibility

BEFORE WE DISCUSS this most crucial fundamental in detail, let me tell you about Arturo.

The Story of Arturo

Arturo's parents were very pleased to have gotten him into a school that used the Training and Education of Autistic and Related Communication-handicapped Children (TEACCH) model. They thought that this school would provide a great alternative to ABA, which they felt had been counterproductive for their son.

One of the aspects of the school that they really liked was that it claimed to respect the "culture of autism." With this model, the school felt that everything should be built around what children on the spectrum already had a knack for. One of the key tenets of the school was that "children on the autism spectrum need structure." (I'm sure you've heard that statement before.)

Everything was conducted according to a clearly defined schedule. The children were taught this schedule in-depth. They learned every single thing that happened at every single time throughout the day. They were shown pictures (PECS cards) for each aspect of the day and given as few transitions as possible (since "children on the autism spectrum have a hard time with transitions").

And in some ways this system really worked. Most of the children in Arturo's new school became very proficient at following the schedule, and there were fewer meltdowns than at most special schools.

So Arturo became adept at following schedules.

But what happened when the schedule changed?

Arturo's parents came to our Start-Up program chiefly because of a significant challenge that lay at the center of Arturo's autism: he was very rigid and inflexible and prone to meltdowns. If there was a deviation from the schedule at home, Arturo would have a screaming meltdown. If they took a different route to the park, Arturo had a meltdown. If his little sister was around him for more than a few minutes, Arturo would have a meltdown.

If anyone tried to get Arturo to play a different game than the one he wanted to play—or if anyone tried to change any aspect of a game he was playing—Arturo would refuse. He would play a small selection of regimented games with his parents, but the games had to be played the exact same way every time. His parents—and others—often described the experience of playing with Arturo as not really playing but rather as having to be a robot that Arturo controlled absolutely.

For example, whenever Arturo's parents would try to do a puzzle with him, he would snatch all of the larger pieces away from them. If they tried to use a larger piece, he would grab it or scream. They could put smaller pieces into the puzzle, but only beginning at the right-hand side of the puzzle; otherwise Arturo would grab those pieces or scream.

In the Start-Up program, we taught Arturo's parents how to build their son's flexibility by utilizing Arturo's motivation and by giving them some specific additional strategies.

When Arturo's parents returned home, they implemented what they learned, and they were elated to see the rapidity of the changes in their son. He hardly ever had meltdowns when the schedule changed or during transitions. He began to tolerate—and sometimes play with—his little sister. He became much more flexible within his games, allowing others to contribute and suggest changes. His repertoire of games and activities broadened considerably. Often, he would really play the games instead of having to simply repeat the exact same steps.

Most importantly, people who played with him actually had the experience of playing and interacting instead of feeling like controlled automatons.

One time, when Arturo's mom got his favorite puzzle out, he once again snatched up all of the larger pieces. Arturo's mom gently put out her hand and asked, "May I have one of your big pieces?"

Arturo stared at her. She smiled at him and continued to hold out her hand.

Arturo looked down at the puzzle pieces in his hand. He looked back up at his mother's outstretched hand. Then back to the pieces in his hand.

Then, with deliberate slowness, Arturo took his empty hand, plucked one of the big puzzle pieces from his hand, and held it out to his mom.

His parents found that Arturo would, more and more often, be flexible and have wonderful back-and-forth interactions, which allowed his parents to arrange and then witness something they had long been awaiting: Arturo's first playdate.

WHY FLEXIBILITY IS SO IMPORTANT

Flexibility is by far the most underappreciated of the four fundamentals. In fact, as in Arturo's story, most of us prize the opposite of flexibility: structure. Is it a bad thing for a child to know the day's schedule? Certainly not. But, as with math, it is utterly beside the point. And, as with math, it just helps our children to be better at being autistic. Remember: the rigid, structured part of your child's brain is just peachy. *You want to work the weak muscle.* You want to develop the part of your child's brain that's having difficulty. Then scores of doors open up for her.

Realities to consider:

- There will *always* be changes in the schedule (as well as routes, routines, the order in which things happen, the meals that are served, etc.).
- There will always be other people around your child, whether they be peers or adults, who want to have their say as to how a game is played, what activity to do, etc.
- A child who is different or who isms a little can absolutely succeed in school. A rigid child prone to frequent meltdowns cannot.
- Your life will be a thousand times easier if you can do things with your child and with the family without fights and meltdowns. So will your child's.
- *Every other area of your child's development* is profoundly affected by your child's level of flexibility.

Okay, let's take a few minutes to discuss that last point. The amazing thing about flexibility is that it doesn't just affect flexibility. For instance, let's say that your child is having difficulties with language. Now, certainly, there are cases where this is due purely to apraxia (difficulty using the muscles of the mouth to form words), and such a child will really need our help to build up the basic ability to form his mouth to make sounds.

However, we see so many cases where a child says a word or phrase with perfect clarity on Monday but seems unable to say it on Tuesday. How do we explain this? After all, if the child has, for instance, low oral muscle tone or is completely unable to use language, how did he use it yesterday?

This is where flexibility comes into play. Flexibility entails your child going your way. (Any time your child is being asked for anything, he is being asked to go your way.) For most of our kids, this is very, very challenging. It is a relinquishing of autonomy that can feel really tough for a child whose world feels out of control and unfathomable. Most of the time, when it comes to language (if your child is not already fluently verbal), someone is asking your child to speak. This may be overt ("Say 'water'") or more natural ("Which toy do you want?"). Either way, when it comes to the vast majority of instances, speaking requires your child to go someone else's way—in other words, it requires flexibility.

So, if your child lacks flexibility, then getting speech is going to be quite a challenge—*even if your child already has speech capability.* If, on the other hand, you address your child's flexibility issues, you remove a gigantic obstacle to language. And language is only one example. When you help your child to become more flexible, you remove an enormous obstacle to *everything.* Every other area of your child's development is freed to move forward.

STRATEGIES

I know I've said this many times with respect to the other fundamentals, but it bears repeating one more time: you don't want to attempt to work on your child's flexibility when your child is isming, not looking, not responding, etc. Work on flexibility when your child is engaged with you.

With that said, here are some flexibility-building strategies:

1. Start by being super user-friendly.

This means *you* being very flexible and responsive to your child. If she wants all of the toy cars to herself (and takes your toy cars from you), let her have them. If she says "Don't touch that," then don't touch it. If she wants you to stand on one foot, stand on one foot. This helps to set the stage because it helps to build trust and to relax your child.

2. **Explain it in advance.**

When there is a change or transition coming (dinner is later, we are changing rooms or activities, etc.), explain to your child what is going to happen in a nice, relaxed tone. Also briefly explain why. Example: "Hey, sweetie, in a half-hour, we are going to put our shoes on and get in the car. We have a dentist appointment." Do this again fifteen minutes before and again five minutes before.

3. **Get it "wrong."**

If your child usually requires a game or activity to go a certain way, make a "mistake" and do it "wrong." For instance, if the getting-ready-for-bed process typically begins with brushing teeth followed by getting into pajamas, get out the pajamas first. If the puzzle always gets put together in the same order, try beginning the puzzle in a different order. When your child calls you on it (whether he does this in a verbal or nonverbal way), say something like, "Ooops! I did it a different way!" You can add, "It's so fun to try things a different way!"

4. **Role play.**

In a fun way, play out a scenario in which your child would usually have difficulty, such as a transition. For example, if your child has difficulty transitioning out of the house, play a game inside where you two *pretend* to get ready to go outside. (Your child needs to be at a high enough stage in her overall development for you to be able to do this. For instance, if your child is totally nonverbal or only minimally interactive, you'll want to save this strategy for later.)

5. **Be silly.**

Normally, when something happens that is outside our children's comfort zone, we get uneasy and tighten up (because we "know what's coming"). This makes things worse. Instead, when your child seems to get a bit agitated over a change, transition, or someone wanting to do something a different way than he does, act silly and goofy about it. If dinner is served early, and your child is attached to having dinner at exactly six o'clock, you can say something like, "Holy moly, the wind is blowing me over to the dinner table!" or "I'm so weird! I'm eating before dinnertime!" You can also do things like bouncing over to the dinner table or falling down in slow motion as you go to the table.

QUESTIONS TO ASK, REQUESTS TO MAKE

It is surprising just how many opportunities we have (and often don't notice) to turn an activity that's already happening into one that challenges our children in the area of flexibility. It makes perfect sense that we tend to not notice these opportunities. No one ever tells us to pay any attention to our children's level of flexibility!

Here are some examples of questions we can ask and requests we can make (as long as your child is not isming) that will gently challenge your child to be more flexible during any activity:

- "That was fun watching you go the last few times. Now I want a turn!"
- "Oh my gosh! You have to try my game! It's so cool!"
- "I have an idea! Let's see what it's like to do it in a different order this time!"
- "Parking your car in that slot is cool! Let's try putting it in the other slot now!"
- "You're right—we usually have dinner at six. If we could have dinner at any time later than six, which time would you want it?"

- "Yeah, I know you like your piece to be the blue one. This time, let's try it a different way. What other color do you want to try instead?"

ACTIVITY TIME!

Table 7 is designed to be filled out over a three-day period. On day 1, choose something in your child's day that you will do differently—and invite her to enjoy it. For instance, change the time of one meal. Encourage your child to get dressed in a different order (pants, then shirt, instead of shirt, then pants). If there is a card game you usually play, change one rule, such as having each person get two turns in a row. On day 2, choose a different item to change. On day 3, choose another item to change. Remember to use the five strategies.

In each instance, use Table 7 to track what change you tried and how your child responded. In the first column, write the name of the game or activity. In the second column, simply circle "yes" or "no" according to whether your child agreed to the change or not. (She can refuse the change by saying no or simply by ignoring it.)

Reminder: don't get caught up in getting all yes answers. Even a no helps to stretch your child's flexibility.

Flexibility	
Item That You Endeavored To Change	Did Your Child Agree To The Change?
1)	YES / NO
2)	YES / NO
3)	YES / NO

Table 7

ONLINE RESOURCES

For some help with the principles of this chapter, please go to www.autismbreakthrough.com/chapter9. Have a great time!

STARTING POINT

Start practicing being silly in the face of change. Any time anything does not go the predicted way, respond in a fun, easy, silly manner. If Aunt Maria doesn't arrive when she says she will, you can jump around, exclaiming, "Whoo-hoo! Aunt Maria's not here yet! Now we have fifteen extra minutes to wrestle! [or draw, play, etc.]" If your child wants food that he cannot have, you can pretend to eat his arm—and maybe sneak in a tickle. There's no one perfect way to be silly, so give yourself permission to experiment!

Note: These past five chapters will powerfully jump-start your child's social and interpersonal development. However, these chapters are just the beginning of The Son-Rise Program Developmental Model, not the end. We spend much time in the Start-Up and advanced programs helping you to utilize the model step-by-step, including tracking exactly where your child is and implementing activities to bring your child to the next level. As noted in Chapter 5, you can download the full version of this model from my Web site. These Four Fundamentals of Socialization are trackable and understandable because of the insightful model that Bryn and William Hogan developed—and I thank them heartily!

experience: her sensory-processing challenges (how all sights, sounds, smells, and touches can be very challenging, overwhelming, or nonsensical to her) and your child's pattern-recognition problems (making her world feel unpredictable, haphazard, and out of control).

When people—not just people with autism but *all* people—are in the throes of an experience where they don't have control, don't have understanding, and have too much input to process, they react in very particular ways. They put everything they have into gaining a sense of control. They seek out situations where they can exert their own autonomy, rather than having their experience dictated to them. And they powerfully resist any efforts to impose control upon them.

When people move to a totally new area, attend a brand-new school, go through a harrowing divorce, lose a longtime job, undergo a life-changing injury, or experience the loss of a loved one, they often become very controlling for a while. They may fall back on familiar routines, seek out only the most familiar people, seek time alone (where they can control everything), obsessively clean their house, watch familiar movies or TV shows, engage in very regimented or controlled eating habits. At the same time, they will often vehemently avoid new situations or people, push back hard if you try to alter their behavior, and push you away altogether if you keep persisting.

As I mentioned in Chapter 2, when your child seems resistant, rigid, or routinized, he is not behaving abnormally; he is behaving normally, given the situation that he's facing. So it is not at all surprising that many of our children are highly controlling.

Most people's first response when dealing with a controlling child is to try to "break" the child of his controlling behavior by wresting control back from him. Some of you might think: *To function in the world, my child has to get used to doing things the right way, so I have to get him to do this particular thing the correct way* now.

TEN

How Giving Control Generates Breakthroughs

So we just finished talking extensively about setting and pursuing social goals for your child. And yet, paradoxically, the be way to enable your child to hit more goals is to *prioritize intera tion with your child over any particular goal that you have.*

Remember: interaction is of primary importance when yo child has a social-relational disorder like autism. Building tr and increasing interaction doesn't just address trust and inter tion. *It addresses everything.* Are specific goals important? Do we want to be persistent and consistent in pursuing th with our children? Absolutely.

You love your child and value your child's progress. Th wonderful and important. And I know that sometimes it's to get single-mindedly caught up in achieving a particular n stone with your child. In your pursuit of your child's prog though, *it is essential to temporarily relinquish any goal as as it causes a control battle with your child.* In fact, control b are one of the most disabling dealings you can have with child. You want to avoid them whenever possible (except safety is involved, of course).

THE PROBLEM WITH CONTROL BATT

Remember the analogy from Chapter 2 about reading park bench, when we talked about your child's experienc world? I detailed two primary factors governing your

For others of you, the situation may be more in-the-moment pragmatic. You might think: *I just have to get my child to brush his teeth* (for example), *and we'll be done. I know he's fighting me now, but soon it will be over, and it will be worth it because he'll have clean teeth.*

If either of these scenarios resonates with you, it's not only normal, it is totally understandable. You love your child, and you are trying to help him fit in with a world that will not necessarily understand or cater to his differences. On top of that, you have a million things you are juggling at once, and sometimes you may just be trying to get through the day.

The problem is that going down this road with your child will end up being highly counterproductive. Asserting control over someone who is controlling leads to that person becoming *more* controlling, not less. You see, when your child's control is challenged, he will feel compelled to dig his heels in and fight to reestablish that control and personal autonomy.

Think of a rope with a knot in it. I am holding fast to one end and you to the other. The harder you pull, the tighter the knot gets—'cause I ain't letting go. You can never release the knot by pulling harder. The only way to release the knot is to let the rope go so that there is enough slack in it for the knot to loosen.

The key to understand is this: if you want your child to be less controlling (and thus more flexible and able to learn more, grow more, and ultimately achieve more goals), *you have to give your child as much control as possible.*

Have you ever hugged your child when she didn't really want to be hugged (she was squirming or pulling away)? Have you ever physically moved items that your child was playing with, such as blocks, to show her the "right" way to play with them? Have you ever pressed your child to shake hands with someone—or to say "hello" or "thank you"? Have you ever held your child so that you could brush her hair, wash her face, etc. while she was trying to get away?

It's totally okay if you've done any or all of these things. I have rarely met any loving parent who *hasn't.* Most parents aren't aware of the cascade of unintended results that occur when these types of actions are taken with a child on the autism spectrum. You may address the issue in the moment (clean teeth, brushed hair, etc.) but you compromise interaction and learning long-term because you get a child who is not only more controlling but also *associates learning or doing something that you want with coercion and unpleasantness.*

The Story of Michael

Michael's mom felt that it was very important for him to have clean teeth. The problem was that Michael, a lanky seven-year-old with a little bit of language, didn't have the same enthusiasm for his oral hygiene. Not to worry. His mom came up with a solution.

Every night before bed, she would, as gently as she could, put Michael in a headlock and forcibly brush his teeth for him. She took no pleasure in this. In fact, she hated it. But she couldn't see any other way to get his teeth brushed. Was she supposed to let all of his teeth fall out?

This was one of the first issues we addressed when Michael and his mom came to the Autism Treatment Center of America for their Intensive program. Although tooth-brushing is rarely at the top of our agenda, it was with Michael because this nightly ritual had destroyed the interpersonal trust necessary for him to progress. (Early on, his mom said to us, "He's always running away from me. I don't understand it.")

To be clear, Michael's mom was a loving and caring mother who only wanted the best for her son. She simply hadn't been able to come up with a better solution, and she felt that abandoning the tooth-brushing altogether would make her a bad mom, so she felt like she was locked into this scenario.

We began a lengthy discussion with Michael's mother about her son's tooth-brushing situation. After hearing all of her reasons for doing what she was doing, we explained to her why forcing Michael to brush his teeth was so detrimental to him and to what she really wanted for him, which was his forward development. (We also highlighted the difficulty she would have attempting the tooth-brushing ritual when her son was fifteen.)

Then, our child facilitators, who were to work one-on-one with Michael all week, addressed tooth-brushing with him directly. To be sure, we didn't feel that Michael brushing his teeth was in and of itself his number one priority. However, we wanted to help Michael while, at the same time, showing his mom that, through The Son-Rise Program, we could enable her son to do things such as brush his teeth without using any force or coercion whatsoever (and without using any nonphysical pushing such as disapproval). Then *she* could do the same with Michael in the situations that she would encounter at home.

Our first child facilitator went into our playroom with Michael. In his back pocket, the child facilitator had two brand-new toothbrushes. After spending some time bonding with Michael and being very user-friendly (responding quickly to Michael, doing exactly what he wanted), our child facilitator said, "Hey! Guess what, buddy! I've got something fun for us to play with!"

With that, he enthusiastically pulled out the two toothbrushes. As soon as Michael saw them, he ran to the other side of the room, threw his hands up, and said, "No!" very loudly.

Without a moment's hesitation, our child facilitator put the toothbrushes down on a little table (which was low enough for Michael to easily see the toothbrushes).

"No problem, Michael," our child facilitator said, "we can play with them later. Thanks for telling me what you wanted!"

He then began to offer Michael rides on his back, which was something that Michael really enjoyed. After several minutes of giving rides (with Michael saying "ride" and giggling each time he wanted another), our child facilitator paused dramatically.

"Oh my gosh! Michael, do you know what I just remembered?" He leapt over to the table, picked up the two toothbrushes, and presented them to Michael with a flourish, "I got toothbrushes, buddy! They're so much fun!"

No sooner had the child facilitator finished his sentence than Michael again scampered to the other side of the room, saying "No!"

Our child facilitator didn't miss a beat. "Oh, okay. I thought you might be ready for some toothbrush fun. Not a problem. We're not going to do anything with the toothbrushes until *you* want to. Okay, Michael? Not until *you* want to."

He put the toothbrushes back on the table.

Then he smiled at Michael impishly. "I gotta tell you, though, Michael, those toothbrushes sure are fun!"

Once again, the two went back to playing the ride game. After several more minutes, our child facilitator, as if realizing that the toothbrushes are on the table for the very first time, grabbed them and introduced them again (with great enthusiasm!).

Michael responded the same away again.

The child facilitator again put them back on the table, explaining to Michael that he was going to keep trying because the toothbrushes are so fun—but also that they would not play with them until Michael wanted to. (We have a saying in The Son-Rise Program: "No means no . . . for the next five minutes. Then I get to ask again.")

This continued for over an hour, with our child facilitator offering the toothbrushes enthusiastically every five to seven minutes. Eventually, Michael began to see—and really believe—that our child facilitator was not going to use force with him.

The tenth or eleventh time that our child facilitator offered up the toothbrushes, Michael didn't back away, and he didn't say "No."

Instead, he just stood there, looking at the child facilitator—and at the toothbrushes.

Our child facilitator was ecstatic. Toothbrush liftoff! He cheered Michael fervently. Then, slowly, he offered Michael one of the toothbrushes. Carefully, Michael took it. The child facilitator jumped up and down, cheering, "You're doing it, buddy! You're holding the toothbrush! You are the man, Michael!"

Our child facilitator put his toothbrush in his mouth and began to brush his own teeth. As he was doing this, he spoke excitedly to Michael.

"Holy macaroli! This is awesome! This feels so good!" He continued brushing his teeth with huge enjoyment. "Michael, you gotta try this, man! Watch what I'm doing!"

He took the toothbrush out of his mouth, put it back in, and resumed brushing. "Oh, this feels terrific!"

Slowly, Michael brought his own toothbrush up to his lips.

"That's perfect, Michael!" the child facilitator said, "Now put it in your mouth like me! See?"

He showed Michael again.

Michael held the toothbrush an inch from his lips but made no further moves.

It was at this point that our child facilitator glanced at the time and realized that he had three more minutes to his session with Michael.

This is exactly the type of situation where most people might think, *three minutes left! We're so close! Why don't I just guide Michael's hand the rest of the way to his mouth.*

That would be the ultimate mistake because it would obliterate all of the trust that had just been built up. And here's the thing: it's not just about the tooth-brushing. After the tooth-brushing, we have a hundred other things we want to help Michael learn. If we violate trust now, each milestone becomes successively harder because Michael now sees each one as being accompanied by force and coercion.

What if, on the other hand, we were willing to take our time, build trust, and give control? Then the first milestone (say, toothbrushing) might take longer, but everything else will be downhill from here because now we have trust. Now Michael associates learning with fun and with personal safety and control. Now he will work *with* us. Plus, we've preserved the cornerstone upon which all autism progress rests: interpersonal relationships and interaction.

The question you want to ask yourself, at every point where you feel the urge to push for something even though your child is resisting, is this: *Is it going to make any difference whatsoever in my child's life a year from now if he learns this skill on Thursday instead of Friday?*

I call this question the return-to-sanity question because asking—and answering—it will always wake you up and remind you what's really important as you endeavor to teach your child new things. You want your child to trust you and to enjoy human interaction. *And you want your child to come back for more.* That *will* make a difference in his life a year from now.

Of course, our child facilitator did not guide Michael's hand (and the toothbrush he was holding) to his mouth. He simply spent those last three minutes cheering Michael on and having fun with him, and they ended the session on a high note—but without having gotten Michael to actually brush his teeth.

As it turned out, it was the *next* child facilitator who got Michael to brush his teeth. She started a game called "Tickling Your Teeth," which inspired Michael to put the toothbrush in his mouth and brush his teeth.

From then on, Michael brushed his teeth nightly before bed—of his own volition and without having to be pushed, prodded, or put in a headlock.

So, remember: you want to be persistent and enthusiastic in pursuing goals with your child. But when your child says no or resists or you feel a control battle coming on, remember to *stop* what you're doing, put it aside and come back to it in an hour or a day or a week.

Your child needs to feel safe and in control before she can bond with you or anyone else. Once she *does* feel safe and in control, you will find that, in addition to being able to bond with you (the most important thing), she will become much less controlling, more flexible, and more willing and able to learn new things.

CONQUERING CAR WASHES

Just after my recovery from autism, when I was still getting used to the world, there were certain things that I found very scary. (This was actually a testament to my recovery because when I was autistic, I wasn't scared of—nor even aware of—much of anything. Once I had recovered, I was absorbing my environment fully for the very first time.)

One of the things I was afraid of was automatic car washes, and another was stopped-up toilets. Yes, I know that second one sounds strange, but I'll explain (after which, it will probably still sound strange).

Naturally, I did not know that I was scared of either of these two pieces of our everyday existence until I experienced them for the first time. I remember being in the car with my father, and him telling me I was about to go through a car wash, which would be really fun.

The car was on the tracks that take it through the car wash, and the car slowly began to move on its own, which I thought was pretty cool. Then, all of a sudden, these things started slamming against the car. (At least, that's how I perceived it.) I remember seeing these giant, monster-like arms crashing loudly against the windows.

Needless to say, I commenced screaming bloody murder.

My dad gently stroked my head. "I know this is new for you, Raun. It's going to be over in another two minutes."

I kept screaming.

My dad continued stroking my head, telling me that I was okay, letting me know when the wash was halfway done, then almost done, then finished.

And then it was over.

Now, there are two ways that parents tend to handle this kind of occurrence. One is to get really agitated when their child is agitated—and then promise him that they will never take him on that scary thing again. The other is to insist that there is nothing to be afraid of and keep trying to get their child into the car wash again so that he can "get over it."

My dad chose neither of these alternatives. First, once the wash was done and we got out of the car, he explained that it was okay if I didn't want to go in a car wash again (giving me control). So I immediately calmed down, knowing that I wasn't going to be pushed to do something that I felt was scary.

Second, he took me around to a big window where we could watch what was happening in the car wash, and he sent the car back through the car wash, this time with both of us watching what was happening to it from the outside. As this was happening, he explained to me exactly what was going on in the car wash.

As it turned out, I found it fascinating to watch from the outside—and to hear how it worked. My dad asked if I wanted to see it from the inside again, now that I'd seen what happened from the outside. I answered with an enthusiastic yes.

We got back in the car and took another ride through the car wash. This time, I really enjoyed it.

Funny as it sounds, this event was pivotal for me, and I actually became, henceforth, a kid who loved going through car washes!

SURMOUNTING STOPPED-UP TOILETS

As I mentioned earlier, one of my other fears was stopped-up toilets. Why, you ask? A valid question. Let me tell you in the context of a story.

I came running into the kitchen and wrapped my arms around my mom's leg. (Yes, I was that little.) She asked me what was wrong, and I explained that I had just flushed the toilet, and now it was stopped up (probably because I used too much toilet paper, a common rookie mistake). I told her that I was afraid to go near the bathroom.

She didn't get annoyed, she didn't say "Oh, poor baby," and she didn't try to make me go back into the bathroom (thus giving me control). In fact, the whole manner in which she helped me is an homage to the idea of giving control.

She asked me why I was afraid of stopped-up toilets. I replied that, when I saw the water rising in the toilet, I felt like it was going to keep overflowing, and I was going to drown. (In this case, the toilet wasn't actually overflowing. I was just afraid that it would.) She didn't laugh or do anything that communicated that what I had said was silly or not worthy of serious consideration.

Then she asked me to bring her some of my little people. (These were little toy people that I used to play with.) I brought three of them back to her. She put them in the empty kitchen sink and propped me up on the counter so that I could see into the sink. Then she told me to imagine that the sink was the bathroom and the drain was the toilet. Finally, she asked me to turn on the faucet so that the water was coming out full force. (I could see the water coming out much harder than it had from the toilet.)

We sat there, watching the sink slowly fill until the water reached the neck level of my little people. It took several minutes.

"See how long that took?" my mom said.

"Yeah," I said.

"Well, if you were one of those little people, what would you do during all those minutes while the bathroom was filling up?"

"I would just leave the bathroom," I said, realization dawning.

All of a sudden, I could see that even in an absolute, bathroom-filling worst-case scenario, I would have plenty of time to just walk out of the bathroom.

The conquering of this fear was so momentous for me that I became Mr. Stopped-Up-Toilet Fixer in my house. Whenever the toilet got clogged for any reason, I was the person who would volunteer to plunge it!

As you can see, because my parents understood the importance of giving control, they were able to use this principle to help me overcome challenges even after my recovery from autism. You can use this principle to help your child today.

The stories in this chapter bring to light a core concept of The Son-Rise Program:

YOU ARE OUR WORLD'S AMBASSADOR

Have you ever met someone from a foreign country? Have you ever noticed that you attribute the characteristics of that person to the country from which he hails? If the person is pushy, you think. *People from that country are pushy.* If the person is loud, you think, *People from over there are loud.* If the person is respectful, you think, *That country has a very respectful culture.*

Every single second that you are with your child, you are, for better or worse, our world's ambassador. You represent the world of human interaction. Everything that you do tells your child what it's like to be a part of our world.

If you force or push, that tells your child that our world is one where she will be coerced. If you disapprove, that tells her that our world is a disapproving world. If you give control, that tells her that the interactive world is one in which she can feel secure and have autonomy. If you are approving, that tells your child that our world is an approving one.

You are asking your child to permanently join you in your world. For this reason, it is critical that you remain extremely aware of the messages you are sending about what that world is like.

REAL-WORLD RULES AND CONSTRAINTS

When I speak at autism conferences, I sometimes get asked how children who are given control will ever learn to deal with the "rules and constraints" of a world where they don't have all the control and can't say no to whatever they want.

I remind these questioners that they are not giving this control forever. Rather, they are giving control for the duration of their child's Son-Rise Program.

Our children cannot yet handle the sensory and social circumstances of the neurotypical world. Therefore, for now, we want to provide them with a situation that they *can* tolerate and then help them to stretch, bit by bit, in a welcoming atmosphere of trust and fun, toward being able to successfully handle greater and greater social connection.

When our children have crossed all or most of the bridge from their world to ours—they are interactive, enjoy relating to people, are flexible, can communicate effectively—then we can work on helping them with the rules of the "real world."

I can tell you from experience that, by and large, Son-Rise Program graduates are exquisitely sweet, easygoing kids who do really well with real-world constraints and don't expect everything to revolve around them. Quite the contrary: they tend to be extremely caring and attentive to other people. (For some outstanding videos of these kids that illustrate exactly what I am talking about, go to www.autismbreakthrough.com/recoveredkids.)

ACTIVITY TIME!

Take a look at Table 8. Think of five situations where you tend to have control battles with your child. You don't have to think of them all at once; you can fill out one or two and then come back later to do more.

Also, these don't have to be giant battles that you have with your child. For instance, maybe when you come home from work, you hug your child even though he is squirming a little to get out of the hug. Definitely not a battle, but still an area where you do something that takes control away from your child.

For each of the situations you come up with, write down what you might usually do, and then write down what you will do now.

Table 8 is designed to be simple; there is no hidden complexity here. Just keep it basic, and it will continue to be a guide and a reminder to you.

Control Battles	What you usually do	What you will do now
1)		
2)		
3)		
4)		
5)		

Table 8

ONLINE RESOURCES

For more in-depth help with the principles and techniques of this chapter, please go to www.autismbreakthrough.com/chapter10. Wishing you much delight!

STARTING POINT

Spend fifteen minutes doing whatever your child wants. (Of course, this does not include anything that might be unsafe or destructive.) Let your child be the boss. If she wants you to run around, run around. If she wants you to stand still, stand still. If she wants you to play a particular game or activity, do it. Don't do *anything* to influence what's happening. Just enjoy yourself and see what that feels like. And notice how your child responds.

ELEVEN

The Good-Tryer Principle: Turning Your Child into a Learning Powerhouse

MOST CHILDREN ON the autism spectrum are fairly poor tryers. What does that mean? For most of us, in most situations, it takes multiple attempts, or "tries," to master something new. This, I'm sure, comes as no shock to you. To be a good basketball player, you have to take thousands of shots at the basket, most of which don't go in. To become a good cook, you have to make hundreds of dishes, many of which end up tasting disgustilicious, at least in the beginning. Learning to weave entails doing it "wrong" first. Learning to read involves messing up lots of words first.

The point is, you have to try many times—and make many mistakes—before you can master almost anything.

WHAT THIS MEANS FOR YOUR CHILD

Your child is missing a whole host of skills that you would like to help him to master. The only way for this to happen is for him to make many, many attempts at every single thing that he is learning.

If your child remains unwilling to try things that seem difficult more than once or twice, there is no way for him to learn and master the skills he is missing—*especially* the social ones because those are the most challenging.

This is crucial to understand because most children on the spectrum are not good tryers, do not like trying, and thus hit various walls in their development. There are some very logical reasons for this, including our children's difficulties with flexibility and interactive attention span. However, the part of this equation that I want to address first is the most essential variable: you.

There are all sorts of little things that you may be doing unwittingly that exacerbate your child's trying problem. Let's discuss them one by one. (These aren't things you need to feel in any way bad about. If you do any of them, that just makes you a normal parent!)

BEING A POOR TRYER

Most of us like to succeed at the things we do. If we're not going to succeed, why do it, right? So we often go through life avoiding doing things that require several uncertain attempts where we are likely to make lots of mistakes.

It is impossible to operate this way without inadvertently communicating an anti-trying message to your child.

Maybe you don't believe me. Maybe you think that how you live has nothing to do with what you do with your child. Let me ask you this: Have you ever not tried a treatment with your child because you didn't want to "get your hopes up"? Have you ever cringed when your child keeps attempting something but seems unable to do it? In which situation do you show more excitement—when your child *attempts* something or when she does it successfully?

If any of these ring true for you, there is nothing to beat yourself up about. You're a human being. Most people, including some very confident parents, operate this way.

The important thing is to recognize any fears of trying that you have and focus on changing them so that you can be the most useful beacon for your child. One of the first steps I would recommend in starting down this road is to use any opportunity you get to practice trying. Deliberately attempt things when the likelihood is high that you will make mistakes. This applies even to the most minor circumstances, such as trying to fix something in the house that you don't know how to fix (if it's not dangerous, of course), attempting to cook something you have no experience with, learning a new skill (such as a language or a hobby), playing a game you've never played, etc.

Get so used to trying that it feels like the natural thing for you to do—so that you cease even noticing that you're "trying."

SABOTAGING YOUR CHILD'S TRYING

Because many of us feel bad about trying and "failing," we often don't like to see our children repeatedly trying without "success." Therefore, we do all kinds of subtle—and not so subtle—things to avoid or cut short such a situation.

When your child is repeatedly trying to say a word, you may find this difficult—and either finish the word for your child or give him what he is asking for. You might avoid playing a game that you know he finds challenging. You may make comments like, "It's okay, honey," when your child is struggling to do or say something, as if there were some reason why his attempts or "mistakes" were *not* okay.

It's so important that you not avoid, curtail, or "smooth over" your child's many attempts at whatever. Your child keeps trying and not getting it? Good! That's what you want because this is a muscle that he needs to work.

Just so there is no misunderstanding, I am not saying to deliberately make things more difficult for your child. I'm only talking about not taking away or undermining the trying that is already occurring.

THE IMPORTANCE OF CELEBRATION

Celebration plays a large role in any Son-Rise Program. Most children on the spectrum are highly undercelebrated, even when they do "get it right." We work with parents, grandparents, family members, volunteers, and professionals all the time who regularly miss literally hundreds of opportunities to celebrate. A child will look in someone's eyes. No celebration. A child will say a word or phrase. No celebration. A child will do something he is asked to do. Nothing.

One reason for this is that we are not taught to notice and be grateful for all of the things that our children are already doing well. We're taught, in countless direct and indirect ways, to look for what's wrong and what's missing. This not only deprives our children of being celebrated, but it also deprives *us* of the chance to see, appreciate, and build upon everything that our children are doing.

So the first order of business is to shift your focus. You want to actively seek out every little interaction or accomplishment that your child makes throughout the day—even if she has done it a thousand times before.

Your child looks at you the same way she has many other times. Celebrate her. Excitedly thank her for looking at you. Your child asks for water. Celebrate her, enthusiastically thanking her for telling you what she wants, even if she has done it hundreds of times previously.

Celebrating more will make you much more aware of—and grateful for—what your child is doing well. It will also have a profound effect on her. Whenever you want more of something, celebrating—giving a big reaction—will maximize the likelihood of your child repeating it. (In Chapter 14, we'll talk about the less convenient aspect of this phenomenon, but for now just think: big reaction—repeat action.) Celebrating shows your child that you are excited by what she did, it highlights it, it makes it fun, and it gives your child a sense of control by giving her a way to influence your reactions.

When you celebrate, it's important to make it sincere and big. I've seen many people celebrate as if they are going through the motions. "Nice job, Johnny," or "Nice look, Juanita" with barely a change in their voice.

When the staff at the ATCA say "celebrate," we mean: react as if you have just won the lottery. Celebrate as if something truly amazing has happened—because it has. "Holy cow! I love when you look at me!" or "Thank you so much for telling me what you want! Whoo-hoo!"

Doing this is not frivolous. Celebrating this way has an enormous impact on how responsive your child is.

CELEBRATING TRYING

You want your child to learn to do it the "right" way. Fair enough. There's no reason why you shouldn't want that. But many parents are told to praise their child *only* when he says the "right" word, does the "right" task, etc.

From now on, you'll want to take a different approach. The good-tryer principle says that you want to do everything you possibly can to encourage your child to be a good tryer—to be willing to make many attempts, even if he isn't getting it. This is a keystone for growth and change.

As we just discussed, you will want to celebrate much more than you do now—including when your child "gets it right." However, you want to add another component to your celebration: give big, bold celebration when your child *tries*. Celebrate every attempt, even if it's way off base.

If you ask your child to say "water" and he says "ba," go crazy with celebration. If you ask your child to touch his nose and he touches his belly, celebrate big. If you are working on toilet training, and your child goes to the toilet and pees—but totally misses the potty, cheer him for trying to pee in the potty.

I have heard some voice concern that learning to do a particular task or skill correctly is vital for our kids, so it might be unwise to treat everything a child does as the "right" answer. But that is why it is important to understand that *we are not talking about pretending your child's answer is correct when it isn't.*

In fact, the good-tryer principle is the best way I've seen to help every child get the "correct" answer. In The Son-Rise Program, when we ask a child to say "water" and he says "ba," we don't say "That's perfect! You said 'water'!"

On the other hand, we don't say, "No, that's not it. Say 'water,' " because this type of response is precisely the reason why many children don't like to try in the first place: they don't want the disapproval (even if mild), and they don't want the "no."

What we would say is, "That was close! Nice try! You are awesome! Now let's try again!" We enthusiastically celebrate the attempt while encouraging the child to try again. We are seeking to make it appetizing for your child to keep trying. We want to build a little bridge of encouragement from the first try to the second, from the second to the third, etc. We know that every additional try we can get from your child brings him one step closer to being a child that can learn anything.

Whenever your child has difficulty with something or gets something "wrong," don't feel bad, feel good! Think to yourself: *Yes! This is another opportunity to help my child be a good tryer. Getting it "right" won't help him with that. Only his striving plus my encouragement can make it happen!*

For your child, trying is actually a form of engagement with the outside world. You want to make *any* engagement as appetizing as possible for him. This leads to a concept that is central to The Son-Rise Program.

THE THREE Es: ENERGY, EXCITEMENT, AND ENTHUSIASM

Displaying energy, excitement, and enthusiasm isn't brain surgery, I know. But having the three Es is essential. We talk about it over and over in the Start-Up course and in all our advanced courses. If you look at circuses, Disney characters, *Sesame Street,* and *Teletubbies,* what do they have in common? They all appeal to children (with or without autism), and they all have the three Es.

Energy, excitement, and enthusiasm always have been and always will be compelling for children. Use this fact. Bring the three Es to every aspect of your interaction with your child

Bring it to your celebrations, yes. But also bring it to taking a walk with your child, giving her a bath, eating dinner, making a request of her, etc. Unless your child is isming (and you are joining) or she is tantruming (to be discussed in Chapter 14), you want to be using the three Es whenever you are with her.

This means making your face and voice super expressive. It also means moving your body more—jumping up and down when you're cheering your child, tiptoeing toward her with the sponge in an exaggerated manner during bath time, etc.

Why is this so important? Remember, you are the ambassador of your world. You want your child to be interested and compelled to be a part of that world. The most vital part of that world is *you*. You want your child to be excited to be with *you*.

The Story of Aeesha

Aeesha's mom attended the start-up program with great trepidation. She was worried that she might hear the same thing from us that she'd heard from her diagnosticians—that her daughter would not improve in any significant way and hoping for more was unhealthy for both of them.

Of course, we told her no such thing, but we weren't surprised when she told us that Aeesha would try something once, and if she didn't get it the first time, she was done. If her mom endeavored to get her to try again, Aeesha would "flip out" (her mom's words), screaming and sometimes hitting or scratching. Aeesha's mom had mostly stopped asking more than once.

As a result, Aeesha had, at this point, made very little progress, which also didn't surprise us, since it's very hard to learn anything new when you never try more than once. When we asked Aeesha's mother how she felt whenever she asked her daughter to try something (saying a word, for instance), she said that she felt uncomfortable and afraid. We asked her why.

Now you might think that her main reason for this was because of her daughter's reactions, but this wasn't the case. (That's why we always ask.) In fact, her discomfort *preceded* Aeesha's reactions.

The *actual* reason was that a part of her believed what the diagnosticians had told her about Aeesha. Because of this, she felt bad about asking Aeesha for more. She felt as if she was simply putting her daughter through more difficulty by challenging her further.

One of the biggest shifts that parents make in the Start-Up course—before they go home, and thus before their children change—is in the way they see their children. They see their children with new eyes and a new attitude. (We'll focus on the importance of our attitude in Chapter 17.)

Aeesha's mom made just such a change in her Start-Up program. Over the course of the week, she began to shift her view of Aeesha. After being shown example after example of children just like Aeesha who made huge progress, she saw the possibilities for her daughter. As she connected with other parents in the same boat, facing the same fears, she found that she felt less alone, and thus less scared. After being armed with an arsenal of tools and techniques to help Aeesha, she started to feel competent. And as she learned that Aeesha's reactions were not a product of trying but rather a consequence of *not* being challenged to try, she no longer felt sorry for Aeesha and didn't see encouraging her as "putting her through more difficulty." By the end of the week, she saw her daughter as capable of sweeping growth and herself as capable of inspiring that growth.

Before her Start-Up, she had been working on Aeesha's language—without much success, since Aeesha wouldn't try a word more than once at a time. Aeesha's mother had heard her say parts of words but never whole words. However, armed with her new perspective on her daughter, she believed that more was possible.

Aeesha loved her Teletubbies, and her favorite one was Tinky Winky. (*Of course*, thought Aeesha's mom, *the Teletubby with the longest, hardest-to-say name.*) Aeesha's Teletubbies were on a shelf beyond her reach, so when she wanted one, she would start by pointing and making some sounds.

This time, Aeesha's mom said, "Oh! Thanks for pointing! I'm not sure which Teletubby you want, Aeesha. Can you tell me?"

Aeesha said, "Kee Kee," which was her way of saying Tinky Winky.

"Hey, thanks for telling me that!" her mom said, "That was a great try! Tell me again nice and slow so I can understand you."

Aeesha screamed and started walking away.

Aeesha's mom knew that this was her moment. Instead of feeling bad or giving up, she stepped it up a notch. "I can't believe it! You are so smart, Aeesha! I know you can say it! Say 'Tinky Winky.'"

Aeesha paused. Her mom had never done this before. "Ickee Ickee," Aeesha said.

Her mom jumped up and down some more, cheering her

daughter. "That was amazing, Aeesha! You're so close, girl! Let's try again. Say 'Tinky Winky.'"

Aeesha let out a short scream, circled the room, and then returned to her mom.

"Inky Inky," she said loudly.

Aeesha's mom decided to stick with it. "That's the best ever! We're almost there! One more time, honey. Say 'Tinky Winky.'"

Aeesha screamed again but stayed exactly where she was. A little smile had crept across her face. "Tinky Winky," she said.

Her mom immediately leapt up, grabbed Tinky Winky, and handed it to her daughter. "You did it, Aeesha! You did it! Your first whole word! I knew you could do it!"

Aeesha held fast to her Teletubby, but her eyes were riveted to her mom, who was still jumping up and down, celebrating her daughter.

ACTIVITY TIME!

For each column of Table 9, simply follow the instructions in the top box of each column. Have fun!

CELEBRATING	TRYING	THE 3 E'S
Something your child does that you can celebrate more (eye contact, language, etc.)	Something your child struggles with where you can celebrate his or her trying more	An activity you already do with your child (baths, meals, etc.) to which you can add the 3 E's

Table 9

ONLINE RESOURCES

For more in-depth help with the principles and techniques of this chapter, please go to www.autismbreakthrough.com/chapter11. Celebrating you!

STARTING POINT

Choose one activity that you already do with your child (from column 3 of Table 9), and really focus on bringing the three Es to this activity. Actively look for any opportunities to cheer your child on. For instance, if you are giving him a bath, be hugely excited about the bath. Cheer your child for getting in the bath (even if he does this every day). If your child picks up a washcloth, celebrate that. You will be astounded at how much this transforms the entire experience—for both of you!

TWELVE

The Big Picture: The Son-Rise Program ABCs

IF YOU CAN'T SEE YOUR CHILD, YOU CAN'T HELP YOUR CHILD

What if I told you that there is an entire element of your child's existence that you have never seen? And what if I told you that I could give you a special pair of glasses that would instantly enable you to see what you've been missing?

If you aren't able to see what's truly going on with your child in a given moment, you can't make decisions about the best way to help her. Being able to see what is actually happening with a particular child from moment to moment is what's missing when most therapists work with a child on the autism spectrum. They see the child's skill deficits, but when they are working with a child from 2:00 to 3:00, they often don't see that the child they are working with at 2:00 is a different child than the one they are working with at 2:45.

At 2:15, the child may be completely encapsulated in her world, shutting out everything and everyone else, including the therapist. At 2:45, the child may be totally connected—participating, receptive, looking at the therapist, etc. But in most cases, the therapist's overall curriculum and methods continues unabated from 2:00 to 3:00. This is unfortunate, because the two modes described above require two completely different approaches.

Wouldn't it be great to be able to clearly see which mode your child was in so that you could use the approach that works best with her in each moment?

Now that you have the arsenal of principles, techniques, and approaches from the previous chapters, wouldn't it be terrific to be able to know exactly when a principle such as joining is optimal and when challenging your child using her motivations is ideal?

Get ready. Here come the glasses.

WHY TIMING IS EVERYTHING

Children—both with and without autism—are typically taught according to the schedule of the adult. We learn *X* from 9:00 to 10:00, *Y* from 10:00 to 11:00, etc. At home, it's no different. We do such-and-such activity in the morning, before bed, whatever. The point is, we (the adults) determine what happens when.

We can pull this off with neurotypical children. Sure, some of them might complain, but we have a guaranteed base level of interaction with them,. They will, in general, respond to their name, follow instructions, and react to cajoling, threats of punishment, or promises of rewards.

We have no such luxury with our special children. Since they occupy a world all their own, free from the constraints of customary interpersonal dynamics, it is up to us to follow the ebbs and flows of *their* internal process. Of course, we can ignore this, as almost everyone does, but then we must live with the side effects: a constant push-pull with our children, damaged trust, a compromised relationship in which our children lack interest in our world, and a dramatically slowed pace of learning.

What ends up happening is that we push our children to learn, interact, or process incoming information during the times they are unavailable to do so. What we don't do is use this "unavailable" time to bond and relationship-build (by joining, for instance). On the other side of this same coin, we don't optimally utilize the small windows of connection, engagement, and availability that we *do* get to help our children to grow, stretch, communicate, and learn new things (by utilizing the motivation principle, for example).

The solution is to be able to accurately see when our children are in their own world, and thus unavailable for teaching or interacting, and when they are connected with us, and thus available to learn, interact, and go our way. Once we do this, we can then cater our interactions with our children to bond with them when bonding is most useful and to challenge them to grow when they are most ready to do so.

THE EXCLUSIVE-INTERACTIVE CONTINUUM

Every waking minute of every day, your child is somewhere on the exclusive-interactive continuum. Sometimes your child is isming, making no eye contact with you, and unresponsive when you call his name. In this instance, we would say that your child is all the way over on the exclusive end of the continuum. He is planted firmly in his own special world, which is "exclusive"—as in, he is excluding you and everyone else.

Other times, your child might play with you, look at you, laugh, talk to you, and you may notice that he is more flexible, more willing to go your way. In this instance, we would say that your child is all the way over on the interactive end of the continuum. He is participating in your world. He is "interactive"—as in, willing and able to interact with you and others.

Of course, there are many times when your child isn't all one or the other. That's why we call it a continuum. Throughout the day, your child probably oscillates up and down the continuum. If you can see where he is on the continuum, then you will know exactly what to do to reach him. You will know precisely which Son-Rise Program technique to use and when to use it.

RED LIGHTS AND GREEN LIGHTS

A simple and easy-to-remember shortcut to these concepts is something we call red lights and green lights.

- Red lights = signals that your child is on the exclusive end of the continuum.
- Green lights = signals that your child is on the interactive end of the continuum.

One other term I want to throw at you: micro-assessments. The word sounds more complicated than it is. When you take your child to be evaluated, they are given an assessment. The double flaw with these assessments is this.

- They only measure your child at one snapshot in time, even though long-term decisions about her are made from this one snapshot.
- The chances are high that your child will behave atypically when confronted with a stranger making her do unfamiliar tasks.

With a micro-assessment, *you* take a moment to observe your child and make a quick assessment as to whether she is giving you a red light or a green light. So how can you tell whether your child is giving you a red light or a green light?

Red Light Signals

- My child is stimming.
- My child is excluding me from what she is doing.
- My child seems rigid and controlling.
- My child does not respond when I speak to her.
- My child moves away when I touch her.
- My child is making sure to move or turn away from me.

Green Light Signals

- My child is looking at me.
- My child responds when I call her name.
- My child seems flexible (i.e., willing to change or alter her activity).
- My child is being physically affectionate with me.
- My child is involving me in her activity.
- When I make a request, my child responds.
- My child is speaking to me.

Now, are you ready to put it all together?

THE SON-RISE PROGRAM ABCs

I developed the ABC model to make it easier for parents and professionals to make moment-by-moment decisions while working with their children. This model is outlined in Table 10.

A stands for Assess, which we've just discussed. It simply means that the first step in the model is to take a moment and do your best to gauge whether your child is giving you a red light or a green light, based upon the criteria above.

B stands for Bond. If you detect that your child is giving you a red light, you'll want to focus on bonding and relationship-building with him.

C stands for Challenge. This refers to the times when you get a green light from your child. These are the times to challenge your child—to teach, promote more interaction, introduce a new activity, etc. In this section of the model, you are asking your child for more.

Assess	Bond	Challenge
Is my child isming? Is my child excluding me from what he or she is doing? Does my child seem rigid or controlling? Is my child non-responsive if I speak to him or her? Does my child move away when I touch him or her? Is my child making sure to move or turn away from me?	Join Give control Be user-friendly Celebrate Don't ask for anything	

Table 10

Assess	Bond	Challenge
Is my child looking at me? Does my child respond when I call his or her name? Does my child seem flexible (i.e. willing to change or alter his or her activity)? Is my child being physically affectionate with me? Is my child walking or moving over to me? Is my child involving me in his or her activity? If I make a request, does my child respond? Is my child speaking to me?		Use the Motivation Principle Play dumb Request something of your child Use the 3 E's Encourage trying Focus on the 4 Fundamentals of Socialization

Table 10 continued

ACTIVITY TIME!

Spend five minutes with your child. However, instead of trying to do something with her (or getting her to do something with you), just *observe* your child. Using the assessment questions, see if you can figure out whether she is giving you a red light or a green light. Important: Once you've figured this out, *don't do anything!* Don't try to bond if you see a red light or challenge if you see a green light. This is about observing your child. As you are observing, fill out Table 11 by writing yes or no in answer to each question.

Assessment Question	Yes/No
Is my child isming? Is my child excluding me from what he or she is doing? Does my child seem rigid or controlling? Is my child non-responsive if I speak to him or her? Does my child move away when I touch him or her? Is my child making sure to move or turn away from me?	
Is my child looking at me? Does my child respond when I call his or her name? Does my child seem flexible (i.e. willing to change or alter his or her activity)? Is my child being physically affectionate with me? Is my child walking or moving over to me? Is my child involving me in his or her activity? If I make a request, does my child respond? Is my child speaking to me?	
Red Light? Green Light?	

Table 11

ONLINE RESOURCES

For more in-depth help with the principles and techniques of this chapter, please go to www.autismbreakthrough.com/chapter12. Happy assessing!

STARTING POINT

Spend five minutes with your child. Determine, as best you can (without using the chart above), whether he is giving you a red light or a green light. Repeat this throughout the day anytime you like. The whole point here is to practice and get used to looking for red lights and green lights whenever you are with your child. Eventually, you will see what signal he is giving you without having to pause and think about it. The "glasses" you're learning to wear will become permanent contact lenses! And, whenever you are with your child, you will have a feel for whether it's time to bond with or challenge him.

THIRTEEN

Sensory Overload: Optimizing Your Child's Environment

EARLIER IN THE book, we discussed what your child's daily experience is like. Let's return to a large component of that experience: your child's sensory-processing challenges. For simplicity's sake, allow me to reproduce a few paragraphs from Chapter 2.

> Your child has difficulty processing and making sense of sensory input. This means that he sees, hears, smells, tastes, and feels things very differently than you or I do. When your child hears something, for instance, it sounds louder, softer, or just plain different than when you hear it.
>
> If you take a moment right now and just listen in silence to any background noise, you may notice a lot of little sounds—cars, wind, the heater or air conditioner, a TV or conversation in another room, etc. You probably didn't notice all of these noises until just now. That's as it should be.
>
> The human ear is bombarded by a continuous cacophony of sounds. One of the brain's chief tasks is to filter out irrelevant sounds and filter in the important sound, such as your spouse/boyfriend/girlfriend talking. (Well, at least we'd call that sound important *most* of the time!)
>
> With your child, all of those noises are coming in at the same volume! (It doesn't work in *exactly* this way, but this is the closest approximation to your child's experience that we can get into right now.) So, when you tell your child to pay attention and listen, what, exactly should he listen to? Which of the twenty-five sounds is your child supposed to pay attention to?

This is your child's experience day in and day out. You know how you feel after you've spent the day at an airport (tired, overwhelmed, like you just want to veg out)? Well, your child wakes up, has breakfast, lunch, dinner, then goes to sleep—in the middle of a busy airport. Even if it's just your living room, it's an airport to your child.

For a deeper understanding of our children's sensory and self-regulation systems, MarySue Williams and Sherry Shellenberger, the creators of the Alert Program® and authors of several books, including *"How Does Your Engine Run?"® A Leader's Guide to the Alert Program®*. They are very knowledgeable and competent when it comes to the ins and outs of sensory integration and self-regulation. I've attended one of their courses, and they have visited ours. They do wonderful work, and they also send parents our way because they understand both the significance of our children's sensory systems and the importance of trust and interpersonal relationships. They wrote an article for parents using The Son-Rise Program available under "Free Resources" at www.alterprogram.com. These two women are also deeply caring and magnificent people!

Because of your child's sensory-processing challenges, addressing your child's environment is essential. Often, an overstimulating environment (at school, at home, or elsewhere) can serve as a major obstacle to a child's progress and interaction. So you want to do everything you can to reduce overstimulation and make your child's immediate environment as conducive to successful sensory processing—and thus, to interaction and learning—as possible.

CREATING AN OPTIMIZED ENVIRONMENT

How do you do this? You set aside a room in the house to be a special playroom or focus room, where much of the momentous work with your child can occur. These are the characteristics of such a setting.

1. **Distraction-free**

Most rooms in which your child finds herself are riddled with low-level distractions—murals and pictures on the wall, items strewn across the floor, phones ringing, people talking, televisions blaring, people walking in and out, windows to look out of and let in blasts of light, etc. Even a single one of these distractions can be very overstimulating to someone with sensory challenges. Choose a totally enclosed room in the house with closable, lockable doors (you could use your child's bedroom if that works), and do whatever you can to eliminate from that room as many of the above distractions as possible. In fact, do your best to create a room that a neurotypical child might find boring. (It won't be boring to your special child.)

2. **Free from control battles.**

Remember our discussion in Chapter 10 about the importance of avoiding control battles? For this room to be a place where you can get extraordinary interaction and progress from your child, it needs to be a place where he feels totally safe and secure. Control battles obliterate that safety and security, to say nothing of how they compromise your child's trust and relationship with you. This means that you want to make this room a "yes" room. You want the room to be so safe that you don't have to say no to *anything*—for instance, "don't touch that," "don't climb on that," "don't do that"—unlike in the kitchen, for example, where you have to say no to many things—sharp knives, hot stoves, and so on.

3. **Toys are on a shelf that your child cannot reach.**

The goal here is not to make things difficult for your child. The idea is to foster communication. Your child can have anything on that shelf that she wants. But she will need *you* to get it. This arrangement sets you up as a partner and friend to your child (rather than an obstacle). Remember, this room is a "yes" room. This is a place where your child will have a huge sense of control and autonomy. However, she still cannot reach what she wants on the shelf without your help. And what a help you will be! You will be there, ready to move, ready to get her what she wants as soon as she asks for it.

4. No electronic toys, televisions, or computers.
I know that your first instinct might be to object to this guideline. I understand. I know that you may feel that your child enjoys these items—or that they serve as a short-term babysitter while you are making dinner. But it is essential to understand that *these items help your child to be autistic.* First, they are self-creating isms. (As we talked about in Chapter 2, there's nothing wrong with isms when your *child* creates them, but that doesn't mean *we* want to provide machinery that creates them.) Second, no matter how educational a video, toy, or computer program is, it can never teach your child to interact and be social. (In reality, these items make it easier for your child to be *less* interactive.) And, third, as long as these items are in the room, you will always be playing second fiddle to a machine. After all, you can't make multicolored lights come out of your eyes (or do anything else a machine does), and machines don't challenge your child to be social. So, in the short term, your child will always prefer these items to you. The bottom line is: less electronics, more interaction.

5. One-on-one.
For now (not forever), you want only one person at a time in the room with your child. This is to prevent overstimulation and promote interaction. You are trying to build a bridge from your child's world to yours. At first, this bridge needs to be from person to person—from your child to another individual. This is the simplest way to forge an interpersonal connection.

6. If possible: a window of one-way glass or two to four mini-cameras.

At the Autism Treatment Center of America, we have this in our playrooms, but of course our playrooms are set up to be perfect. Yours doesn't have to be, but you will want a way to see what is happening in your child's playroom or focus room. This is important both so you know how your child is doing and so you can tell how the person working with your child is doing.

WHY LOCKING THE DOOR CAN BE HELPFUL

I often get asked why Son-Rise Program parents often lock the door to their children's playrooms.

To be clear, we are not talking about locking your child in his room by himself. Remember, there is always an adult in the room.

With that said, it bears stating that I have never, in my life, heard anyone ask this question about the fact that front and back doors to houses are routinely locked (with the child and at least one adult inside). No one I know is advocating for an open-door house policy, where children with autism can simply leave the house when they please and go marching down the street.

I bring this up to highlight the fact that there is *always* an enclosed environment around every child. It's just a question of where that enclosure is. You cannot really work with a child that is running from room to room (*your* child may not do this, but many do).

And it's not about locking anyone up. It's about giving your child some relief—and providing him with a loving, nurturing, and helpful environment.

So, if you believe that it could be useful or important for

your child to have a one-on-one environment that is free from control battles and is not overstimulating, then being in a playroom or focus room where the door is not a revolving one might be what you choose. At the end of the day, it is, of course, your decision.

TAKING YOUR CHILD TO THE SUPERMARKET, PLAYGROUND, OR AMUSEMENT PARK

Many parents feel that it is very important to take their child to the playground or similar venue where their child can "be a regular kid." They feel that to skip this is to deprive their child of vital experiences.

It is essential to understand, though, that your child, right now, is not a "regular kid." Your child is different. Your child has special challenges. If having your child in a typical environment solved these challenges, you wouldn't be reading this book, and we wouldn't have an autism epidemic, because we could just take our kids to typical environments with neurotypical children, and—poof!—challenge solved.

You know better than anyone else that this isn't the way it works. I completely understand that you might sometimes *want* it to work this way. I really do. And I would never begrudge you wanting that. But I also know that you love and care about your child and would go to the ends of the earth to help her.

So, please, take this in: because of your child's sensory-processing challenges, she *can't* have a "regular" experience at the park—not right now. Your child can't experience success in these public arenas when she is overstimulated and cannot take the experience in.

However, wouldn't it wonderful to be able to reintroduce

these types of experiences to your child later—when she *can* process them and be successful? This is possible! It doesn't require perfection on your part. It just takes some investment now. It takes some concentrated time now—time where you limit excursions as much as possible—in order to get years of payoff later.

I have heard parents adamantly exclaim that their child loves being out of the house and in these public environments. I always respond with one of my favorite quotes from my sister Bryn: "Heroin addicts really like heroin. That doesn't mean that it's good for them." (This quote is so good, I'm going to bring it back in Chapter 16, when we talk about diet.)

When children have sensory-processing challenges and they enter an environment where their nervous system is overwhelmed, one of two things happens. Many children become reactive and prone to meltdowns. Some, however, enjoy and become addicted to the rush of adrenaline and cortisol that courses through their fragile systems.

If your child is of the second variety, she will appear to love being in overstimulating environments. That doesn't mean it's good for her. It doesn't mean that her nervous system isn't compromised and that her ability to interact and learn is not severely impaired by that environment.

Can I say for sure, without ever meeting your child, she cannot handle these public, highly stimulating environments that she appears to enjoy? No. But I can tell you this: For 99 percent of the children we see, these environments are detrimental to learning and interaction. Unless your child is already highly interactive with other people, flexible, tolerant of all sounds and lights, does not ism or have meltdowns on these excursions, and does not ism or have meltdowns within two hours of returning home from these excursions, your child is probably a member of that 99 percent.

FROM THE PLAYROOM TO THE "REAL WORLD"

The fact that the playroom or focus room is a "yes" room doesn't mean that your child will never get challenged. Quite the opposite. In that room, your child will be more directly and clearly challenged on the core aspects of his autism than anywhere else on earth.

When your child isn't trying to juggle a million other sensory inputs, he can actually move forward on the four fundamentals: eye contact and nonverbal communication, verbal communication, interactive attention span, and flexibility.

Once you eliminate overstimulation and get your child out of the fight-or-flight mode that accompanies that overstimulation, everything changes. I don't just mean that your child becomes more interactive, although this is certainly what we see. I also mean that children in focus rooms learn to adjust their sensory input systems. Slowly, they begin to tolerate more and more stimulation—*if* it is added piece by piece and not all at once.

If I tell you to lift two hundred pounds, you probably can't do it, even if I have you try all day (or all week). But if I start you off at thirty pounds, then build up to forty, then fifty, then sixty, eventually we can get to two hundred pounds.

Over time, we make the playroom more and more like the outside world until, eventually, there is no difference. Then your child doesn't need a special environment anymore. He can be successful in any environment.

I was in a playroom for three and a half straight years. Now I spend my days in crowded, crazy places in a host of countries worldwide. That distraction-free "yes" room that my parents set up way back in 1974 has proved to be a godsend to me now.

The Story of Jordan

Several years ago, a boy from the United Kingdom named Jordan came to the Autism Treatment Center of America. (I'm using his real name because his story was broadcast on TV internationally.) The BBC aired a documentary entitled "I Want My Little Boy Back," which followed Jordan and his parents as they traveled to the ATCA and then continued their Son-Rise Program at home. (Contact the ATCA if you would like a DVD of this documentary.)

Jordan's story is rather amazing; he changed quite radically. I'll let you see the documentary and experience it for yourself, but I wanted to highlight one part of Jordan's story because it so clearly applies here.

Before Jordan came to the ATCA, he was in perpetual sensory overload. He screamed and cried much of the time. He was overwhelmed. If someone was mowing the lawn near his house, he would cover his ears with his hands, screeching.

This was Jordan's parents' day-in, day-out experience. They often found it difficult just to get through the day.

After one week in our playroom environment, Jordan noticed one of our property maintenance workers mowing the lawn outside his window. He strolled to the window and calmly watched the lawn being mowed. He neither cried nor covered his ears.

Jordan's parents were shocked, but we weren't. We see the effect of the focus room environment every day.

AN EXTREME ENVIRONMENT

If setting up a playroom or focus room for your child, including all of the guidelines and recommendations in this chapter, feels extreme to you, I want you to know that I agree with you. The

Son-Rise Program playroom *is* extreme. Your child has autism. Extreme is called for. The focus room is an extreme *temporary* environment designed to get extreme *permanent* results. If that is something you want, then taking the steps outlined in this chapter is worth considering.

ACTIVITY TIME!

As a way to get yourself started, take some time to fill out Table 12.

Five Things You Can Do To Optimize Your Child's Immediate Environment
1)
2)
3)
4)
5)

Table 12

ONLINE RESOURCES

For more in-depth help with the principles and techniques of this chapter, please go to www.autismbreakthrough.com/chapter13. Delve in!

STARTING POINT

Before you set up any kind of official playroom or focus room, you can take some very basic steps in your living room, your child's bedroom, or another room in the house where you will be with your child today. First, clear away any items on the floor, countertops, and tabletops. Close any open doors in this room as well. Unplug any appliances (other than the lights, of course!). Bring in three nonelectronic toys or games that you think your child likes or might like, such as a set of stuffed animals (counts as one item), a ball, a musical instrument—or, if she is more sophisticated, a card game, a board game, or paper and markers (counts as one item). Now you have a temporary focus room! Spend thirty minutes in this room with your child today and focus on enjoying this time with her.

FOURTEEN

Tantrums and Other Challenging Behaviors: How Changing Your Reactions Changes Everything

I'M SURE YOUR child doesn't have any behaviors that you find challenging, right? Okay, dumb question. If your child is a human being, then he does things that you, at times, find tough to deal with. That's all right. You're in good company, and so is your child.

What may surprise you is the outsized role you have in your child's tantrums (crying, hitting, biting, etc.) and other related behaviors. In fact, chances are extremely high that you are unwittingly teaching your child to do *more* of the very behaviors you most want him to cease.

How in the world could that be possible?

AN ANALOGY

Have you ever spent a significant amount of time in a foreign country where English was not spoken? On the other hand, have you ever spent time in a country where English is not the first language spoken but everyone can still speak English fluently?

Allow me, if you will, to walk you briefly through two of my foreign escapades. You may recall from Chapter 1 that I spent some time living in Stockholm, Sweden.

Now, the Swedes speak Swedish, of course. But they also speak superb English, and many of them enjoy practicing their English on native English-speakers. During the year that I lived in Stockholm, I took Swedish language classes five days a week. On top of that, I'm pretty good at languages, so I fully expected to be fluent by the end of the year.

I was utterly mistaken.

Swedish, as a language, is not particularly difficult. However, what I noticed, when I was out on the town in Stockholm, is that I would stop someone to ask for directions. I would begin speaking in Swedish, but as soon as I found myself stumbling the tiniest bit, I would fall back on my English. The moment I did so, whomever I was speaking to would respond to me in crystal clear English. It was awesome!

The only problem was, since this was a regular occurrence, I found that, by the end of the year, I was very un-fluent in Swedish. How come? As long as I knew that people understood English, it didn't matter how much Swedish I took or how many times my teacher told me to "Tala Svenska, du skit!" (That is: "Speak Swedish," followed by an expletive that I decline to translate.) I would fall back on my old language, never fully making the transition to the new one.

However, I also spent some time in Spain, where most people did not speak English. If I wanted to find a restroom I really, really had to ask in Spanish. Even though I had taken Spanish in high school, I was nevertheless shocked at how quickly I picked the language up in Spain. The key was: Spanish was the only language that anyone understood. Communicating in Spanish was the only way for me to get anything across to anyone. So, Spanish it was, and pronto.

TANTRUMS: THE OLD PARADIGM

The analogy above illustrates a concept that applies very powerfully to your child. Most of the time, when a child on the autism spectrum tantrums, hits, screams, cries, etc., parents take one of two roads. Option one: They get angry and reactive, scolding their child. Option two (most common): They try to "fix the problem." They ask, "What is it, sweetie-pie?" and then proceed to dash around frantically, trying to figure out what their child wants so they can give it to her—so that the tantrum will stop.

The driving, overriding question in most parents' minds is: How do I stop this tantrum? I call this question "the indentured-servitude question" because, once you ask it—congratulations! You are now a servant to your child's tantrum. You will do whatever it takes to bring that tantrum to a blessed end. Both types of reactions outlined above (option one and option two) fall under the heading of "big reactions." Big reactions are emotional, fast, animated, loud (usually), and action-packed.

The reason for these big reactions is that most parents see the tantrum as a kind of alarm system. When it goes off, they are immediately on high alert. They want to find and fix the emergency. What's more, there is usually a direct emotional connection between their child's tantrum and their own discomfort. They feel instantly agitated (which doesn't help their child to calm down).

This is not difficult to understand. Most parents feel agitated because they see the tantrum as something wrong, and every minute that the tantrum continues is a signal that they are not being a good mom or dad. After all, "good" mothers and fathers solve their children's problems and stop the tantrum, right?

But, wait! I haven't gotten to the best part yet!

Not only are you now an indentured servant, but you will, for sure, get more and more tantrums from your child. Why? Take a look at Figure 2, on the following page, which shows what most of us do when confronted with a challenging behavior—and how this affects our children's behavior over time.

As we can see, a big reaction from a parent leads to more challenging behavior from the child. And each time a parent (or teacher, therapist, family member, etc.) reacts this way, the

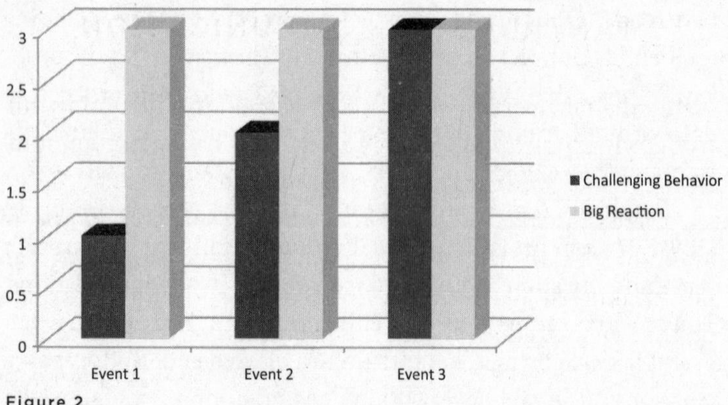

Figure 2

challenging behavior grows successively more frequent, more extreme, and longer in duration.

Furthermore, the term "challenging behavior" doesn't just refer to tantrums. It also refers to instances where your child does something such as pulling a painting off the wall, speaking loudly, being disruptive in a public place, breaking a household item, running into the street, or using profanity.

What happens when our child behaves in one of these challenging ways? In most cases, we light up like a Christmas tree. For instance, if our child pulls a painting off the wall, we might sprint over to where our child is (with a shocked or exasperated expression on our face) and exclaim, "Honey, what did you do?! You're not supposed to touch that!" For some of us, we may feel a bit guilty for reacting and say, "I know you didn't mean to. Let's take you into the other room." By this time, though, it's too late. We've already given a big reaction, and thus lived out the above graph.

Whether it is a tantrum or something else, the results of that graph are the same: *more* challenging behavior.

I'll explain why this is in a moment, but first let's explore a brand-new paradigm.

TANTRUMS AS COMMUNICATION

Here's the new paradigm: When your child is tantruming, hitting, crying, pinching, screaming, etc., he is trying to communicate! Terrific! You *want* him to communicate!

There's just one problem: Your child is speaking to you in Swedish! Speaking in Swedish is much more communicative than not speaking at all, but the downside of this—from your child's point of view—is that no one around here understands Swedish.

Your child can't go into a store, scream, and get a pack of gum. No one will know what he wants.

So it is important to understand that when your child is doing anything that resembles a tantrum, it's not an alarm bell. It's not a statement about you as a parent. It's just an attempt to communicate. (This is why we don't join in with tantrums. Joining is what we do when a child is exclusive and disconnected. A tantrum is the opposite. A tantruming child is specifically endeavoring to communicate with us, not to disconnect.)

Using this paradigm, let's return to the graph above. Why would your big response encourage your child to do more of the challenging behavior over time?

Two reasons: First, recall from Chapter 11 that big reactions lead to repeat actions. This serves your child when it applies to big celebrations—the type of big reaction discussed in that chapter. When you celebrate your child looking at you, you get more looks. But it doesn't serve your child (or you) when your big reaction acts as a highlighter for exactly what you don't want.

Remember that your child lives in a world in which he often feels no control or predictability. He is therefore always on the lookout for predictability and control. If you light up like a Christmas tree every time he does behavior X, he will do it more, if only to restore that predictability and control.

The second reason your big response results in more challenging behavior is that *your reaction tells your child that you understand Swedish*—especially if you are running around trying to "fix" things. Your child is no dummy. Why on earth would he work his tail off trying to speak in full sentences when he could just scream and be understood (at least generally)? Why should he do the heavy lifting required to formulate words when a tantrum sends everyone scurrying?

But wait! I *still* haven't gotten to the best part!

Not only are you now an indentured servant who is teaching your child to increase his or her challenging behaviors because you understand Swedish, but you have also helped to decrease your child's useful, productive communication.

Let's explore why this is.

Let's take another look at Figure 2.

Okay. Now what happens when your child engages in a sweet, communicative behavior? If you're like most people, you deem this a nonemergency, and you don't fall all over yourself trying to respond.

Suppose that you are making dinner and your child comes up to you and quietly says a word or two. Or gently tugs on your sleeve. If you're right in the middle of cooking, you probably say something like, "I hear you, sweetie. I'll be there in just a few minutes. I just need to finish dinner."

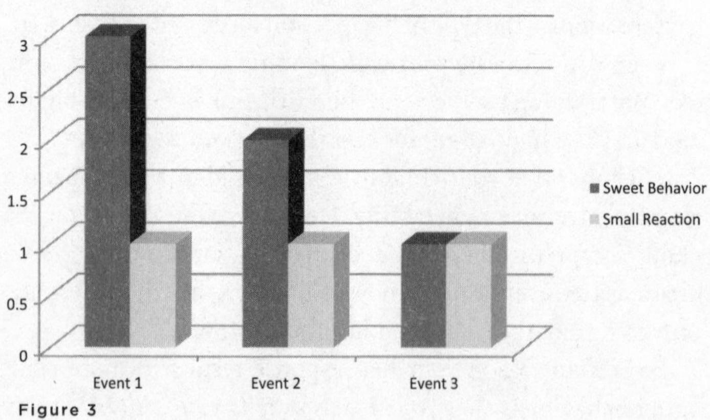

Figure 3

The results of that scenario are depicted in Figure 3.

Ah, but how do we react when we are making dinner and our child starts screaming? Dinner can wait—we have a crisis on our hands! Aaaaand we're back to Figure 2.

What does your child take from all of this? Any intelligent child would surmise the following: communicating sweetly gets me the slowest, most mellow, least urgent response, and screaming get me a fast, big, urgent response. When your child really wants to communicate something important, which method is he going to use?

All right, so now that we know this, what's the way out?

TURNING THE TABLES

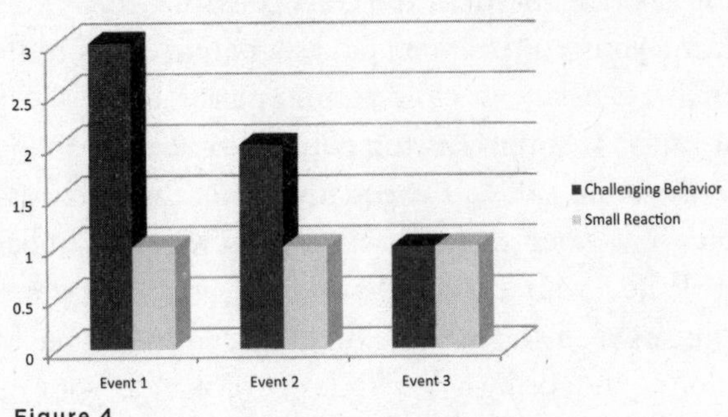

Figure 4

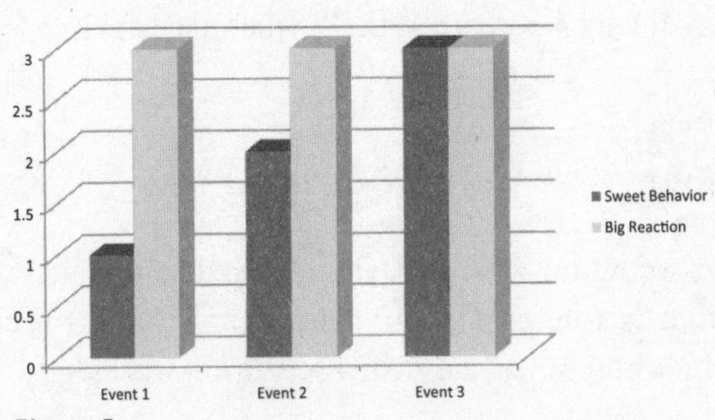

Figure 5

Take a gander at Figures 4 and 5. Do you see? You can turn the tables by reversing your reactions. When your child yells, cries, tantrums, whatever, you want your response to be slow and flat. (This is one of the very few times when I would advocate *not* using the three Es.) I'm not saying to ignore your child—or to be punitive and say something like, "Listen, buddy, I'm not going to help you when you whine and carry on." This isn't about punishing or "teaching her a lesson."

I'm talking about communicating to your child that you understand English, but you don't understand Swedish. The next time she tantrums, you want to immediately relax. Instead of asking yourself the indentured-servitude question ("How do I stop this tantrum?"), ask yourself this: "How can I help my child communicate more effectively?"

If you ask that question, you can't go wrong.

Remind yourself that your job as a parent is not to stop the tantrum, it's to help your child communicate. In the short term, that may mean that the tantrum goes on for *longer*.

One the other side of the equation, it is absolutely essential that you show your child that you really, really understand English. When your child behaves in a way that is sweet or communicative (using words, tugging gently at your sleeve, taking your hand, using a nice tone of voice, etc.), your mission in life is to respond quickly, urgently, and enthusiastically. The running-around-like-a-chicken-with-its-head-cut-off that used to happen during a tantrum—that's what needs to happen here instead.

To recap:

Tantrums, crying, screaming, hitting, biting, pinching → slow, flat, mellow.

Sweet, communicative behavior → fast, big, urgent, excited.

So, what do you actually do? Let's outline that in the context of a specific child so you can really see how it works.

The Story of Michelle

I was working with Michelle at an outreach I did some years ago, and she wanted one of her toys from the shelf. (You may recall from Chapter 4 that an outreach is when a Son-Rise Program teacher or child facilitator spends a couple of days in a family's house helping them implement their program.) I was more than happy to get it for her, and I had a good idea which one she wanted, but she was screaming a blue streak. ("Screaming a blue streak" is an expression I happily steal from William Hogan.)

Michelle was crying and yelling. One of her hands was pointing up at one of the shelves. The other was being ferociously bitten—by her. (Every time she jammed her hand in her mouth and bit down, she would look right at me.)

Knowing from her parents that this was a common response of Michelle's (she was very fluent in "Swedish"), I was quite glad that she was doing this with me. I thought to myself, *This is the perfect opportunity to help Michelle communicate more effectively!* (Sincerely, that's really what I thought. I know this may seem far-fetched to you, but we'll address how it can be totally doable for you in Chapter 17.)

I squatted down so that I wasn't standing over her. "Hey, Michelle, I really want to help you get what you want, but I can't understand you when you scream." I paused for a moment, then clapped my hand to my mouth. "Ooh, you know what? I can understand you when you use your words! Tell me what you want, and I'll *run* and get it!" I paused again, this time for a while.

Michelle screamed some more, bit her hand again, and threw something at me.

"Hmmm," I said, putting on my best "confused" look. "I don't know what that means." I very slowly wandered toward the shelves. Michelle continued screaming.

"Huh. I know you want something, but I can't understand screaming." I finally reached the shelves.

"I'm just not sure." Slowly, I reached up and plucked something down—a toy that I was fairly sure was *not* what she wanted.

I walked slowly back to her and handed the toy to her. "Is this the one you want?"

Michelle flung it across the room, continued screaming, and bit her hand again.

"Okay, so it's clearly not that one. Cool." I wandered back toward the shelf.

"I can't understand screaming, so I'm still not sure. If you use your words, Michelle, I'll know exactly what you want."

She continued screaming.

I picked another toy from the shelf—not what she wanted—made my way back to her, and said, "Is this the one you want?"

Michelle grabbed the toy and pitched it at the bowl of soup on the shelf. Missed.

I squatted down again so that I was at eye level. "I'll tell you what, Michelle. Since I can't understand you when you scream, I'm going to be over in that corner playing with some toys. If you want me, just use your words, and I will *run* and get you what you want so fast!"

I took some toys and went to the corner to play.

Michelle screamed for a while longer. Fifteen minutes passed.

Suddenly, from the other end of the room, I heard, barely audible: "Want doll."

I sprang up, bounded over to the shelf, grabbed the doll, ran over to her, and held it out to her. She snatched it.

"Hey, Michelle! You did it! Thank you so much for using your words! Now I can understand you!"

For the rest of my session with her, whenever she would so much as glance at the shelves, I would jump up and stand poised at the shelves, ready to follow her command, happy to show her how much she could get if she used her words.

She actually started to get a kick out this, ordering me to do various things, sometimes even laughing at my darting to and fro.

For the rest of my time in her home, she didn't tantrum at all. Her parents, who, of course, had been watching everything, were very excited because they saw a clear, effective way forward—and they took it.

GROWING UP TANTRUM-FREE

You can imagine what it was like growing up in my house. We all knew from the get-go that tantruming, screaming, crying, etc. was just never going to work with my parents.

I must admit that sometimes, as a little kid (post-autism), I found this annoying. But in the end, guess what? I didn't tantrum! Not as a kid, not as a teenager.

It's not that I never tried to cajole my parents into giving me something. It's just that I did it by talking and convincing, not by crying, whining, or complaining. And I certainly didn't always get what I wanted, but when I didn't, I still saw no point in flipping out about it because I knew that it wouldn't change anything anyway. (I will tell you that, one time, when I was little, after being turned down in my request for a family trek to get some ice cream, I went through the house, made all of the beds, vacuumed all the rooms, and then put up a sign for my parents to see, asking yet again. I got it!)

A NOTE ON THE WORD "MANIPULATIVE"

I have, in the past, been asked whether the explanation of tantruming as something our children do in an attempt to communicate what they want means that our kids are being manipulative. To say that our children are being manipulative is to believe that our children are being insincere or deceptive in order to maneuver us to their ends. It has a somewhat sinister connotation.

When I say that your child is crying, yelling, screaming, hitting, biting, or pinching in order to communicate, I mean that quite literally. Your child may find communicating with words to be difficult, cumbersome, and, as we discussed earlier, not terribly useful in getting a fast response.

Your child is thus doing his level best to communicate. He's coming from a totally sincere place. Just because your child may be, for instance, using crying to *communicate* rather than because they are *upset* does not in any way impugn his motives.

Your child is doing the very best that he can to communicate in a topsy-turvy world. There is absolutely nothing wrong with that. "Manipulative" would be the very last word I would use to describe your child.

We help our children to communicate more effectively when we don't judge their current behaviors. In fact, you will find that following the guidelines in this chapter without any annoyance or judgment on your part will be enormously helpful in enabling your child to switch gears.

SENSORY OVERLOAD OR PHYSICAL PAIN

It is possible that your child may be crying because she is in a state of sensory overload or because she is physically hurting (bumped her head, has a stomachache, etc.).

If you clearly see that your child is hurt or hurting, of course you'll want to do what you can to help or soothe. James was prone to severe stomachaches, and there are many times when I or Charlotte would rub James's stomach as he was crying.

But even here, using our reactions to foster communication makes sense. Partly because, from the get-go, Charlotte used the "reactions" approach with James, he can now tell us what part of him is hurting. Don't you want your child to be able to communicate what is hurting? It will always be helpful to her if you give big and fast responses to language and slower, calmer responses to crying. Even if your child is hurting (or scared, etc.), wouldn't you want to send the message that it's okay—rather than sending the message that something scary and stressful is occurring (which is exactly the message we send when we react in a panic to crying)?

With respect to sensory overload, we have spent a great deal of time on this issue because of how important it is. The playroom or focus room described in Chapter 13 reduces meltdowns precisely because it eliminates sensory overload. Joining also helps in this regard. Keeping your child out of overstimulating situations will, without question, also reduce crying and meltdowns.

So, as much as possible, take your child out of overstimulating situations and environments, whether or not she is crying. If you see a sensory issue, such as a sound that's disturbing your child, and you can address it, then by all means do so, whether or not she is crying.

Here again, this chapter's principles apply. You want to communicate that nothing scary is happening, even when your child is overstimulated. And you want to show her that you understand English, not Swedish, precisely so that she can better communicate if something is overloading her.

In addition, letting your child work it out herself yields all kinds of benefits to her self-regulation and self-calming.

I certainly experienced this with James.

JAMES: MONTH ONE

Although James loved the ladies, he was very reactive to men. When I first began to work with him, he wasted no time in communicating this fact to me. I would enter his playroom, and the second he saw me, he would fall over like a toppling tree and start wailing and crying on the floor.

I had seen other people endeavor to talk to him and calm him down when he did this, and the result was always the same: the more they talked to him (regardless of what they said), the louder and more insistent his crying became. His agitation seemed to increase with each second that these people spent attending to him. Furthermore, if someone got too close to him during this period, he would push his chin into that person with quite a bit of force and sometimes dig his nails into the person's skin.

When he fell over and started crying as I entered his playroom, I honestly wasn't sure whether he was trying to communicate something (like maybe "Raun, get out!") or whether he was just overwhelmed and agitated because I was a man. Here's the thing: it didn't matter.

What I did was this: first, I would *very* briefly tell him, "Hey, bud, I'm going to be over in that corner when you want to play or use your words." Then I would go over to the corner and begin drawing something on the wall. (His playroom had special walls that you could draw on.)

Every time this occurred, I would feel genuinely relaxed, with zero urgency to stop James from crying. I knew that he needed to regulate himself, and I wanted to give him a chance to do that—without me judging him, pushing him, or placating him.

Another note: while I was drawing in the corner, I would deliberately position myself so that my side (profile) was toward him. Let me tell you why. I have found with many children—including James—that when they are in a tantrum or on a crying jag, if you sit (or stand) facing them, they can feel your attention and focus upon them, and they often become more agitated. On the other hand, you don't want to sit with your back to them because then you can't see them.

So I would sit facing the picture I was drawing (the hardest part of this whole endeavor, given the sad state of my drawing skills), and every so often I would give a quick sideways glance over at James to see what he was up to.

Before I tell you what happened, let me explain that I had seen James wail for *forty-five minutes to an hour* on a regular basis when certain people entered his playroom.

For the first month that I worked with him, James would fall to the ground and cry every single time I entered. I had never had a child cry like this more than once or twice when I entered, so I had to be very clear in my own mind that James was doing this for his own reasons (i.e., because I was a guy)—and not make it mean anything about me.

However, even though James did this for the first month, do you know how long he would cry after I entered each time? *Four minutes.* At most. Sometimes two. Out of a session that lasted between ninety minutes and three hours.

After a few minutes, James would stop crying, walk over to me, and spontaneously begin playing with me (wrestling, taking my hand, asking for something, falling into my lap and laughing).

At that point, I would immediately reciprocate, and that would set the stage for the rest of the session.

After that first month, James never again cried when I entered.

THE IMPORTANCE OF CONSISTENCY

This works only if done with total consistency. It *can't* not work because it plays to your child's intelligence *and* to your child's motivation to get what he wants.

For those who think you've implemented this strategy and believe it hasn't worked, I give you the following anecdote.

The Story of Hassan

We had a mom in the Start-Up course who had a son named Hassan who tantrumed *a lot*. This little guy really loved cookies (understandably). His mom would often let him eat cookies (a problem for separate reasons that we will go over in Chapter 16). However, there were certain times, such as just before bed, when Hassan's mom did not want to give him any cookies.

As she explained to us in class, oftentimes when she would refrain from giving Hassan his cookie, he would scream, cry, etc. When we explained the above principle, she immediately cut in, "Yes, I know, but that doesn't work with my son."

We had heard that response many, many times, so we asked her to take us through exactly what transpired the last time this situation popped up.

She recounted that the night before she flew to the ATCA for her Start-Up, she was getting Hassan ready for bed, and he said "I want cookie" (a phrase he knew quite well).

"And what did you do then?" the teacher asked.

"I told you," Hassan's mother said, "I told him that I was sorry, but that he couldn't have a cookie right before bed."

"Okay," the teacher replied, "and what did Hassan do then?"

Hassan's mom threw her hands up. "Well, that's when he started his routine. He began crying, saying, 'I want cookie!' over and over."

"All right," the teacher continued, "and what did you do then?"

"I told him that he could cry all he wanted, but that he wasn't going to get a cookie right before bed," Hassan's mother said in a tone that implied that she had just spoken the most obvious truth known to humankind.

The teacher followed up again. "And after you told Hassan that, what did he do then?"

"Oh, he really went for it then. He started screeching, rolling around on the floor, kicking his feet, and yelling "I want cookie!" over and over," Hassan's mom explained, looking exasperated.

"And what did you do at that point?" the teacher asked once more.

"Well, of course, this can go on all night, and I have to get him to sleep at some point, so, you know, eventually, after a long while, when there was no other alternative, I had to . . ." She mumbled the last few words of her sentence with her head down, so the teacher couldn't make it out.

"I couldn't make that last bit out," the teacher said gently. "What was it you said you had to do?"

"Give . . . him . . . the . . . cookie," Hassan's mom said hesitantly. She looked disheartened.

Allow me to chime in for a moment. I don't recommend showing your child that you understand Swedish by giving into the tantrum. However, I recommend even *less* the practice of holding out, holding out, holding out—and then giving in an hour later. Why? Because now you've just communicated the following to your child: if you want to get the cookie before bed, you need to speak Swedish (tantrum) *for an hour* before you get it.

Returning to our story, the teacher explained to Hassan's mother exactly what to do, and she went home and really did it. She made sure everyone else in the house did it. And she never wavered. She was slow, flat, and "confused" when Hassan tantrumed (and, of course, never ever gave him a cookie before bed), and she was fast and excited when her son communicated sweetly.

After being back for a couple of weeks, she told us that she was astounded by what she'd seen. The first few days, Hassan screamed, cried, and tantrumed even more than before. But after that, Hassan's mom said it was as if someone had flipped a switch. His tantruming went from several times a day to only once the entire past week. Hassan also became much more communicative, as he saw the power of using his words.

His mother told us that, although she certainly was happier and calmer, what was most exciting was to see that her son seemed so much happier and calmer, too.

One final note on this point. Once in a while, we'll get a parent who absolutely swears that he or she *never* gives his or her child the cookie, and yet the tantruming continues unabated. In response to this, I will, once again, quote my sister Bryn: "Then *someone's* giving your child the cookie."

If you are 100 percent sure that you never give in and never "understand Swedish," then the only other possibility is that someone else in your child's life is responding to crying, hitting, etc. There is no other way for the tantruming to continue. Your child is smart. There is simply no way that your child will, day in and day out, continue to use a mode of communication that never, ever works. It's just not possible.

NOT HITTING VERSUS BEING GENTLE

Don't think of a banana. Whatever you do, don't think of a ripe yellow banana. How'd you do? If you're like the rest of the world, you probably thought of a banana. Then, maybe you tried to imagine a piece of paper or a cloth or maybe just blackness covering the banana.

What does this prove? It illustrates something very important about the human mind: it cannot *not* think of something. If

I tell you *not* to think of a banana, this is impossible. What *is* possible is to *think of something else instead*—an orange, for instance.

Most of us say things to our children such as, "Don't hit," "Don't pinch," or "It's not nice to scratch your sister." For almost everyone, this seems like the most natural thing in the world.

The problem is that when we say "Don't hit," our children hear "Hit." When we say "Don't pinch," our children hear "Pinch." We are inadvertently taking the thing we don't want and making it bigger. We are focusing all of our children's attention on the behavior we *don't* want them to do.

Instead, let's focus on helping our children to *be gentle*. How often do we jump up and down and cheer when our children are gentle? We can show our children what being gentle looks like (touching a hand or shoulder gently). Even better, whenever our children do anything gently (touch our arm, take our hand), we want to make a *huge* deal out of it. Celebrate. Cheer. Clap. Sometimes, when a child who hits touches my arm gently, I run around the room rubbing my arm and exclaim, "Ooooh! That feels so awesome when you're gentle!"

In most cases, our children see us giving large reactions when they hit, pinch, or bite us—and very little, if any, reactions when they are gentle. We want to turn the tables in dramatic fashion!

Remember: our children can picture being gentle, but they cannot picture *not hitting*. Rather than thinking to ourselves, *I need to get my child to stop hitting*, we want to focus our energy and attention on *encouraging our children to be gentle*.

ACTIVITY TIME!

All you're going to do here is to compile a list of all of the behaviors and situations to react *less* to and all of those that you will react *more* to. This list—Table 13—will then serve as a very helpful guidepost going forward!

To React LESS To	To React MORE To

Table 13

ONLINE RESOURCES

For more in-depth help with the principles and techniques of this chapter, please go to www.autismbreakthrough.com/chapter14. Relax and relish!

STARTING POINT

This starting point has two separate parts.

Part 1

The very next time your child hits, cries, or tantrums, focus all of your attention on relaxing yourself. Take a few deep breaths. Remind yourself that what he's doing says nothing about you as a parent. He's just trying to communicate. Nothing terrible is happening.

Until you are relaxed, don't move (unless something unsafe is happening). When you are totally relaxed, say the following to your child: "I love you and want to help you, but I don't understand what you want." Then invite him to use his words to say what he wants. If your child does not yet have any language, invite him to point to what he wants.

If your child speaks or points (without screaming or hitting), then cheer him exuberantly and do your best to give your child what he wants.

Part 2

Find any excuse throughout the day to celebrate your child being gentle or communicating clearly. We're talking about *any* instance. It doesn't have to be right after a time when he was hitting or crying. Look for and notice any times when your child is gentle or communicating clearly, and cheer each instance with great gusto!

FIFTEEN

Asperger's Syndrome: Applying the Son-Rise Program Principles

At the Autism Treatment Center of America, we work with a large number of families who have children or adults with Asperger's syndrome or deemed "high functioning." All of the principles of The Son-Rise Program are just as effective (in some cases, more so!) with these unique individuals. In this chapter, we'll talk about how to apply these principles to your "extra-sophisticated" child.

I strongly recommend scanning back through each chapter before reading each section below. For instance, it will be of great help to you to scan back through Chapter 2 before reading the joining section below. Then, the suggestions below will be easier to understand and apply.

JOINING

When it comes to kids and adults with Asperger's syndrome, there are variations both in what we consider to be an ism and in how we join.

People with Asperger's syndrome will usually not engage in a traditional ism, such as hand-flapping, spinning, tearing off tiny strips of paper, etc. More often, they will either talk profusely about a particular subject (or set of subjects), or they will engage in a hobby in a very focused and intense manner. These are the two main types of behaviors that you want to think of as isms. When your child does either of these two things, you want to join like there's no tomorrow.

At the same time, the way you join with these behaviors will look different than joining a behavior that is less complex. We spoke earlier about how someone unfamiliar with the concept of joining could mistake, for instance, joining in with hand-flapping for copying, mimicking, mirroring, etc. Joining with your child with Asperger's syndrome, though, could never be mistaken for mimicking. With more sophisticated isms, you join by becoming an active participant in your child's interest.

Let's say your child loves trains. She talks about trains, reads about trains, and can name every type of train built within the last hundred years. What most often happens is that, at some point, everyone makes it very clear that they've really had enough of the train conversation and they want to move on. Parents (or teachers) will tell their child, "This isn't the time to talk about that," "Sam doesn't want to hear about that right now," "We've already talked about trains enough today, sweetie," or "Why don't you tell us about what you did with your dad yesterday."

Trying to move our children off their topic of choice ends up being very counterproductive, often resulting in their becoming more rigid about their subject, not less.

On the other hand, when it comes to the train conversation—and other similarly sophisticated isms—you do *not* want to simply copy whatever your child does (repeating everything she says, doing whatever she does). Instead, you want to join by becoming a fascinated student of your child's favorite subjects.

If your child likes to talk about (and read about, build, etc.) trains, your job is to become a train *freak*! If she wants to show you a picture of a train, look at the picture with great enthusiasm. When she talks about trains, listen intently. If she asks you a question about trains, answer it.

Answer as best you can, based upon your own knowledge. If

this is the twelfth time you've been asked the exact same question, great! That means you probably know the answer, so go ahead and answer, even if that means giving the same answer you gave the first eleven times.

Take some time on your own and read up on trains. When your child next brings up the subject, you can contribute your train knowledge (only if your child gives you space to do so).

I'm just using trains as a simple example. Many variations are possible based upon what your child actually does. If your child likes to build model airplanes, then go ahead and participate in this with her. If she does not want you to mess with what she's doing, get your own model airplane set and work on it in the same room as your child.

There are all kinds of ways that this type of joining can play out. I worked with a boy who loved post offices. He would put together envelopes and packages and then would want me to stamp them. So I joined him in that way, him putting together a package and me weighing and stamping it.

The key here is to look for an ism (an intense and rigid interest in a subject of conversation or hobby) and then join by participating as best you can (even if that means just listening intently).

MOTIVATION

There really is very little you need to do differently when applying the motivation principle to children or adults with Asperger's syndrome. As with any other child on the spectrum, you will want to observe your child and note what his interests and motivations are. In many cases, this will be very clear because your child will be talking quite often about whatever interests him. For example:

- Airplanes
- Characters from his favorite movie
- Buildings
- A particular country
- Illnesses that people die from

You will want to begin with a game or activity (or conversation) centered around one of these motivations, such as:

- Talking about airplanes, reading about airplanes, etc.
- Pretend you are characters from your child's favorite movie.
- Build models of your city's tallest buildings.
- Take a pretend trip to your child's favorite country
- List illnesses, talk about differences between them, etc.

Once the game, activity, or conversation is under way, you can introduce a challenge or educational goal. Naturally, the goals or challenges that you choose may be fairly sophisticated. For instance:

- Focus on having a social conversation about what you each like to do.
- Set a goal of fifteen minutes of total flexibility, where you are seeking to inspire your child to play a game or have a conversation completely on your terms for that time.
- Work on your child asking you questions as a way to practice being interested in another person.

- Ask your child to teach you something—encouraging him to make sure you understand.
- Trade topics, where you talk about something your child loves for ten minutes, then something you love.
- Talk with your child about a subject he likes—say, spaceships—and eventually connect that topic to a social topic—such as, if you met an alien on another planet, how would you introduce yourself, what would you ask, etc. You could even role play, where you are the alien, or you could write an info sheet together, explaining everything your child would want the alien to know about him and about Earth.
- If your child loves trains, you might talk about different types of trains. You could then morph this into a conversation about who you'd want to take on the train with you, where you'd want to go with them, etc. You could even create an in-depth activity where he calls or talks to each one of his friends ("friends" could be people who work with him), finds out where each person would like to go and why, and makes a list of who would go where on what train. Later, you might even take a field trip to a train museum with some of your child's friends, with the understanding that it is his job to explain the trains to his friends and answer any questions they might have.

Take a look at this next story to see just how powerful the motivation principle is when it comes to children and adults with Asperger's syndrome.

The Story of Sandra

Sandra was a fifteen-year-old girl with Asperger's syndrome. While her verbal and academic skills were equal to those of you or me, she still had great difficulty with the simplest of social interactions. Her parents attended the Start-Up program, and right away they explained that, despite their daughter's advanced skills in many areas, she seemed unable to engage in basic, everyday conversations.

One of the chief goals that Sandra's parents had for her was to be able to have a conversation about what she—and the person with whom she was talking—liked to do on weekends. To these parents, who had been struggling with this for quite some time, this goal seemed to be a million miles away.

During the Start-Up course, we have special sessions just for parents of children diagnosed with Asperger's syndrome or deemed "high functioning." It was during one of these sessions that Sandra's parents brought up the difficulties they were having with their goal for Sandra.

Naturally, we began to explain the motivation principle to them, and we asked them what one of Sandra's interests was. They both immediately chimed in with an answer—the *same* answer. Sandra liked daytime talk shows. But not just any daytime talk show. Sandra absolutely loved *The Jerry Springer Show*. Sandra did not simply enjoy *watching* Jerry Springer. She liked to *be* Jerry Springer.

Sandra would walk down the streets of her neighborhood, brandishing a short stick or a spoon (which she would use as her "microphone") and approach random people in the street, asking them questions such as: "So, Bob, why did you sleep with your wife's sister?"

Sandra's very straitlaced parents were horrified! They felt that this behavior was inappropriate and deeply embarrassing. They embarked upon a full-fledged crusade to eliminate it.

Not surprisingly, the more they endeavored to clamp down on

Jerry Springer, the more rigid and controlling Sandra became about Jerry Springer—and conversations in general. By the time Sandra's parents had arrived at the Autism Treatment Center of America for their Start-Up program, the situation had escalated to the point where Sandra would *only* have conversations according to her own prescribed steps and rules. Only she could ask questions; others could not (because, of course, Jerry *asked* the questions; he didn't *answer* them!). Furthermore, all conversations had to follow the format of *The Jerry Springer Show*, with others giving only particular types of answers and discussing only specific types of subjects.

We explained to Sandra's parents that Jerry Springer wasn't the problem, he was the solution. *No, no,* they insisted, *trust us—Jerry Springer really is the problem!* We totally understood why they might see it this way, but we further clarified that Jerry Springer did not have to be the obstacle in Sandra's way. Rather, he could be her doorway out! *After all,* we continued, *you've already told us that you don't feel that the current way of addressing this with Sandra is working.*

They nodded, intrigued.

We helped them come up with a simple activity that they could do with Sandra when they returned home from the Start-Up course. And, indeed, the day after returning home, they made it happen.

They went into Sandra's room and set it up with a real microphone in the center (which Sandra had never had before!). Then they set up four chairs against one of the walls—one chair each for Sandra's mom, dad, aunt, and a family friend. (This, of course, was the Jerry Springer panel.)

When Sandra entered, she was ecstatic. This girl, who rarely expressed emotion and often had a flat facial expression, looked openly excited! She eagerly grabbed the microphone and began firing Jerry-Springer-esque questions at them. This time, though, whenever anyone was asked a question, they enthusiastically answered—no matter how outrageous the question.

As the "show" continued, Sandra's parents began to notice a change in Sandra's demeanor. She seemed not only happier, but more relaxed, less intense, less controlling, and more flexible. Sandra's father decided that it was time to try an experiment. So he asked Sandra a question. (Remember, asking Sandra a question was previously not allowed and would not result in getting an answer.) To everyone's surprise, Sandra answered her dad's question without the slightest fuss or hesitation. Her parents glanced at one another, doing their best to conceal their shock. A few minutes later, Sandra's mother tried asking her a question. Sandra answered it. A breakthrough!

As they all progressed further into the activity, Sandra's mom and dad found that they could push the envelope of the conversation more and more. They were slowly able to alter the entire direction of the conversation. An hour and a half later, the five of them (the four adults and Sandra) were all sitting around having a conversation about what each of them liked to do on the weekend and why. This was the exact goal that Sandra's parents had asked about during their Start-Up course!

SOCIALIZATION

As we've discussed, The Son-Rise Program Developmental Model runs a full five stages—from severely autistic all the way to socially successful and neurotypical. So of course it includes children and adults with Asperger's syndrome. Someone with Asperger's syndrome, for instance, might be at stage 2 in Fundamental 1, eye contact and nonverbal communication; stage 5 in Fundamental 2, verbal communication; stage 4 in Fundamental 3, interactive attention span; and stage 3 in Fundamental 4, flexibility.

You want to build forward from wherever your child is now.

Prioritizing social goals (rather than academic ones) is *crucially* important here. Many people with Asperger's are rock stars when it comes to academic subjects—at least the ones they like. And I'm not suggesting that you take what they love away from them or stop them from doing these subjects. What I am suggesting is that when you are with your child, focus especially on the social areas. Remember: if your child or adult has Asperger's or is high-functioning, *the entirety of what is holding her back is social in nature.*

Of course, you will want your approach to match your child's sophistication and maturity level. For instance, for eye contact, you may say something like, "Hey, bud, could you look at me when you say that?" Then, if your child looks, you might simply say, "Thanks, man," or "Awesome. That really helps me get what you're saying" (unlike with a younger, less sophisticated child, where we might jump up and down, shouting "Whoo-hoo! You are such a great looker!").

Eye contact and nonverbal communication is often an area that people with Asperger's really struggle with, so it is important to remain cognizant of this area even though your child may be very sophisticated in other areas. Most communication happens nonverbally. This means that no matter how advanced her language is, your child will be missing most communication unless you work on this.

You may think that your child is at stage 5 in verbal communication because she has a large vocabulary and perfect sentence structure. But your child may have difficulty talking about social things—what others think, how he feels, how you feel, joking, etc. This is why you want to relentlessly pursue this area when conversing with him (in a fun way!). Utilizing the motivation principle, you might begin with a subject that your child loves, and, as she becomes more relaxed and engaged, you might bridge that subject with a more social subject, as we already discussed. Another simple verbal strategy is, rather than peppering your child with questions all the time, sometimes it can be helpful to simply make a statement and see if she responds, such as, "I had so much fun with Kelly today!" or "I love having my friends over to hang out!"

When it comes to interactive attention span, again, you are still going to encourage your child to keep sticking with interactive, interpersonal activities (not video games!) for longer and longer periods of time. The strategies discussed in Chapter 8 work with all developmental levels.

Flexibility can often be a major issue for people with Asperger's syndrome. When playing a game or having a conversation, here are some examples of what you might say:

- "Wow, you sure explained how you built that train really fast! I've never built a model train before. Can you explain it more slowly and clearly so that I can understand how to build one?"
- "Oh, I had so much fun playing that game your way! Now let's try playing again, but this time with *my* rules!"
- "I know you love taking Seventh Avenue to the park. Thank you for describing it to me. What's a different route we could take to get there?"

Again, using the flexibility strategies is helpful regardless of your child's verbal sophistication. The "be silly," "get it 'wrong,'" and "role play" strategies from Chapter 9 are particularly useful.

The Story of Deshawn

Deshawn's mother could not understand why her son would ask her the same question over and over, even though he knew the answer. In fact, he *wanted* to hear the same answer. For instance, Deshawn might ask, "What time is lunch?" His mom would answer, "Twelve thirty," thinking, *He already knows this—why is he asking?* Then, Deshawn would ask again. His mom would answer again. And he would ask again. And she would answer again. After enough iterations of this scenario, Deshawn's mother's frustration would reach the point where she would either yell at him—telling him to "Stop asking, already!"—or just ignore him.

When she came to the ATCA for her Start-Up course, Deshawn's mom brought this issue up during the special question-and-answer session for parents of Asperger's and high-functioning children. As she related her recurring scenario—and her reaction to it—many parents nodded in agreement and understanding.

We explained that, first, Deshawn (and the other children and adults who do this) was not trying to be difficult or to annoy his mom. However, what he was doing *did* provide a fantastic opportunity to work on his flexibility—in a way that would be helpful to him and fun for his mother.

We told her to bring in the "be silly" and "get it 'wrong'" strategies. (We, of course, explained that this would only be useful if she actually felt relaxed and silly, not if she was tense and annoyed. The other parents nodded again, this time with guilty smiles on their faces.) We detailed very specifically how to do this.

At the end of the week, Deshawn's mother returned home excited to use her new Son-Rise Program techniques. When her son asked her what time lunch was, she answered him happily. When he asked again, she got silly.

"Lunch is at twelve thirty-two and fourteen seconds," she said with a smile. Her son looked startled. He asked her again.

"Lunch is at three little piggies o'clock." She put her hand over her mouth as she said this, looking at her son slyly. Deshawn stared at her. He asked her again.

"Lunch is at four in the morning. Oh, no! We'll have to eat in our sleep!" She looked at her son, throwing her arms up in an exaggerated manner. Deshawn blinked. Then he smiled.

"We can't do that," he said.

Deshawn and his mom then had a conversation about whether people could eat in their sleep and why people had lunch during the day.

Deshawn never asked what time lunch was again.

GIVING CONTROL

Many people with Asperger's syndrome can seem very controlling. Often, because those with Asperger's can be so verbal and sophisticated, we assume that they should "get" that they can't always have things their way. But it's not a question of "getting" it. It's a question of how in control of their environment they feel.

I'm not suggesting that you make your sixteen-year-old with Asperger's syndrome the boss of the house (or school). But there are a whole host of areas where you could give more control than you do. And there are almost certainly unnecessary control battles that occurring in your home.

So step back and take an honest look at your child's day-to-day existence. Where can more control be given? Does it matter whether he sleeps on the floor instead of the bed? If he wants to wear clothes that don't match? If he prefers to eat his soup with a teaspoon? If he wants to sit in the backseat of the car even when the front seat is available? If he enjoys doing his work standing up? (I recently had a consultation with a very sweet mom who asked for my help in getting her son—who wanted to study an area of biology in college that had "low job growth"—to change his major! It will not shock you to learn that I suggested that we focus on helping him with his difficulty making friends and relating to people first!)

Also, ask yourself this: how often do you get so preoccupied with the "goal" that you compromise the interpersonal connection and interaction? Since social interaction is sometimes the only area where people with Asperger's syndrome are behind, this makes it all the more vital to prioritize the human interaction over any goal or task. For these children and adults, nothing on earth is more important for their development.

This might be a useful time to bring up a separate but related subject. I have met adults with Asperger's syndrome who tell me that they desperately want to be able to communicate and relate more with others and to operate more adeptly in the neurotypical world.

However, I have also met people with Asperger's who explain that they like and value who and how they are, and they don't want to change—and they don't want others to try to change them, either. I would never advocate trying to change these adults against their will. Like all of us, they have the right to be who they want to be and the desire to be respected and loved for who they are. Different does not equal worse. In fact, it often means talents and perspectives that are missing from the neurotypical community.

What I really appreciate about The Son-Rise Program is that using the principles we've been discussing is win-win when it comes to people with Asperger's syndrome, regardless of which of the above camps they might place themselves in. For those who want help overcoming their challenges and connecting with others, using these principles and techniques can really help them. For those who say that they don't want to be any different than they are, using these principles is the best way I can think of to respect them and to create the closest, most meaningful relationship possible with them. (And for those with Asperger's who are somewhat skeptical of "neurotypicals," experiencing someone helping them without disapproval, without pushing, and without saying that there is something wrong with them will often provide the crucial turning point for them.)

HELPING YOUR CHILD TO BE A GOOD TRYER

Celebrate your child's achievements, celebrate her attempts, and use the three Es—energy, excitement, and enthusiasm—but adapt all of this to your child. We've worked with kids with Asperger's syndrome who really enjoy it when we are loud, bouncy, and high-energy.

We've worked with just as many who really don't want us to jump around cheering them on; it's not "cool." No problem. In these cases, we calibrate our reactions to what resonates for them. For instance, I might give a thumbs-up and say calmly, "Dude, you rock. That was awesome." I might whisper "Nice job" while keeping my face very expressive. I might even fall out of my chair—and then explain that what they just did was so awesome that I couldn't keep my balance.

You could try various responses out. You could even ask your child what she would prefer. There isn't one right way to do it; just make it maximally digestible to your child.

Most important, you want to cultivate a feeling inside yourself of excitement and gratitude with regards to your child.

THE SON-RISE PROGRAM ABCS

You will want to continue to follow the ABC model with your child, but the specific red light signals are a little bit different. (The green lights are the same.)

Here is a red light list for a child with Asperger's syndrome:

- My child's eye contact plummets.
- My child is doing something that looks neurotypical, but he is excluding me from participating.
- My child seems rigid and controlling around the activity he's doing, the subject he's talking about, the arrangement of the room he's in, or the schedule for the day (or morning, afternoon, evening, etc.)..
- My child responds when I speak to him, but he does so in a rigid or repetitive way.
- My child is saying no a lot.
- My child is talking about one of his favorite subjects in a rigid or repetitive way and does not seem amenable to any alteration in the conversation.

As you can see, unlike less verbal children whose red lights may include obvious repetitive behaviors (bouncing a ball, repeating the same word, stacking blocks, lining up objects, flapping hands, etc.), people with Asperger's syndrome often have more subtle red lights. You want to keep your eye out most especially for rigidity.

OPTIMIZING YOUR CHILD'S ENVIRONMENT

If your child is, say, a sixteen-year-old with Asperger's syndrome, you may want to modify the focus room environment. (I wouldn't call it a playroom. Just stick with "focus room.") You will, of course, want much more sophisticated items in the room. Locking the door may not work, unless you get your child's permission. (This is actually doable. We've done it.)

I would still keep the electronics out of the room, even if it is just for the times when you two are working together. Keeping the room distraction-free and control-battle-free remains very important. Keeping all toys on a shelf usually isn't as important. (That's okay because you aren't working on language in the same way, anyway.)

In short, use common sense, but endeavor to preserve as many aspects of the focus room as possible. You can even feel free to explain to your child exactly what you're doing (for example, "For the next couple of hours, while you and I hang out, I'm going to clear out some things so we can both concentrate and not be distracted. Wanna help?")

DEALING WITH TANTRUMS AND OTHER CHALLENGING BEHAVIORS

Some people with Asperger's syndrome tantrum the old-fashioned way (as do most neurotypical kids), and others tantrum not by kicking and screaming but by looking really angry, cursing, clenching their fists, calling their parents names, saying "I hate you," or finding the one thing to say that will push their parents' flip-out button.

In either case, it is important to hold fast to the principles from the previous chapter. Relax. Stay comfortable. Don't make your child's behavior mean anything about you. Ask, "How can I help my child to communicate more effectively?"—not "How do I stop this behavior?"

No matter how sophisticated, your child is still just trying to communicate what she wants as best she can.

The *only* difference here is that you can be more sophisticated in how you word your responses—both to tantrums (i.e., "Swedish," according to our analogy) and to sweet, communicative behavior (i.e., "English").

For instance, in response to "I hate you!" you can say, "That's okay, I love you. But saying that doesn't help me understand you, and I don't respond to that. If you want to ask me nicely, though, I am ready to get you what you want!" Or, if you cannot give your child what she wants, offer an alternative: "We can't do that now, but maybe later. You know what, though? We can do this other thing instead if you ask me nicely!"

You can also give your child a coping mechanism—a way to feel comfortable in the face of challenge. The best way to do this is to suggest a perspective; for example, if she says, "I'm very angry!" you can say, "It's okay to be angry, but you can also feel okay when you don't get what you want and find something else to be excited about," or "When I don't get what I want, I tell myself that it's okay, and I find something else fun to do."

If you feel that your child is experiencing sensory overload, you can say something such as, "If you're feeling a little overloaded, you don't have to get angry or push. You can just say, 'I'm overloaded' and leave the room," or "If you're feeling funny, try pushing your hands together as hard as you can for ten seconds. Let's try it!" (Then, you can do it together.)

When your child *does* communicate nicely, it is absolutely imperative that you thank her, cheer (in a way that she thinks is "cool"), and *immediately* do whatever you can to help her get what she wants. (Again, if it's not possible for that to happen, offer an alternative, and make it very clear that you are willing to move heaven and earth to help her.)

Remember: it is okay for your child to raise her voice, seem agitated, act out, etc. She is going to be okay. *Your* job is to help her so that she can find a way to cope and communicate differently.

Charlotte's son, James, doesn't have Asperger's syndrome, but one thing that Charlotte taught him, which is both very useful to him and very cute, is to say soothing things to himself. So, now, when James gets agitated, he says things like, "It's okay," and "No big deal." Saying these phrases out loud helps him to relax and self-regulate.

ONLINE RESOURCES

For more in-depth help with the principles and techniques of this chapter, please go to www.autismbreakthrough.com/chapter15. Have fun!

STARTING POINT

Become a student of one aspect of your child's world, and join him in it. If your child loves old-fashioned cars, read a book about old-fashioned cars, and talk about it with him. If your child likes telling people about space travel, enthusiastically listen when he's telling you about this subject. If your child loves sea creatures, get posters of sea animals, hang them up, and ask your child which ones are his favorites. Not only will your understanding of your child's world increase, but he will find it easier to connect with you—and to be more flexible!

SIXTEEN

The Recovery Mode: Addressing the Biology of Autism—Especially Diet

DISCLAIMER

I want to make sure that I am totally clear: nothing in this chapter should be construed as any kind of medical advice. This chapter is not intended to prevent, diagnose, treat, or cure any illness. I am not a medical doctor, nor do I play one on TV.

I have spoken at many autism conferences, listened to and conversed with many autism doctors, and seen many children respond to various biologically oriented interventions. In fact, quite a number of our families implement The Son-Rise Program alongside and in conjunction with biomedical and biological interventions.

AUTISM: THE BIOMEDICAL CONNECTION

We all know that autism is a neurological condition. But it is not *only* a neurological condition.

Many of our children face immunological and digestive challenges that are intimately connected to their social, relational, sensory, behavioral, and learning difficulties. At autism conferences nationwide, I've heard doctor after doctor discuss the biology of autism, particularly how many children on the spectrum have difficulty with digestion, with elimination, with fighting off pathogens, and with a host of other biological processes.

Some of you are already aware of this, and many more of you

may be reading this information for the first time. If this is the first (or second) time you are hearing this, you may be thinking that your child doesn't have these other challenges. You might be thinking that your child doesn't have food allergies, doesn't get sick often, and doesn't seem to have any physiological problems. And this may, indeed, be the case.

At the same time, with autism spectrum disorders, our kids' behaviors and overt difficulties can take up so much of our attention that many less obvious challenges can be hard to see. This is especially true if you've already been told by your doctor or others to focus exclusively on your child's behaviors (that is, your child's *symptoms*).

It is essential to understand, though, that your child's internal biological issues may be affecting her behaviors—possibly a great deal. The interaction between your child's physiology and her autism can be direct or indirect.

A direct interaction is when chemical reactions throughout your child's body are impairing or interfering with your child's developing brain. (I'll give you an example of how proteins in wheat and dairy can cause this in some children later in this chapter.)

An indirect interaction is when a physiological problem is giving your child a stomachache, a headache, lethargy, etc. Think about how a severe headache affects your ability to work, converse, and interact. Imagine how an intense stomachache, for instance, might impact your child as she is being asked to listen, look, interact, and learn new things.

So you can see why it might be important to look into your child's biology, if you haven't already done so.

One phenomenon that will become clear by the end of this chapter is that the principles of The Son-Rise Program and biological interventions (often called biomedical interventions or treatments in the autism community) affect one another. A child in The Son-Rise Program will often progress faster if she is responding well to biomedical treatments. Removing or lessening a child's physiological challenges can accelerate her Son-Rise Program.

It is equally true that, by shifting children from fight-or-flight survival mode to recovery mode, the principles of The Son-Rise Program can actually improve and enhance their bodies' capacity to respond favorably to biomedical interventions. More on this later.

CHOOSING THE RIGHT DOCTOR

I would strongly encourage you to see a doctor who specializes in autism, if you are not already doing so. Such a doctor can administer blood, urine, and other tests to get a better picture of your child's biological situation. He or she can then address problems with your child's digestive or immune system. These issues can be multifaceted, but they can also be as simple as a mineral deficiency.

Note: I have also worked with parents who have seen improvements in their children from seeing naturopaths, homeopaths, and other nonallopathic practitioners. Your child's situation may be quite complex, so it will always help to keep an open mind.

If you are going to take your child to an autism doctor, it is incredibly important to choose one who has vast experience with autism and knows what he or she is talking about. To my astonishment, I still hear from many parents who report that their pediatrician makes statements such as, "Changing your child's diet is not going to have any effect whatsoever on his autism." (Other ill-informed statements of this nature include, "That rash covering your child's body is not related to your child's autism," and "Your child's constant diarrhea and constipation is just a phase. Nothing to do with your child's autism.")

Consider this: what we eat and drink affects our energy levels, our susceptibility to infections, our propensity for certain kinds of cancers, the onset of type 2 diabetes, the symptoms of Crohn's and celiac diseases, and the condition of our arteries and thus the likelihood that we will have a heart attack or stroke. Eating foods to which our body overreacts (if we have an allergy to peanuts, for example) can cause an immediate, and sometimes deadly, physiological response. Drinking a relatively small amount of alcohol impacts our brain function in short order. None of these facts are controversial. We know that what we consume affects us physiologically. So why is the fact that diet can affect the extrasensitive brains and bodies of children on the autism spectrum still in dispute?

I don't know a polite way to say this, so I'll just say it: any doctor who tells you that there is no way that what your child eats can have any impact on his autism does not really know or understand autism. In such cases, they are dispensing advice without knowledge, which is both unhelpful and potentially dangerous.

If your child has chicken pox, and you ask me for advice, I'm not going to give you any. You know why? Because I know nothing about chicken pox. Your pediatrician may know a lot about fevers, strep throat, whooping cough, and hundreds of other conditions, but if he or she makes this kind of comment to you about dietary intervention, go elsewhere for your autism help. There are plenty of doctors out there who *do* know a lot about autism. I meet them all the time at conferences—and in the Start-Up course.

Charlotte's son, James, has many physiological challenges that directly affect his autism. One of his big issues is his inability to properly digest a vast array of foods. When James was much younger, Charlotte and her ex-husband went to a doctor because James had not pooped in two weeks. He frequently held his stomach and screamed. The doctor said, "He's holding it in on purpose."

These types of statements represent such a profound lack of understanding of the biology of autism, it can seem a bit breathtaking. (In fact, once Charlotte—drastically—changed James's diet, he began pooping regularly and stopped holding his stomach and screaming. He also improved in a myriad of other ways.) My heart goes out to those of you who are still running into doctors who flatly deny the existence of occurrences that you can see with your own eyes. Trust me when I tell you, if you have a truly informed autism doctor, you won't have these types of experiences.

Another big factor to keep in mind when selecting an autism doctor is how long the doctor has been helping children with autism. You don't want your child being a guinea pig, even if the doctor has the very best of intentions. I recommend a minimum of five years' direct experience with autism. (Keep in mind that a doctor can take a three-day seminar and claim that he or she has been "trained" in autism treatment.)

Also, ask the doctor why he or she got into autism treatment. This question can often give you great insight into where the doctor is coming from. Because autism rates have been increasing so rapidly in recent years, some physicians have jumped on the bandwagon as a way to expand their practice. On the other hand, there are an increasing number of wonderful doctors who are parents of children on the spectrum. They began focusing their medical expertise on autism to help their own children. I tend to trust these people the most, and I often find that, as autism parents themselves, they treat other parents with more respect.

THE DOCTOR CHECKLIST

When selecting an autism doctor, it is crucial to choose one who will support, not undermine, what you are doing to implement the principles of The Son-Rise Program. In this regard, here are ten questions I always recommend asking when choosing autism doctors.

1. Do they deeply and sincerely respect your role and your knowledge as the parent?

2. Do they see the value in building a bonded relationship with your child and in helping your child to connect with others? (It's okay if this isn't *your doctor's* focus, but they have to get why it's important.)
3. Do they seem interested in *your* emotional state?
4. Do they see your questions as inquiries and not challenges?
5. Are they gentle and relaxed with your child?
6. Do they value your child's emotional state—rather than seeing her as merely an immune system and digestive system to be fixed?
7. Do they value aspects of your child other than the areas they are treating directly?
8. Do they value other treatments (including interventions such as The Son-Rise Program) besides the ones they are providing?
9. Do they recognize that *how* an intervention is administered to your child can be as important as *what* intervention is administered?
10. Since any intervention only works if it can be administered, do they check in with you to find out how you are doing with delivering their treatment protocol?

THE IMPORTANCE OF YOUR CHILD'S DIET

What your child is eating might be having a gigantic effect on him. A child's behavior, level of interaction, frequency of isming, and his autism in general, can be greatly impacted one way or the other by diet. This is to say nothing about food's impact on his pooping, cravings, rashes, sleep, skin tone, autoimmunity, and sensory processing.

We will spend the bulk of this chapter discussing dietary intervention for two reasons. First, biologically speaking, it has the best chance to have the most immediate effect on your child's development. Second, dietary intervention is something that, like the rest of The Son-Rise Program, you can implement at home.

A great many children on the autism spectrum have food sensitivities. (I say "sensitivities" and not "allergies" because, often, these problems will not show up on a traditional allergy test, for reasons we will discuss in a moment.)

It will greatly help your child if you think about what he ingests in the following way: *to your child, food is either medicine or poison.*

Way back in 1974, long before our current understanding of the connection between autism and diet, my parents implemented dietary interventions with me. This was yet another arena in which my parents proved to be decades ahead of their time—so much so that even now I have trouble getting my head around just how far ahead of their time they really were.

They felt that I was being affected by what I ate, and they sought to remove any foods they could think of that might be hindering me. (In fact, as a way to make things simpler, improve everyone's health, and prevent accidental contaminations, they removed the offending foods from the diet of the whole family.)

First, they removed dairy. Interestingly, I was prone to chronic, sometimes life-threatening ear infections as a child. When my parents removed all dairy, my ear infections ceased.

Then, they went about removing sugar, artificial colors and flavors, red meat, and processed foods from my diet. They fed me only organic foods. (Remember that this was decades before every supermarket had an organic foods section.)

This dietary intervention was an important component of

what my parents did to help me. It accelerated the pace of my Son-Rise Program by removing biological obstacles so that the program could do its work. Fortunately or unfortunately, depending on how you look at it, I am now able to eat a completely regular diet—that is, the standard diabetes-, stroke-, cancer-, and heart attack-inducing American diet—without any deleterious effects. Ain't life grand?

At the Autism Treatment Center of America, these are the very first food items that we tell parents to begin looking at.

- Casein (a complex protein found in milk and milk products)
- Gluten (a complex protein found in wheat and many other grains—and also often added to nonglutinous foods such as potato chips because it prevents them from sticking together)
- Caffeine
- Sugar

Let's look at these four items more closely.

GLUTEN AND CASEIN

The biological process I am about to describe has been outlined by many physicians in the autism field and explains why something as simple as eating wheat or dairy can affect brain function and brain development. (For the sake of brevity, I will not go into the biological processes behind why these foods can also cause diarrhea, constipation, and other nonbrain side effects.)

Some children on the spectrum are missing enzymes that break down the complex proteins gluten and casein. On top of that, these children have something that many doctors call leaky gut syndrome, which is when the walls of the small intestine (where most digestion takes place) are too permeable.

A simple way to think about what this means is to imagine that, for some children, the walls of the small intestine have little swiss cheese–like holes. (The walls of the intestine are extremely important in keeping undigested or partially digested food from getting into the rest of the body.) Undigested or partially digested gluten and casein particles then enter the bloodstream through these "holes" in the small intestine.

These gluten and casein peptides circulate around the body and cross the blood-brain barrier. Once in the brain, they act as opiates, binding to the same receptors as morphine and heroin.

So, essentially, for many of our children, ingesting gluten or casein is like getting high on drugs. Moreover, when these foods are initially removed from a child with this issue, it is like suddenly removing drugs from a drug addict. At first, she ain't gonna thank you. She is powerfully addicted to these substances. Not only will a child going through the withdrawal process most likely have a very strong craving for gluten and casein; her body will go through all sorts of intense reactions—sometimes for as long as two weeks—from diarrhea and vomiting to tantrums and sleepless nights.

However, when it's over, what a beautiful day! We get reports of children making vastly more eye contact, sleeping regular hours, using more language, isming less, and overall, responding even more quickly to the principles of The Son-Rise Program.

It is absolutely critical, if you are going to remove gluten and casein from your child's diet, that you do it 100 percent; 99 percent is almost like not doing the diet at all.

You might be reading this and thinking, *There is no way I can do this because all my child eats is grilled cheese sandwiches and milk* (or some other wheat and dairy combination)! If so, I am extremely happy for you and your child! This is one of the surest signs that gluten and casein are a big problem for your child. Voluntarily eating a narrow list of foods like this is the behavior of an addict.

Why would I be happy about that? Because we tend to see that the kids who have this severe an addiction—this big an issue with gluten and casein—are the ones who respond most dramatically to the removal of those foods.

If you are feeling freaked out and intimidated by this revelation, hang on! I will shortly get to how to change your child's diet using the principles of The Son-Rise Program, and it doesn't have to be hard or scary.

CAFFEINE

Of course, we know that coffee has caffeine. (Decaf does, too. It just has less.) Caffeine is also in colas and a host of other sodas. (There are a thousand things wrong with sodas from an autism point of view. Caffeine is but one.)

Remember, too, that caffeine is also present in chocolate. This is a big way that it enters the diets of our children. As I said earlier, I am a chocolate freak. So I deeply, passionately understand the desire for it.

The problem is: caffeine is a nerve stimulant. We don't want to be giving our children nerve stimulants. 'Nuff said.

SUGAR

Sugar is a tough one because it is added to almost everything. I'll tell you right now, you won't be able to remove all sugar from your child's diet. Luckily, this is okay, for two reasons. First, we need some sugar in our diets (though, ideally, it would be the naturally occurring type that is present in, say, an apple). Second, the biological mechanism that makes sugar a problem for many of our children is totally different from the one that makes gluten and casein problematic. This means that, although you would need to reduce gluten and casein down to zero for that diet to have its intended effect, this is not the case for sugar. With sugar, the goal is just to get intake as low as possible.

The way that many autism doctors describe it, there are two biological issues happening with some children that make sugar a problem. The first is that some children on the spectrum secrete too much insulin in response to relatively small amounts of sugar. This causes blood sugar levels to crash, making them sluggish and irritable—and causing more sugar cravings. Then the child eats more sugar, blood sugar spikes, and, again, too much insulin is secreted, resulting in another crash and more cravings. We end up with a constant seesawing of blood sugar levels, which plays havoc with a sensitive child's brain and body.

According to the autism docs, the second, and most pernicious, biological challenge around sugar is that many children on the autism spectrum have candida yeast overgrowth. What this means is that, in some cases, children will have a higher than normal amount of yeast—a fungus—growing in their intestines. This can exacerbate the leaky gut problem outlined earlier and cause "brain fog"—which, for a child with autism, can be especially consequential.

And what does candida yeast live on? You guessed it: sugar!

In fact, there is some evidence to suggest that a big part of the powerful sugar cravings that some of our children experience is actually coming from the yeast itself. *The yeast* is craving the sugar, and as it begins to die off from lack of sugar, it gives the body an increased craving.

There are some autism doctors who prescribe antifungal medications for candida yeast overgrowth, but the first order of business is to simply reduce sugar intake, which, according to the professionals, reduces candida yeast levels.

If a child has high candida yeast levels, and sugar intake drops suddenly, this can cause what some call a "die-off." This term is used to describe the dying off of a lot of the candida yeast at once. When this fungus dies en masse, it is believed that the dying and breaking open of these organisms releases toxins into the body. This is used to explain why, at first, when some of these children have their sugar intake reduced, they can have symptoms such as nausea, vomiting, headaches, and low-grade fever for a few days.

I can tell you, from personal experience, that this phenomenon still appears to happen to me. I can eat whatever I want and be fine, but when I drastically cut down my sugar intake (as I do every time I want to drop a few pounds), I have two days of nausea, headaches, low-grade fever, swollen glands, and mild diarrhea. (I am fully aware that this may be more information than you wanted to know about me!) It is truly a delightful experience. However, afterward, my sugar cravings go way down, and so does any bloating I had. (Note: consistent bloating is another symptom of candida yeast overgrowth often cited by the professionals.)

DIETS TO LOOK INTO

There are a host of autism-friendly diets out there—and more and more foods available at the supermarket that are autism-safe. There are also a plethora of terrific books detailing these diets, so I won't seek to do that in a comprehensive way here. What I *will* do is give you three places to start.

The three diets below are my personal favorites. They are listed in order from least to most restrictive, and they build on one another. (This means that the second diet listed, for example, excludes the foods I mention *in addition to* gluten or casein.) If you decide to implement the gluten- and casein-free diet, and it doesn't "work"—you don't see any difference in your child—that does not necessarily mean that diet is not an issue for your child. It might mean that *you haven't removed enough foods and found the culprits yet.* This is the reason why many parents then escalate to the next diet on the list.

I am not telling you to do these diets. Rather, I am advocating that you do some research and look into them.

1. The Gluten- and Casein-Free Diet (GFCF)

As we've already discussed, the gluten- and casein-free diet involves the total removal of all foods containing gluten and casein—milk products, wheat, and a myriad of other products with gluten in them. For most parents, this is the place to begin. This diet is *much* easier now than it was years ago because there are tons and tons of GFCF foods out there. Almost anything (milk, yogurt, bread, pasta, cookies, etc.) is available in a GFCF version. Note: it is not recommended that you simply replace milk products with loads of soy products. Soy is highly allergenic and difficult to digest, and some physicians and dieticians believe that it can mimic the female hormone estrogen in the body.

2. The Specific Carbohydrate Diet (SCD)

Invented by Dr. Sidney V. Haas and popularized by Elaine Gottschall, the specific carbohydrate diet is predicated on the idea that, in some people, incomplete digestion of certain complex carbohydrates and sugars results in the growth of harmful bacteria in the gut—which then causes inflammation and autoimmune responses (where the immune system attacks parts of the body). Many parents who found that their kids did not respond strongly to the GFCF diet have reported that their children have changed greatly with this diet. It has many more guidelines than I can go into here, but a cornerstone of the diet involves removing potatoes, corn, and rice (in addition to gluten and casein). If you are wondering what there is left to eat, look this diet up. You'll be surprised! (Also, bear in mind that many cultures have existed over the millennia without those three foods.) There is a diet similar to the specific carbohydrate diet called the gut and psychology syndrome (GAPS) diet, created by Dr. Natasha Campbell-McBride.

3. **The Body Ecology Diet (BED)**
Invented by nutritionist Donna Gates, the body ecology diet has many similarities to the SCD, but it focuses more on achieving and maintaining a balance of gut flora (intestinal bacteria). There is a strong focus on reducing candida yeast overgrowth. Rather than focusing only on eliminating certain foods (sugar, grains, etc.), this diet puts a healthy emphasis on replenishing missing gut flora that are crucial to digestion by adding "cultured" foods such as fermented vegetables and young coconut kefir, a fermented drink. This diet could be considered the highest rung on the ladder in terms of strictness and comprehensiveness. A much smaller number of parents have their kids on this diet (which takes a lot of work), but many report significant improvement in their children after they've tried other diets.

Although it may seem that much of our dietary focus thus far has been aimed at removing substances, *adding* items can also make a difference. Sit down at any autism conference, and you will likely hear doctors discussing a variety of significant deficiencies that they see in children on the autism spectrum. Although all children are different, here are some items that are well worth exploring:

DIGESTIVE ENZYMES

In order to digest food, our bodies secrete a plethora of digestive enzymes. Without these enzymes, we could not digest anything. Since we require enzymes to extract nutrients from our food, food without enzymes is not food. For instance, the reason that wood is not food for us is because we lack the enzymes to break it down. If we were termites and we had enzymes to break down wood, it would be food to us. We might start the day with a sawdust sandwich! (Incidentally, we require (nondigestive) enzymes for almost every bodily function, such as fighting infections, temperature regulation, and even thinking.)

Some autism doctors feel that there is a great deal of evidence that many of our children lack the normal quantity and quality of digestive enzymes, resulting in compromised digestion. These doctors talk about the benefits of supplementation with enzymes to help these children digest and extract nutrients from their food, to ease bloating, constipation, diarrhea, and other digestive issues, and to aid the body in other areas such as immune system function. Enzymes are not drugs—or even vitamins; they are considered food products and are sold in health food stores.

A number of Son-Rise Program parents utilize enzymes and feel that they work synergistically with their program. Enzymedica, a company that focuses on making highly potent and very "clean" (i.e., without fillers) enzymes, feels so strongly about this synergy that, since 2009, it has paid for scores of parents to attend the Start-Up course at the Autism Treatment Center of America. Enzymedica helped to found the Autism Hope Alliance (AHA), a nonprofit organization that has also funded many parents' Start-Up course tuition.

As I mentioned earlier, James has a host of physiological challenges, from toxic levels of heavy metals to substantial digestive difficulties. He takes digestive enzymes and has been on all three of the above diets. He also gets mineral, essential fatty acid, and probiotic supplementation. (We'll discuss probiotics shortly.)

For James, enzymes have made a huge difference. He went from being a child with a constantly bloated stomach and dark circles underneath his eyes, who would often scream as he pressed on his stomach and oscillate between extreme constipation and diarrhea, to a kid with no bloating, no pain, no dark circles, and regular poops. As well, this regimen accelerated what was happening in his Son-Rise Program, with language improvements coming faster and big leaps in his interactive attention span.

PROBIOTICS

The term "probiotics" is the catch-all name for the beneficial microorganisms that we require for gut health. Like enzymes, these are also considered food products and are sold in health food stores. If you've ever seen those yogurt commercials on TV advertising the benefits of their product for digestive health, that's because most yogurts contain probiotics. However, for our kids, yogurt is problematic because it is dairy (or soy). Also, a good probiotic capsule or powder that you would buy in a health food store contains far more probiotics than a serving of yogurt.

Again, I'm not telling you to go out tomorrow, buy a bottle of probiotics, and start feeding it to your child. What I recommend is to look into probiotics—and to ask your autism doctor about them.

VITAMINS AND MINERALS

I would certainly not recommend specific vitamins or minerals for your child, but I would strongly advocate that you have your child tested for large deficiencies. Many autism doctors talk about children they've treated with B12, magnesium and/or zinc deficiencies, for example. (As an interesting side note, a deficiency in zinc can make some vegetables taste bad and increase the desire for sugary foods.)

ESSENTIAL FATTY ACIDS

You may be familiar with all the recent research (outside of autism circles) about omega-3 fats and essential fatty acids. It is increasingly understood that the right essential fatty acids provide us with all sorts of health benefits—for the heart, arteries, mood, digestive system, and brain.

Essential fatty acids are often recommended by autism doctors because, among other things, they are used to build and maintain the protective coating around brain and nerve cells. This coating is much like the rubber that coats electrical wires. Some doctors maintain that this can be highly beneficial to some children on the autism spectrum.

Essential fatty acids are sold in health food stores in liquid and capsule form. For now, just look into this. If you do decide to give them to your child, make absolutely sure that you conduct some research into specific products ahead of time. Simply feeding your child large amounts of fish oils, for example, can mean flooding his body with mercury and other toxins if you aren't careful.

USING THE SON-RISE PROGRAM TO CHANGE YOUR CHILD'S DIET

Even if you already knew everything I just explained about dietary intervention, this next section is going to change your life. Really! I find that even people who are very knowledgeable about autism and diet do not necessarily feel knowledgeable and confident about *how* to get their child to stop eating detrimental foods and start eating healthy ones.

So let us talk about the five Son-Rise Program feeding principles.

THE 5 SON-RISE PROGRAM FEEDING PRINCIPLES

Control

Control is a core autism issue—and yet it is highly overlooked as relates to feeding. Our children tend to be very controlling (for good reason, as we discussed in previous chapters). Remember, we want to always endeavor to see everything from our children's point of view. This absolutely includes food and feeding.

Ironically, many parents and caregivers get very controlling around feeding. We decide when our children will eat, what they will eat, how long they will eat for, and even *how* they will eat (at the table, with a fork, etc.).

If we want to change *what* our children eat, we have to give them control in every other area of eating. We need to take all of the pressure off. No more pushing our kids to eat. No more pressing our kids to eat at the table. Even, temporarily, no "lunchtime" versus "dinnertime." Offer the food at various times, and let them eat anytime they want. Let them eat with any utensil that they want. Let them eat anyplace they want.

When you offer food, offer it in a gentle, relaxed, noncoercive, noncontrolling way. Present the food at a distance (rather than right in their face), and let your child come to *you* for it. As soon as your child even looks at the food, you might be tempted to thrust the food at her. It's easy to forget that when we grab a fork and jab it at a child's mouth, it can be startling to that child.

Take a buffet mentality with your child: "Grab anything you want."

Have plates of food around and accessible throughout the day. Touch the food. Fly toy airplanes around it. If your child doesn't want to actually eat it at this point, stay nonpushy about that, too. Also, do your best to avoid feeding your child when she is isming or giving you a strong red light.

Some children will only eat one item per plate; they'll eat peas and chicken, but not on the same plate. Allow this. Start to become aware of the temperature and consistency your child likes. Then adjust her meals accordingly. For now, cater the food to the way your child likes to eat it. (Remember, this does not mean that she gets to eat cookies and ice cream and cake. You're still choosing *what* is on offer for her to eat.)

Giving your child this kind of control over her food removes a big obstacle to her eating what you want her to eat. If your child does not feel that she has control, she will feel a strong desire to go against whatever dietary changes you are implementing.

Giving your child control in this area will also allow her to come to the food of her own volition, which is crucial for sustaining any restrictive diet.

Creativity

Actively seek new ways to present food in a fun way. Present food in a variety of ways. You can have toy cars carrying the food. You can be a witch presenting her magic brew. You can have the food take on personalities. Be a robot who needs the food as fuel, and invite your child to fuel up, too. Put a carrot in your mouth, and wiggle like a worm—and encourage your child to do the same. "Hide" the food, and then focus on finding and eating it.

When Charlotte was first endeavoring to get a reluctant James to eat broccoli, she dressed up as a giant stalk of broccoli and stomped into his playroom singing a broccoli song. He eventually got involved. They would sing the broccoli song and even talk to the real broccoli that Charlotte brought in with her. They did this for quite a while before the subject of actually *eating* the broccoli even came up. Now James eats broccoli regularly—and likes it. (He also happily eats carrots, spinach, kale, and every other healthy food.)

The first time I ever heard James say, "I want my algae," I almost fell out of my chair. Algae is exactly what it sounds like: the green stuff that grows on the bottom of lakes. James's algae is a cultivated version made into a green drink that James imbibes each day. If you ever tasted this drink, you would understand my awe that James would actually ask for it. It is truly a testament to Charlotte's effective use of all five of these feeding principles.

Relationship-building

This principle may appear unrelated to feeding, but it is essential. All of the joining, all of the celebrating, and all of the giving control really pays off here. If you have been building rapport with your child in these ways, he will trust you.

This trust will be the keystone to having food breakthroughs with your child. When your child trusts you, you have much more leeway to present and provide new foods to him. He will be open to what you have to offer.

Attitude

The attitude that you have around food and feeding is an absolutely vital component of any change in your child's diet. Parents, especially, tend to be tense about feeding their children on the spectrum, particularly if they have a child who is a picky eater. This brings a stress and agitation to feeding that will turn your child off at precisely the moment when you want her to be open.

When you are feeding your child, you are asking her to take

something outside herself into her body. That's a big request. It is so very important to have a calm, relaxed, and even excited attitude when dealing with anything food-related.

Really cultivate this attitude around your child's eating. Model eating foods with the three Es. You want your child's experience around food to be like slipping into a warm bath—relaxing, easy, comfortable, and deeply enjoyable. That's how you will get your child to want to jump into it.

Persistence

Okay. So, at the end of the day, changing your child's diet is all about who will persist longer. I know that you may feel that you've really tried to get your child to eat X or Y. But how many times did you try?

Successfully shifting what your child willingly eats is all about persevering. Staying the course. Refusing to get discouraged—even after many attempts. It will take a bit of time to train your child's palate to enjoy healthy foods. You are the key to your child having that time.

REMOVING PROBLEMATIC AND UNHEALTHY FOODS

Persistence applies to both sides of the food equation—to introducing new food *and* to removing unhealthy foods.

While introducing new foods can seem challenging because, ultimately, it is your child who will decide whether to eat them, removing foods should theoretically be far easier. Unless your child spends his days in environments where you are not present and have no say about the food given to him, you can remove any foods you like from the house and simply not provide them. In theory, your child does not get a choice.

From an emotional standpoint, however, removing foods is an entirely different matter. At the Autism Treatment Center of America, we see that removing foods can feel like Armageddon to many parents. There is often a huge amount of fear and anxiety around this issue, and I can understand why. A child who is not eating—while, at the same time, clamoring for food that we are not providing—touches on some very core parental beliefs and emotions. We see nourishment as one of our most basic jobs as parents. Feeding is often an expression of our love.

The first thing to understand is that, in our thirty years of experience, we have never seen a child starve himself to death when his diet was changed. We've certainly seen children go one day, two days, sometimes even three, but eventually these kids get hungry. As we've discussed, persistence is key.

I will say this: the kids who hold out the longest tend to be those determined souls who see cracks in their parents' armor. They see parents who look and feel guilty, who look and feel anxious, who have buckled many times in the past, who beg them to eat, who yell at them to eat, etc. In short, they believe—correctly, in most cases—that their parents are having such a hard time that they will cave after just a bit more waiting.

Children can usually outwait their parents. When Bryn is teaching parents in the Start-Up program, she astutely quotes the thought process of our kids this way: "I can *not* eat longer than you can *watch* me not eat." This factor alone elucidates why our attitude is so very important in this situation. If you believe that you are doing something mean or terrible to your child by removing harmful foods from his diet, then removing these foods will be very, very hard. You will feel guilty, anxious, and scared.

If, on the other hand, you believe that you are doing something very loving and very helpful to your child (which you are), then this process will feel very doable. You will feel comfortable, relaxed, and very clear about staying the course. Equally important, your child will then see that you are clear, comfortable, and free from any wavering, and, in most cases, will come around sooner. This is why, in the Start-Up course, we spend a great deal of time on your attitudes and emotions, not just on techniques.

I know that you may be thinking, "But my child *likes* those unhealthy foods." So, it's time to remind you of Bryn's quote: "Heroin addicts really like heroin. That doesn't mean it's good for them." (By the way, she speaks from personal experience. She and William put their daughter, Jade, on a special diet and stuck to it throughout her program.)

Your child may want "just a little piece of one cookie." If your child wanted to not wear a seatbelt "for just a little bit of the ride," or your child wanted to play with a sharp knife "for just a few minutes," or your child want to drink "just a bit" of liquid drain cleaner, I'm sure you wouldn't oblige. These are nonnegotiable issues.

You want to put your child's diet in the nonnegotiable category. This is your child's health and safety we're talking about. Make it nonnegotiable.

One final point—remember how, in Chapter 3, we talked about the problems with relying on rewards as the main driver of your child's behavior? I used an analogy about how many of us, when we were little, were trained to slog through the "gross" healthy food in order to get the "yummy" unhealthy dessert. In this case, there is no analogy; this *is* the actual situation.

Again, our beliefs about food are central. We think about and then present the least healthy foods as rewards—as "the good stuff." I've heard many, many parents make statements like, "Well, I don't want to deprive my child forever. When can my child get off this diet?" The beliefs hidden in these words will cripple your ability to help your child eat healthily. Why is not feeding your child foods that will harm him "depriving" him?

And the question of "when can my child get off this diet?" is worth examining closely. We are basically asking, "When is the soonest possible date when I can resume feeding my child poison—foods which will give my child heart disease, stroke, diabetes, premature aging, and cancer?" Why are we in such a rush to get these poisons back into our children's bodies?

FIGHT-OR-FLIGHT SURVIVAL MODE

Let's come full circle and return to the key component of your child's autism that I mentioned at the beginning of this chapter. There is a preponderance of evidence showing that the vast majority of children with autism are living in a near-perpetual fight-or-flight state. I first learned about this in detail from a discussion I had many years ago with Dr. Scott Faber, who, at the time, was the Director of Developmental-Behavioral Pediatrics at Mercy Hospital in Pittsburgh (he is now with the Hospital at the Children's Institute), but it has since become a common understanding among many autism doctors. Why is this important?

When your body is in fight-or-flight, you are basically in immediate survival mode. These are some key biological processes of this state.

- Adrenaline (epinephrine) courses through your veins.
- Your heart rate increases.
- Blood vessels constrict (to prevent excessive bleeding).
- Blood flows away from your vital organs and into your arms and legs (to ready you for running or fighting).
- Lymphocytes from your immune system race toward your skin (in readiness for you being cut or bitten).

Also, of particular relevance to your child:

- Major, more vital, areas of your immune system shut down—while other areas become hyperactive.

- Your digestive system shuts down.
- Physiological repair gets put on hold.
- The brain gears up for quick, immediate, reflexive decision-making—rather than tasks such as learning and social interaction.
- And, importantly, cortisol and corticotropin-releasing hormone levels skyrocket. Cortisol is the major long-acting stress hormone in your body. It is secreted by your adrenal glands. Corticotropin-releasing hormone (CRH) is a stress hormone released in the brain—but now found in other areas of the body in children with autism.

Now, let's take a look at what this means. The process outlined above is perfectly natural. It is a system that served our distant ancestors well. When a saber-toothed tiger is chasing you, the only thing that matters is getting away in one piece. In a few minutes, this kind of situation is over. You have either escaped or you were eaten. (What a happy thought!)

However, we are not designed to stew in this state indefinitely. Fight-or-flight survival mode works in a short burst. *Fight-or-flight survival mode for hours or days begins to cause detrimental breakdowns in the human body.*

Take this physiological situation and apply it to our children, and what do you get? Let's have another look at the last five bullet points above. Think about what happens if major areas of your child's immune system shut down, and she already has a compromised immune system (or if a child with an autoimmune disease keeps triggering immune system overreaction). Or if your child's digestive system shuts down, and she already has digestive issues. Or if you are administering biomedical interventions designed to help your child's digestive, immune, and other systems rebuild—and major physiological repair is on hold in her body.

Now also imagine trying to help your child to learn and interact socially when her brain is in this fight-or-flight state. Learning and social interaction are exceedingly difficult for our children when they are in this mode. Attention span is affected, interfering with learning, and the child is in a highly self-protective state, shutting down her ability to interact socially.

And then we have the cortisol issue.

THE PROBLEM WITH CORTISOL

During my conversation with Dr. Scott Faber, he told me that he found that children with autism often have chronically elevated stress hormone levels, particularly cortisol. This is a key sign of someone in fight-or-flight survival mode.

Dr. Theoharis Theoharides (yes, that really *is* his name), scientist, professor of internal medicine, and professor of pharmacology at Tufts Medical Center in Boston, has also found elevated levels of CRH in children on the spectrum. He has found it in areas of the body outside the brain (a fairly big deal, as it is thought to be released only by the hypothalamus inside the brain), and he believes it can exacerbate inflammation throughout the body, which is an issue that some of our children face. This presence of CRH is yet another sign of a body in fight-or flight mode.

I would add that, although I didn't know all of the biology surrounding this scenario, I didn't find this at all surprising when I heard it. If a child is in a constant state of sensory overload, surrounded by an environment that seems totally unpredictable, and then pushed and pulled in a myriad of directions against his will, the fight-or-flight response would seem the most likely result.

What is increasingly well understood is that chronically

elevated levels of cortisol cause the atrophy of cells in the hippocampus—and prevent the genesis of new hippocampal cells. The hippocampus is a small area near the center of the brain that is responsible for the formation of new memories, something of obvious and crucial importance to our children. Interestingly, the hippocampus is one of the first regions of the brain to suffer damage in people who have Alzheimer's disease. (See books such as *The End of Stress As We Know It*, by Ewan McGowan and *Social Intelligence*, by Daniel Goleman for more on stress, cortisol, and their effect on the hippocampus.)

These are the key points to take away from this discussion.

- We do not want our children to have chronically elevated levels of cortisol (or CRH).
- We do not want our children to be in a perpetual fight-or-flight state.
- We want to do whatever we can to enable our children to shift *out of* the fight-or-flight survival mode and *into* the recovery mode.

THE RECOVERY MODE

There is good news here. Everything described above is reversible. The most promising thing that Dr. Faber discussed with me was why he felt The Son-Rise Program was so effective. He found that when the children with autism were joined, given control, handled with a nonjudgmental and welcoming attitude (all of which he termed "emotionally attuned intervention"), and placed in an environment that was not overstimulating, their stress hormone levels (adrenaline, cortisol) *dropped to normal ranges.*

I cannot tell you how excited I am about this. It explains an important aspect of why The Son-Rise Program works and gives us all a concrete way to help our children biologically, physiologically, neurologically, and developmentally.

You have the ability to powerfully impact the core biology of your child's autism. When your child shifts out of fight-or-flight survival mode and his stress hormones return to normal ranges, the door is open for breakthroughs on several fronts.

- Your child is relaxed and can think.
- Your child's digestive system springs to life.
- Your child's immune system is given its best chance to function optimally.
- Your child's brain is in a nonthreatened state that allows for learning and social interaction.
- When cortisol levels are not elevated, the process of hippocampal atrophy ceases and reverses itself, with cells growing and reproducing in the hippocampus again. (Remember, the hippocampus is crucial for learning, since it is the part of the brain responsible for the formation of new memories.)
- Your child's body can now engage in sustained physiological repair (SPR). This means that your child can make maximal use of his biomedical interventions. If your child is getting treatments designed to aid and rebuild his digestive, immune, neurological, and elimination systems, he needs a body that is actually going to respond, repair, and rebuild.

We call the state in which the above factors are present the recovery mode. Using The Son-Rise Program to enable your child to shift from fight-or-flight to recovery mode gives your child every chance to progress and grow.

It also provides your child with something most children on the spectrum lack: treatment synergy. Biomedical interventions can work more powerfully together with The Son-Rise Program than individually.

It is thus absolutely essential that we administer any biological interventions (diet, enzymes, biomedical treatments, etc.) in a manner that is relaxed, noncoercive, and fun. This must be done with our children's cooperation rather than their resistance. For this reason, utilizing The Son-Rise Program techniques outlined in this chapter (and others) is imperative. We want to do all that we can to shift our children from fight-or-flight survival mode to recovery mode. This is what really matters.

ACTIVITY TIME!

To begin, you will just do two simple things. First, decide on one food item that you can safely say is unhealthy for your child. This does not refer to an entire food group, such as dairy, but rather to a single food item, such as soda, chocolate chip cookies, doughnuts, grilled cheese sandwiches, or pizza. Second, choose one food item that your child does not now eat which you will introduce, such as spinach, squash, or asparagus. Once you have decided, fill in Table 14.

One Food Item To Remove	One Food Item To Add

Table 14

ONLINE RESOURCES

For more in-depth help with the principles and techniques of this chapter, please go to www.autismbreakthrough.com/chapter16. Enjoy!

STARTING POINT

As a first step, let's just focus on removing that one food item on the left-hand side of Table 14. It is important not only to remove this item from your child's diet but to remove it from your house. If, for instance, you choose soda, you will want to make your house soda-free. Look back over the five Son-Rise Program feeding principles and the section on removing problematic and unhealthy foods. Then, when you have one hundred percent conviction behind the need to remove this one food item, you're ready to go!

SEVENTEEN

Attitude: The Critical Element

THIS IS THE most important chapter of the entire book.

The subject of this chapter is, without question, *the* most overlooked area of autism treatment. Moreover, without this chapter, none of the other principles, techniques, and strategies of this book will work.

Did that get your attention?

WHY YOUR ATTITUDE IS THE CRITICAL ELEMENT

People like to learn hard skills. I don't mean hard as in "difficult." Rather, a hard skill is a skill that is physical and easily seen and measured. Joining, for instance, is a technique based on a hard skill. You can see if someone's joining a child. You can see if someone *isn't* joining.

Most parents, when I first speak with them, want to hear all about the hard skills and techniques of The Son-Rise Program. They want me to tell them about joining. They want to know how to use one of their child's interests in a skill-building game. They want to hear about the four fundamentals of socialization and how to teach them.

What they don't show as much interest in at first is learning about the importance of attitude and how to utilize it. Attitude is considered a "soft" skill. To many people, it feels mushy or touchy-feely. I cannot count the number of instances that I have heard a parent make this statement: "Look, I think The Son-Rise

Program will really help my child. I want to learn the techniques, such as joining. But, attitude? Attitude, shmattitude. I don't need to spend loads of time looking at my emotions and stuff like that. Just teach me the techniques."

In the same vein, I still occasionally hear the old and deeply misinformed critique: "The Son-Rise Program says that if you just love your child enough, your child will come out of his or her autism." This statement, at its core, is not a criticism of The Son-Rise Program—since we don't say or believe that—so much as it is a reflection of the far-reaching cultural bias against attitude as a relevant (and, in this case, crucial) component of treatment.

I see this bias all the time in the many psychiatrists, psychologists, psychotherapists, and others in the helping professionals with whom we work. Many of these individuals experience sustained distress and discomfort routinely during their day, including while they are working with people. And yet they don't seem to view the dichotomy between the emotional well-being they endeavor to enable people to attain and their own lack of that well-being as particularly relevant. The idea that the attitude of the therapist bears no relationship to his or her ability to help people still reigns supreme. We believe that it's only knowledge and education that count. We remain married to the idea that, in the therapeutic and educational setting, the only thing that matters is *what* we do, rather than *how* we do it.

Even I, with a lifetime of evidence about the impact of attitude, briefly fell into this trap a couple of years ago; I'll tell you about it a little later.

The attitude of the person working with—or spending any time with—your child is of monumental importance for three primary reasons. Let's take them one at a time.

ATTITUDE HAS AN ENORMOUS IMPACT ON HOW RESPONSIVE OUR CHILDREN ARE

Children on the autism spectrum, as we've discussed before, are highly sensitive to their environment. They are easily overstimulated, they have difficulty processing incoming sensory input, they live in a world that seems haphazard and unpredictable to them, and, in many cases, they are in a continuous fight-or-flight state.

And, remember, autism is a social-relational disorder. Our children have difficulty leaving their own world and making interpersonal connections.

What do these factors mean when we put them all together? When our children are with someone who is uncomfortable or agitated, they perceive it as a threat. As a result, they either become more withdrawn or behave with more aggressiveness. These are both self-protection mechanisms.

When, on the other hand, our children are in the presence of someone who is relaxed, comfortable, welcoming, and truly nonjudgmental, they perceive this as safe and inviting. They respond more, engage more, display more flexibility, connect more, and, in most cases, shift out of fight-or-flight survival mode and into the recovery mode.

Thus, our attitude can provide the impetus for a challenged child to reach out to us, or it can act to drive that child away.

This is not some theory or idea. It is fact. We have seen this phenomenon play out with children for almost thirty years. We have seen children on the spectrum respond to attitude time and time again, moving away from those they perceive as agitated or uncomfortable and toward those they experience as comfortable, relaxed, and welcoming.

In truth, you have probably seen this many times as well. Have you ever noticed that your child will go to a particular therapy (say, occupational therapy or speech language therapy), and will respond quite powerfully to one therapist and not another? This is not a technique issue, since both therapists are doing the same type of therapy. Rather, your child's response is a function of the *attitude* of these two therapists. One of them has an attitude to which your child responds well, and the other doesn't.

An increasing body of research supports the attitude effect (see Appendix 1).

THE GIRL IN THE HOSPITAL

I want to share with you a brief but telling experience that my parents had when I was little. This occurred as they were waiting in a hospital lobby just prior to an important three-hour follow-up examination to be performed on me by the same team of neurologists, doctors, and associates as had performed a previous exam—with a very grim prognosis. Since the previous exam, I had made roughly 90 percent of what would become my full recovery—needless to say, a great surprise to the diagnosticians.

Here is their experience in that hospital lobby, taken directly my father's book, *Son-Rise: The Miracle Continues.*

> Samahria, Raun, and I sat together on the couch. A little girl and her mother came walking past. The child broke away from her mother's grasp and ran directly to Samahria, who smiled and opened her arms to her. The girl had teal blue eyes. Razor sharp! Samahria stroked the child's face gently and began talking to her in a whisper. The little girl just gazed into Samahria's eyes and then touched her head to Samahria's. They were like two old friends saying hello in the most intimate way. Finally, the child's mother came over. Without saying a word, she took the child's

hand and directed her toward the door. All this time, the little girl kept looking back at us.

Later, we inquired about this child. We were told that she was autistic and had always avoided human contact. Hmmm. Perhaps this little girl knew. Perhaps, when a loving and accepting attitude is expressed tangibly in a smile or in the gentle touch of a hand, the invitation might inspire even the most dysfunctional little person. Perhaps, in the face of such safety and encouragement, this child stretched herself beyond her normal limits.

THE AUTISM ONE / GENERATION RESCUE CONFERENCE

In 2011, we at the Autism Treatment Center of America had a powerful experience. I spoke at the Autism One / Generation Rescue conference in Chicago, Illinois, the largest and most broad conference of its kind at the time. (You may know Generation Rescue by its president, Jenny McCarthy.) I had spoken at this conference in previous years, but this year there was a fascinating twist. In a national survey conducted over a period of months by the conference, The Son-Rise Program had won the Best Autism Therapy award, and I had been awarded Best Presenter, which was a huge honor—but this wasn't the twist to which I refer.

For this conference, we had flown our entire team of child facilitators out to the conference to donate free child care to parents who attended the conference with their children on the autism spectrum. We were very excited, but, to be sure, this was also somewhat experimental. The Son-Rise Program is designed for a controlled, one-on-one, very personal environment, and this scenario would entail having two hotel rooms filled with special kids. Each room would have about twenty children and four or five adults.

We knew that, given these circumstances, we were not going

to be able to carefully implement each Son-Rise Program technique customized to each child, as we would normally do. Instead, our child facilitators decided to focus on the very basics. They would, above all, maintain a comfortable, welcoming, completely nonjudgmental attitude toward all of the children. Of course, in following what we all believed in, they would provide a safe and noncoercive environment. They would allow the children to do their isms. They would celebrate them and invite the kids to interact with them. But with a giant group of kids, even these basics had limits. In the end, we all knew that the one thing we could do with perfection no matter what was to maintain The Son-Rise Program attitude. And so that is what these wonderful child facilitators did.

Allow me to pause for a moment for a brief mea culpa. Although I was very excited about this whole endeavor, I was also a bit skeptical about it. How effective could we really be with just The Son-Rise Program attitude? In asking this question, I had fallen into that old cultural bias of valuing *what* we do over *how* we do it. In spite of all of my experience, I had, for a moment, fallen into the trap of failing to fully appreciate the paramount importance that attitude—yes, just attitude—has on treatment, and on our kids, especially. And I was quickly and vigorously disabused of my skepticism.

Over the three to four days the kids participated in our day care, some astonishing changes occurred. Parents would approach us, sometimes in tears, telling us stories about how different their children were in just a few days. They recounted events such as these.

- Jamie's parents told us that he was a very withdrawn child—except when a teacher at school would try to move him or get him to change what he was doing, at which point he would become aggressive. With us, he was extremely sweet, never once becoming aggressive in three days. Jamie would approach us and engage with us at times. His mother told us later that he was so much calmer after his time with us.

- Kaitlin cried the first whole day with us. She also scratched us and didn't want to participate in any way. Two days later, not only did she no longer cry, but she would come to us and insist on holding hands with us the entire time she was with us. She sang with us at times and at other times would continue to sing on her own.

- On the first day, Bianca would climb on everything and try to pull the other children's hair and push them. She would run from us and then look for a reaction. By the third day, she would come to us on her own for bounces, squeezes, and tons of celebrations. In the end, she was easily following directions (come eat your lunch, time to change your Pull-Up, etc.). She became incredibly loving and sweet, and she would watch the other kids, glance at their hair, and then *not* try to pull it. On her last day with us, she came through the door, calmly watched her mom and one of our child facilitators talk, waited until they were all done, *took the child facilitator's hand,* and then walked into the room with her.

- Kahanu's parents told us that his crying, which had been constant at home, decreased hugely after his time with us at the conference.

- Daniel, we were told, had "major separation issues." He had never before gone to a babysitter or to school without crying, tantruming, and becoming aggressive. His mother was used to holding him, both to restrain him from acting out on his teachers and babysitters and because he didn't want to be separated from her. Indeed, Daniel cried for most of his first day with us. On the second day (and every day thereafter), he pushed his parents out the door, saying "Bye-bye!" At the end of each day, he didn't want to leave. Throughout each day, he would smile, laugh, and participate with the other kids, occasionally interjecting, "Daniel's okay."

- Zach's parents came at the end of the day to pick him up and take him to a special "treat"—a trip to the museum that they had previously been looking forward to. Zach a high-functioning boy, explained to his parents that he didn't want to go—he wanted to stay with us. After his parents finally convinced him to go, Zach kept saying, as they were leaving, "But am I going to be able to come back? When can I come back?"
- A parent approached me at my conference booth and said, "After being with you guys, my son is so completely different than how he is every day when he comes home from school. I don't know if I can ever drop him back at school again."
- And many more instances of transformation, large and small: a little boy saying, "I love you" to us, a little girl's language increasing, a boy spontaneously sitting on his mother's lap for the first time, parents telling us that their children were suddenly calmer and happier, verbal children talking about their time with us for the rest of the night.

Keep in mind: this wasn't even from the full Son-Rise Program. This was just The Son-Rise Program *attitude.*

ATTITUDE DETERMINES OUR EFFECTIVENESS AT ENABLING OUR CHILDREN TO REACH NEW HEIGHTS

I know the walls of doubt and denial that you, as a parent, face from others about your child. I am aware of the avalanche of pessimistic messages that are communicated to you in a thousand different ways, subtle and unsubtle. And I am acutely cognizant of the undercurrent of social pressure that you may experience to "be realistic" about your child. To take some of that upon yourself is totally understandable.

That is why it is so important for you and me to spend some time looking at the effect our attitudes have on how we are with our children—and how this affects their development. This is not in any way an indictment of those of us who struggle with feelings of anger, frustration, fear, sadness, pessimism, or hopelessness—and who buy into the barrage of predictions ladled out so copiously about our children.

On the contrary, this is our chance to use this knowledge to change our children's trajectories.

Believing that your child is capable of accomplishing things that she hasn't yet is *the* prerequisite to you making such leaps happen with your child. If we don't believe that our children are capable in these instances, several obstacles of our own making will appear.

- We won't encourage our children to acquire the new skill—certainly not with real sincerity or passion.
- We won't persevere in our attempts over time, which, for many of our children, is necessary for reaching the next level.

- We will communicate to our children, in a plethora of different ways, that we don't believe that they can do it; this discourages them from continuing to try.
- We won't see or recognize when our children actually begin to achieve the goal, sabotaging our ability to build on it in any way.

You may remember the discussion from Chapter 7 in which I recounted a phenomenon we've seen many times at The Son-Rise Program Intensive. (Recall that parents attend this program with their child.) There have been times, while watching one of our sessions with their children in which they spoke for the very first time, when the parents could neither see nor hear this momentous event. These parents, having been told so many times that their children cannot speak, internalized this prediction. And, having internalized it, they remained unable to hear when their children were contradicting the "fact" that they couldn't speak. There have been instances where we have had to play back video footage of a child speaking multiple times before the parents watching could see and hear their child speaking. Although this may sound extreme, smaller versions of this phenomenon happen all the time when we decide in advance what our children *can't* do.

Every single thing you do while you are with your child is determined by your attitude. Let's look back through The Son-Rise Program techniques for some examples:

Joining, at least in its true (and effective) form, comes directly from an attitude of nonjudgmental acceptance and genuine interest in our children's worlds. Let's say that you are lining up toy cars with your child. If you are simply copying your child, you will find joining to be only marginally effective.

Imagine instead that, while you are lining up the cars, you are feeling a sense of nonjudgmental acceptance of what your child is doing, curiosity about his world, and celebration of his uniqueness and ability to take care of himself. Now your joining is imbued with the characteristics that make it work. You are enjoying yourself, communicating love and warmth toward your child, and showing him that you are a safe and integral part of his world.

The *motivation principle* stems from a real excitement about our children's interests. To capitalize on our children's motivations, we need to, first, be interested in what those motivations are (so that we can watch for them). Then we need to engage in a game around one of the interests (say, submarines), which, if that game has any hope of enticing our children, must be created with full-throated enthusiasm.

We can only use *celebration* effectively if we are feeling sincere gratitude for and delight in something that our child has just done. Otherwise, it is simply a rote praise that will have no currency with our children (i.e., our children won't be moved by it to do more of what we are celebrating, thus negating its efficacy). We need the three Es—energy, excitement, and enthusiasm—to make it work. Also, we won't even notice what to celebrate if we aren't focusing on and feeling grateful for the wonderful things that our children are already doing.

When dealing with *tantrums and other challenging behaviors,* think about this: how can we stay truly nonreactive when our child is engaging in some challenging behavior unless we can honestly maintain a comfortable attitude? When our child scratches us and we light up like a Christmas tree (i.e., frown, scold, raise our voice, look agitated), this is because of our attitude—in this case, one of anger, frustration, or fear. When this happens, it isn't because we forget The Son-Rise Program technique that applies here (remaining calm, nonreactive, and playing "dumb"). It's because, *even though we know what to do, our attitude makes it impossible for us to do it.*

You can read this book and memorize all of the techniques

therein, but when you feel agitated or upset, you will not be able to effectively implement the principles you've just committed to memory. Our attitude affects everything we do. We cannot join with love and curiosity when we feel sad. We cannot celebrate with gratitude and excitement when we feel upset. We cannot stay relaxed and help our crying, scratching child to find a different way to communicate when we feel frustrated.

It's not that you have to be perfect and never get upset with your child again. It's just that, once you prioritize your attitude and begin to shift the ways you approach even some of the daily situations and challenges you face with your child, you clear the way for mammoth change to occur in how she relates to you. Each time you take even one event or behavior and approach it with The Son-Rise Program attitude, you maximize your power to be helpful to your child.

You already love your child more than anything. Now you can express your love in the way she can most understand.

ATTITUDE WILL DETERMINE WHETHER OR NOT WE WILL STAY MOTIVATED OVER TIME

This should come as no surprise to you, but it bears mentioning. If you are stressed out, burned out, bummed out, freaked out, or otherwise discouraged, disempowered, despondent, or demoralized, you will not stick with what you are doing. This is true if you are implementing The Son-Rise Program, but it is also true if you are implementing *any* program. For success, you must sustain your program (whatever program that is) *over time*. You will not be able to do this unless you can stay consistently motivated, upbeat, confident, and clearheaded.

Have you ever been at home with your child, when you could take some time to play with him, but you realize that you have a load of laundry to do? Do you ever see your child acting "autistic," and instead of spending some time with him, you put him in front of the TV for a while?

It's totally fine if you *have* done these things. Almost every parent I've worked with has. Many parents have difficulty enjoying their child on the spectrum, which affects the amount of time they spend with their child. And time is the one thing that is absolutely necessary for The Son-Rise Program to work.

When you are comfortable with your child, you will spend more time with your child—not because you think you're supposed to but because you *want* to. When you have real conviction behind what you are doing, you will stick to it. When you feel relaxed on a regular basis, you will *not* feel exhausted, and so you will have energy to give to your child. When you feel a sense of self-confidence with regard to your competence in helping your child, you will maintain the motivation and consistency over time that is critical for the principles of The Son-Rise Program to do their job.

One of the reasons why we spend so much time during the Start-Up program and the advanced programs working with parents on cultivating a comfortable, confident, relaxed, and hopeful attitude is that *nothing else will matter without it.*

BONUS REASON: YOUR PERSONAL RELATIONSHIP

For most of us, just navigating a marriage or similar long-term relationship can be hard enough. Couple that with raising a child—any child—and our lives can feel like a real challenge. That's *before* we have a child with autism.

When we *do* have a child on the spectrum, it can feel like an experience beyond the biggest challenge that we have ever imagined facing. Your child is different. She exhibits behaviors to which others respond with discomfort or confusion. The simplest daily tasks, like eating or taking a bath, are fraught with difficulty. Dire predictions are handed out like candy. The most basic dreams that you and your partner had for your child seem dashed. You must choose from a confusing list of treatment options, or you're given only one option and told to be grateful that you have even that. Stress levels that may already be high often explode. For many, many couples, autism seems to push the relationship to the breaking point.

If there were things you could do to strengthen your relationship and increase the chances of it surviving autism, wouldn't you want to know what those things were? If you are still wondering if attitude is really important day-to-day in a relationship, ask yourself this. Have you ever noticed:

- How different you are with your significant other when you are stressed out about your child?
- How you feel about your significant other when he or she says something that you think means that he or she doesn't value you?
- How much harder it is for you to feel close to your significant other when you are feeling very critical of yourself?

These experiences are all about attitude. If you have a way to change your attitude, these experiences change.

I (and the other teachers at the Autism Treatment Center of America) have conducted a great many couples counseling sessions. This is one of the most satisfying aspects of my work. One of the most moving transformations I witness at the ATCA is seeing couples on the verge of dissolution learn to use their child's autism to grow closer and nurture a more caring, honest, and loving relationship.

For some of you, this may sound like a pipe dream, but it is not beyond the realm of possibility. The only way to turn the ship around, though, is to begin with attitude. You already know that how you are with your child (calm or frustrated, celebratory or annoyed, accepting or critical) affects every aspect of your relationship with him. In the same way, how you and your partner are attitudinally with one another affects every aspect of your partnership.

Even as you read this, you may be thinking that this sounds nice, but it's the *how* that eludes. Fair enough. We haven't yet discussed the *how* of attitudinal change, but we will. This chapter will give you some simple tools you can put to use immediately—with your child *and* your partner.

But, first, you have to be on board for the idea that *if* there were ways for you (and your partner) to face events with your child and each other in a more comfortable, clear, loving, and relaxed manner, it would be to your benefit—it would *matter*—for you to do so. So what do you say? Are you willing to prioritize attitude?

THE COMPONENTS OF THE SON-RISE PROGRAM ATTITUDE

The Son-Rise Program attitude can be summarized as follows: embracing *without judgment* where your child is today—while believing that she can go anywhere tomorrow. Of course, it goes deeper than this, but let's use the two halves of this concept as our jumping-off point.

"Embracing without judgment where your child is today" has profound meaning. It goes way beyond simply loving your child, which we all do. It means loving everything about your child, including the most autistic parts. It involves embracing your child's autism the way you embrace her brown eyes, curly hair, sweet smile, or any other aspect of who she is. It entails seeing your child ripping sheets of paper into tiny strips and falling in love with ripping paper. It means not labeling any of your child's behaviors as bad, wrong, or even inappropriate, which necessitates knowing that, right now, she is doing the very best that she can.

This essential ingredient of The Son-Rise Program attitude is what sets the stage for all relationship-building. We use the word "nonjudgmental," but we could also add the words "welcoming," "loving," "accepting," "caring," "at ease," "curious," and "delighting." You want to cultivate an attitude that involves sincerely cherishing every aspect of your child—especially those traits that make her different.

You may recall, in the first chapter of this book, that I quoted something from my father's book that he and my mom asked themselves upon receiving my diagnosis and the dark predictions that went with it: "Could we kiss the ground that the others had cursed?"

That's what The Son-Rise Program attitude is really about. Others may call your child's condition a tragedy. You don't have to. People might look upon your child with disapproving eyes. You can make your every gaze an embrace. You can kiss the ground that the others have cursed.

"Believing that your child can go *anywhere* tomorrow" is also very important. We can embody this part of the attitude with hope, optimism, anticipatory invitation, excitement, and, indeed, joyful silliness. It means seeing your child's abilities rather than focusing on supposed deficiencies. People will (with the best of intentions) try their best to convince you to be "realistic." They will urge you to "come to terms" with what you child cannot do.

When faced with such naysaying, it is all the more important to be *unrealistic*. This means cultivating a belief in what your child *can* do—unencumbered by the limited, pessimistic, stifling version of reality that others may espouse. After all, you are the parent. Your love is unrivaled, your experience is unmatchable, and your long-haul commitment is unparalleled. You do not have to apologize for believing in your child when no one else does. You don't have to feel embarrassed about seeing what no one else sees.

This vital piece of The Son-Rise Program attitude gives your child every chance to reach new heights. (It's not a guarantee, but it opens so many closed doors!) It allows you to have a child who has not yet spoken and say, "He just hasn't spoken yet, but he can absolutely do this." It enables you to know that what your child has done (or not done) up until now tells you *nothing* about what he can do in the future.

WHERE YOUR ATTITUDE COMES FROM—AND HOW TO SHIFT IT

I can understand how it might, at first, seem a bit pie-in-the-sky to read about the importance of cultivating a particular attitude when, in your day-to-day experience, that attitude may seem far off. You may feel as if events happen throughout your day, and you simply react to them as best you can. Some things happen that appear to brighten your day, while other, more challenging occurrences seem to make you upset. And when you experience a really massive event, such as having your child diagnosed with autism, it can certainly feel as if the event itself is *causing* your unhappiness.

This almost universally accepted model of the human psyche holds that the events and circumstances in our lives determine how we feel emotionally (happy, sad, excited, scared, content, angry). Our child ripping up the pages of a book *makes* us feel upset. Her tantrum *makes* us feel frustrated. A diagnostician telling us that our child will only improve slightly *makes* us feel devastated. On the other side of the equation, our child saying her first word *makes* us feel wonderful. A teacher telling us that our child has made progress *makes* us feel proud or hopeful.

There are two problems with this model, though. The first one is a flaw in logic: how do we explain two people responding in totally different ways to the same events? If events and circumstances really do *make* us feel the way we feel, then shouldn't everyone respond the same way to the same thing? How do we explain that one person feels devastated or worthless when he or she gets fired, and someone else shrugs it off—or even feels excited about the prospect of moving on? How is it that some lottery winners say that winning was the best thing that ever happened to them and others maintain that it was the worst? Since everyone responds differently to the same events—and *we* respond differently to a particular event on different days, there must be something else besides the event that is determining how we feel.

The second problem is a practical one: this model makes us out to be victims. We don't determine how we feel; events outside of us do. If only my child would communicate more, progress faster, not be autistic, not behave that way, etc., *then* I could feel good (comfortable, relaxed, hopeful, etc.).

Given this culturally reinforced paradigm, no one on earth could fault you for feeling distraught, upset, scared, angry, frustrated, or despondent about the challenges that your child—and, thus, you—face. Many of us feel like we are locked in a nonstop battle to get our children to behave a certain way or reach particular benchmarks just so that we can sleep at night. I can understand that. We want to be good parents. And we want our children to have fulfilling lives.

The problem is that when we need our children to be a certain way, it does a lot more than just make us miserable. It also greatly hinders our ability to help our children. Why? Because, as we've been discussing, we are different with our children—and they respond differently to us—depending on our attitude. In fact, if we need our children to behave a certain way or progress a particular amount in order for us to feel good, they will experience this need as a push. And if there is one thing we know about our children, it's that when they feel pushed, they dig their heels in (or push back).

So freeing ourselves from this prison is the very best thing we can do for ourselves and our children. The question is, how?

THE MISSING PIECE: BELIEFS

In reality, it is not the events and circumstances themselves that determine how we feel. It is, rather, our *beliefs*.

What, exactly, is a belief?

I like to think of beliefs as tinted sunglasses. You might have yellow lenses in yours, and, consequently, everything you see looks yellow. I might have green. Someone else might have blue. We might all insist that our color is the "real" color of things, but, in reality, we are all just gazing through our own lenses.

Because our human brains function as belief-making machines, we can never remove our sunglasses altogether. We are always believing *something.* What we *can* do, however, is to switch our lenses—as often as we like. If I feel that my green lenses aren't serving me (they are fueling my unhappiness or making me ineffective), then I can swap them out for blue ones. If those don't work for me, I can replace them with red lenses. My vision will always be colored in some way by my lenses (beliefs), but I get to choose *how* they are colored. Are they rose-colored or mud brown?

So a belief is a conclusion that we draw about ourselves, other people, events, and the world around us in order to make sense of our environment and to take care of ourselves. In each particular situation, we hold a belief which acts as the lens through which we see that situation. Beliefs are perspectives, opinions, perceptions, biases, or preconceptions that provide our frame of reference for understanding what is happening.

Here are some examples of beliefs.

- My child will never change.
- I did something wrong to bring about or contribute to my child's autism.
- If I prioritize myself and what I want too much, I will become selfish and not be there for my child.
- My child isn't capable of doing that (speaking, making friends, etc.).

Alternatively, we could believe this.

- My child is capable of profound growth and progress.
- I didn't do anything "wrong" to cause my child's challenges, but I can be part of the solution.
- If I take time to prioritize myself and what I want, this will leave me with more reserves, more health, and more focus to help my child.
- My child is totally capable of doing that; he just hasn't done it *yet.*

The beliefs we hold determine every emotion we have, from joy to anger, from contentment to fear. It works like this.

- An event occurs in our lives (we are told that our child has autism).
- We filter the event through the belief we hold about it (my child is facing a lifetime of suffering and limited possibilities, this is my fault, etc.).

- We feel an emotion based upon our belief (sad, scared, angry, etc.).

Here are some more examples of our beliefs in action.

- A young boy with autism is lying on the floor and making loud noises in the middle of the supermarket, and his mom feels embarrassed as she sees the disapproving looks of others. The belief causing the embarrassment: If people are judging me, it means I'm doing something wrong as a parent.

- A mom feels proud and excited as she notices that her daughter is repetitively stacking blocks. The belief fueling the pride and excitement: My daughter knows exactly what to do to best take care of herself, and I can use her behavior as a way to connect with my daughter and know her world better.

- A dad feels frustrated as he sees his son with autism watch the same two minutes of a DVD over and over again. The belief fueling the frustration: This behavior means that my son is broken and incapable of change and growth.

- A little boy with autism says his first word, and his parents feel overjoyed. The belief fueling their joy: This is the first step to my child speaking fluently. More language is on the way.

- A mother of a five-year-old with autism feels angry and sad when she sees neurotypical kids. The belief causing the anger and sadness: My child can never turn out like those kids. Autism is bad. It's unfair that my child has autism while others don't.

WHERE DO WE GET OUR BELIEFS?

We are taught a great many of our beliefs from those around us. Throughout our lives, we are bombarded by a never-ending stream of beliefs by our parents, teachers, friends, strangers, the news, movies, and television shows. Most of the time, we are taught beliefs that fuel distress, fear, unhappiness, and ineffectiveness. We adopt and continue to hold such beliefs and the unhappiness they create as a strategy to take care of ourselves. We do, at times, adopt beliefs that lead to contentment, but our belief-adopting bias tends to lean toward "Oh, no!" rather than "Oh, yes!" perspectives. Some examples:

- A child who is told by her parents that she is irresponsible adopts this belief about herself and continues to hold on to it as an adult.
- A husband adopts the belief promoted to him by his father that he must financially provide for his new wife in order to be a good husband.
- A schoolchild is told by his teacher that he is not good at math. He adopts this belief and retains it for decades. (This could work in the reverse direction as well: A college-aged woman adopts the belief promoted to her by her writing professor that she is a good writer.)
- A man is told by a news anchorperson that his favorite candidate has little chance of winning the election. He adopts this belief and does not vote for that candidate. (And, thus, a self-fulfilling prophesy is created.)

In some cases, we develop beliefs ourselves through our experiences. For example:

- A man who is mugged on a city street at night concludes that cities are dangerous and avoids metropolitan areas.
- A elderly man is repeatedly treated in a dismissive manner by people around him, and he concludes that his advancing age makes him less important.
- A middle-aged woman who has been through two divorces creates the belief that she can never find true love.
- A visitor to France is shouted at by someone in French on three different occasions. He creates the belief that the French are rude. (This could operate in the opposite direction, too: A visitor to Italy is treated sweetly by several Italian people and concludes that Italians are nice people.)

How does this relate to you as the parent of a child with autism? Think of how you felt when your child first got her diagnosis—or when you first realized that something was very different about her. Did you feel scared? Angry? Sad? Did you feel like there was a bowling ball in your stomach or a hand around your throat?

For most of us, the second someone gives our child a diagnosis, they accompany that diagnosis with a stream of beliefs about what this diagnosis means about our child—and about us. We are told that our child will not be able to do what other kids can do. We are told that autism is a lifelong condition. We are given a myriad of details about what the next thirty years of our child's life will supposedly be like. And we are told of the many limitations that we ostensibly have as parents, such as a lack of the "proper" training/education or being "too emotional/too involved." Most important, we are told these things—these *beliefs*—as if they are facts.

In many cases we adopt these beliefs without ever really examining or considering them as optional perspectives. And who could blame us? We are surrounded by advocates and proponents of these beliefs and biases. We are immersed in these beliefs at a time when we are least equipped to be discerning. Our child is given a life sentence. We are inundated with pronouncements. We feel a sense of desperation—we know that our child is facing profound challenges, but we don't know what to do to help her.

In the face of this, we don't realize that we get to decide if we want to take on the beliefs we are presented with or not.

As time goes on, we pick up more beliefs (or create them on our own), most of them disempowering and unhappiness-producing. Then, when we're confronted with day-to-day experiences with our child, we face a never-ending torrent of triggers. He pinches or bites. She doesn't speak. He faces criticism from others. *We* face criticism from others. She engages in unusual repetitive behaviors. He doesn't appear to return our affection. She is rigid about how events must transpire.

But, remember: these triggers are only triggers because we're holding beliefs that make these events feel terrible. If, for example, we saw our child's pinching or biting as a temporary instance of our child's most sincere attempt to take care of himself instead of meaning that he will never change or doesn't love us, it would feel very different than it does.

Lest this picture appear gloomy, let us explore the most important part of this whole equation.

THE GOOD NEWS: BELIEFS ARE CHANGEABLE

Since beliefs are learned, we can unlearn them. And since our beliefs fuel our emotions about an event, changing them completely changes how we feel, even when there is no change in the event itself.

We work with many parents who change fundamental

unhappiness-producing beliefs about themselves and their children, often in just the five days of the Start-Up course. They go from seeing their child's autism as a nightmare to seeing the most profound beauty in their child's uniqueness. They shift from seeing themselves as ill-equipped to concluding that they have everything they need to make a profound and lasting impact on their child's trajectory. They change from thinking that their child is capable of only small and slow change to believing that their child is capable of vast and sweeping growth. These transformations are only possible because beliefs are changeable.

Understanding how beliefs work shifts us out of the victim position and into the driver's seat. One of the strongest ways to keep yourself in this driver's seat is to say to yourself, next time you get unhappy or upset: "I'm feeling upset not because of what's *happening* but because of what I'm *believing* about what's happening."

Okay, so if beliefs are changeable, how do we change them? First, we have to uncover them. And if you've never done this before, it can seem tricky at first. That's why we teach parents (and others) to use a special questioning process called the Option Process Dialogue to uncover and then change beliefs, preconceptions, and biases which might be getting in their way—particularly when it comes to maintaining The Son-Rise Program attitude so crucial for helping their child.

Explaining this entire process would entail a book by itself. (In fact, there is such a book. If you would like to learn the fundamentals of the Option Process Dialogue in detail, you can read *PowerDialogues,* by Barry Neil Kaufman.) What we can do here is give you some starting questions that will be enormously helpful to you if you use them regularly. I would recommend that you practice asking yourself these questions each time you find yourself feeling unhappy, upset, annoyed, or frustrated. This can include issues and events not related to your child because, as you get better at uncovering and changing beliefs, you will find that you will get more and more adept at feeling comfortable and maintaining The Son-Rise Program attitude in situations that *do* involve your child.

Okay. Ready?

THREE QUESTIONS TO ASK YOURSELF

1. What am I believing (i.e., telling myself) that is fueling my unhappiness (frustration, fear, sadness, anger, etc.)?
2. Why am I believing/telling myself this?
3. What could I believe instead, and how will believing this help me or my child? (Shortcut question: How can I see this situation as good—or at least okay?)

Wait! Hold on! Before you start using these questions, take a look at the following lists of common parental beliefs. Looking over these lists carefully will make it much easier for you to answer the three questions above. These lists are also essential for completing the vitally important Activity Time! section at the end of this chapter.

TOP SEVEN DISEMPOWERING, UNHAPPINESS-PRODUCING PARENTAL BELIEFS

1. My child's autism is a tragedy, and I cannot possibly feel okay about it.
2. My child's condition is static and unchangeable. (What my child has done in the past tells me a lot about what she is capable of accomplishing in the future.)

3. My child knows that she is not supposed to behave this way. She is doing this just to drive me crazy.
4. I just can't handle this.
5. This situation is going to ruin my marriage.
6. My unhappiness about my child's condition is a sign of how much I care and how much I love her.
7. I have to get other people to agree with me, understand me, or support me in order to feel okay.

TOP SEVEN EMPOWERING, HAPPINESS-PRODUCING PARENTAL BELIEFS

1. I love my child and can enjoy and see the beauty in my child exactly as he is—with all his differences.
2. My child is capable of limitless change and growth. (What my child has been able or unable to do in the past tells me absolutely *nothing* about what he is capable of accomplishing in the future.)
3. My child is behaving this way because it is the only way he knows how to take care of himself. He is doing the best he can.
4. I can absolutely handle this.
5. I can use this challenge to meaningfully enhance, improve, and deepen my marriage.
6. My unhappiness doesn't have to be the measurement of how much I care. I can express my caring through my love and effort.

7. I don't need others to understand, agree with, or support me in order to feel okay. I just need conviction behind what I'm doing.

To get more help with belief and attitudinal change, I strongly recommend reading the book *Happiness Is a Choice* by Barry Neil Kaufman. It is a clear and very easy-to-read book with specifics about how to make far-reaching attitudinal changes in ways that feel easy and doable. Of particular interest are the six shortcuts to happiness. These are simple steps you can take to cut through the craziness and get yourself into a comfortable and relaxed state of mind quickly.

ACTIVITY TIME!

For this section, you will want to choose an issue or area of emotional discomfort or unhappiness that you have concerning your child or your relationship to her. You can choose an issue that you feel unhappy about right now or one that comes up regularly, such as feeling sad about your child's autism, fearful about her future, or worried that you don't have what it takes to help her. Alternatively, you can choose a specific event or occurrence where you got upset, such as a time when you got frustrated about how your child was behaving or an incident where you felt embarrassed in public with her.

Once you've chosen your issue, take a look at Table 15. Now you can plug your event or issue into this table. Then continue to fill out the table from there. When filling out the final two boxes, it will help you enormously to take another look at the seven disempowering and empowering beliefs listed earlier. You can choose your beliefs from these lists or come up with your own beliefs to write down.

When you are filling out that final box, take a few moments

to really consider what alternative belief you want to focus on adopting because it will serve as your ultimate attitudinal goal. Allow it to be your guide, your North Star. Your mission in life, at this point, is to adopt this belief.

Most important: don't be hard on yourself if you don't just drop everything and adopt the alternative belief you've chosen. It will take some time. You've had years to cement your unhappiness-producing beliefs. The most essential step is to start the ball rolling. Tape the alternative belief onto your bathroom mirror, write down a list of evidence supporting this belief, have your partner or a friend remind you about it, write down how adopting this new belief will help you help your child—or do all of the above. But above all, be easy with yourself. That you are even doing this at all is a statement of love for your child and will make a meaningful difference for both of you.

Event or Circumstance	
How You Feel/ Felt	
Belief Fueling This Emotion	
Alternate Belief to Adopt	

Table 15

ONLINE RESOURCES

For more in-depth help with the principles and techniques of this chapter, please go to www.autismbreakthrough.com/chapter17. Enjoy this final chapter's online assistance!

STARTING POINT

For starters, choose one aspect of your child's condition or behavior that you tend to judge or with which you have a hard time. Now, try asking yourself the three questions we discussed earlier. Here they are again for your convenience:

1. What am I believing (telling myself) that is fueling my unhappiness (frustration, fear, sadness, anger, etc.)?
2. Why am I believing/telling myself this?
3. What could I believe instead, and how will believing this help me or my child? (Shortcut question: How can I see this situation as good—or at least okay?)

Next, spend a few minutes thinking about one dream you have for your child that you might have begun to suppress or keep to yourself because you were concerned that people would think it was unrealistic. Now just sit with this dream for a moment. If you feel any part of you internally apologizing for having this dream, just let it go. You are allowed to dream for your child. You are allowed to want more for your child. And you are allowed to give your child every chance to reach new horizons.

A FINAL WORD FROM ME TO YOU

We have taken quite a journey together, you and I. I have put my mind and soul into these pages with the hope that they will find their way into your heart. More than anything, I want these ideas, principles, and strategies to be useful to you and to your wonderful, special, and unique child.

Please, please, do not hold yourself up to some impossible standard of perfection. You're a human being who loves your child. That's enough. As you endeavor to implement the tools and techniques in this book, be gentle with yourself. If you don't utilize these strategies every single second, that's okay. If you feel discouraged or down or afraid sometimes, that's okay, too. Just pick yourself up, dust yourself off, and get back on the horse.

And, whatever you do, don't believe anyone who tells you that your child's future has been written—whether your child is three or thirty-three.

The Story of Jarir

A few years ago, the mother of a thirty-three-year-old man with autism named Jarir came to the Autism Treatment Center of America from the United Kingdom for the Start-Up program. At the time, her son was being cared for in an institution, where he had spent much of his life.

Jarir spent most of his time isming, had minimal eye contact, communicated mainly using single words (though he could sometimes use two words together), and spoke mostly in response to requests rather than spontaneously and unprompted. He preferred being alone and showed very little interest in the activities of others, often rejecting attempts to engage him.

The Start-Up program was transformative for Jarir's mom, giving her new hope and specific strategies to help her son. Upon her return to the UK, she removed Jarir from the institution, took him home, and implemented a Son-Rise Program with him.

Over the next eighteen months, Jarir underwent a spectacular metamorphosis, isming only 10 to 20 percent of the time; his eye contact increased to a neurotypical level and his speech surged forward so that his average sentence length was five to six words, with some as long as ten words. Moreover, his communication was often spontaneous and self-generated rather than only in response to others' requests. And Jarir became a man who *wanted* others around him, joining in and enjoying the activities of others the vast majority of the time.

IT'S NEVER TOO LATE

Jarir's story is a testament to his mom's dedication, to the power of the strategies detailed in this book, and, most of all, to the capacity of Jarir—and all of our children—to change and grow in dramatic fashion, at any age, regardless of the circumstances preceding that transformation.

There are no permanent roadblocks for our children. There is no point of no return. The brain remains plastic throughout our children's entire lives. (This is why a man in his seventies can have a stroke, lose his speech capabilities, and then relearn to speak.) So don't let anyone convince you that it's too late, that it's time to give up, that what your child *has not done* is any indicator of what your child *cannot do.*

When it's late at night, and you're feeling all alone, please know that there is a team of us on a mountainside in a small town in the Berkshires who are rooting for you, cheering for you, and believing that you can help your child reach the stars.

Recommended Reading and Viewing

I strongly recommend that you check out these books and DVDs.

- *Breakthrough Strategies for Autism Spectrum Disorders* by Raun K. Kaufman (DVD)
- *Inspiring Journeys of Son-Rise Program Families* (Free DVD)
- *Autism Solutions* (Free DVD)
- *Son-Rise: A Miracle of Love* (NBC-TV movie, available on Amazon .com)
- Three books by Barry Neil Kaufman: *Son-Rise: The Miracle Continues, A Miracle to Believe In,* and *Happiness Is a Choice*

Go to my Web site at www.autismbreakthrough.com for help applying the principles and techniques in this book, including webcasts, articles, interviews, and some awe-inspiring recovery videos—including some touching interviews with the recovered kids themselves.

Contact the Autism Treatment Center of America for a twenty-five-minute call with one of our Son-Rise Program Advisors at no charge to get your questions answered, inquire about financial aid, or register to attend a Start-Up program.

As a non-profit, charitable organization giving financial assistance to families seeking to come to the ATCA to learn to use the principles on this book, we welcome and deeply appreciate donations, which are one hundred percent tax deductible.

This is how to reach us:

Autism Treatment Center of America
2080 South Undermountain Road
Sheffield, MA 01257
www.autismtreatment.org
sonrise@autismtreatment.org
1-800-714-2779
1-413-229-2100

APPENDIX 1

EMPIRICAL RESEARCH SUPPORTING THE SON-RISE PROGRAM

This appendix is all about the science. I've included it for two reasons: so the very scientific-minded parents and professionals among you can see exactly how the existing literature and research support the principles of The Son-Rise Program; and so you can provide this information to skeptical professionals, schools, etc., whom you are endeavoring to get on board with the ideas in this book and with funding your Son-Rise Program.

First, here is a link to a study in the *Journal of Communication Disorders* demonstrating the effectiveness and efficacy of The Son-Rise Program. This journal is published by Elsevier, one of the world's leading providers of science and health information, serving more than 30 million scientists, students, and health professionals worldwide. The peer-reviewed study ("Promoting Child-Initiated Social-Communication in Children with Autism: Son-Rise Program Intervention Effects"), conducted by Northwestern University in the U.S. and Lancaster University in the UK, showed significant improvements in the social skills and engagement of children who received The Son-Rise Program treatment compared to a control group of children who did not. Especially remarkable is that, even though this study was conducted over a five-day period, the children receiving The Son-Rise Program showed quantifiable results. So if someone asks you whether The Son-Rise Program is an evidence-based program supported by scientific, peer-reviewed research, you can answer with an emphatic, "Yes" and cite the study below!

http://www.sciencedirect.com/science/article/pii/S0021992413000518

Second, the following academic paper compiles an array of published studies that support the principles and techniques of The Son-Rise Program detailed in this book. As an academic, research-oriented paper, it makes for very dense technical reading—*much* less easy to read and to digest than the book itself. I hope that this paper is both informative and extremely useful to you! (You can download copies of it at www.autismbreakthrough.com/appendix1.)

* * *

Since autism was first outlined (Kanner, 1943), an agreed-upon definition of autism has been reached and standardized diagnostic methods produced. To date, however, no clear etiology has been established, and proposed treatments vary widely. Research has uncovered enough about autism's underlying neuro and cognitive psychology to allow us to outline treatment implications to benefit those families seeking help now who are unwilling to wait for the elusive ultimate answer.

The Autism Treatment Center of America has been using The Son-Rise Program *(SRP)* with families since 1983 in order to fulfill this need. The SRP was developed by parents experimenting with ways to reach their severely autistic child (Kaufman, 1976). Science at this time offered no guidance on facilitating the social development of children with autism. Since their son emerged from autism after 3 and a half years of intensive work, the Kaufmans have offered SRP to families internationally. To date, no rigorous longitudinal testing of the efficacy of SRP has been performed yet it can be seen that the key principles of this approach draw support from the current research literature. This paper will discuss some key principles of SRP in the context of current research in autism to create a platform for quantitative investigation.

PRINCIPLE: CREATE AN OPTIMAL PHYSICAL LEARNING ENVIRONMENT

Hyperarousal to sensory input among those with autism (Belmonte and Yurgelan-Todd, 2003; Hirstein et al., 2001; Tordjman et al., 1997) accompanied by an impairment to choose between competing stimuli is widely observed. EEG studies involving tasks requiring people with autism to selectively attend to relevant stimuli and ignore irrelevant stimuli have shown either an abnormal heightened P1 evoked potential to the relevant stimuli or an abnormally generalized response to irrelevant stimuli (Townsend and Courchesne, 1994).

Additionally, the N2 to novel stimuli is heightened in children with autism, even when these stimuli are irrelevant to the task (Kemner et al., 1994). Similar results have been seen using auditory stimuli (Kemner et al., 1995). This supports behavioral observations that children with autism can either be overly focused on one aspect of a task or greatly distracted by stimuli irrelevant or peripheral to the task. During tasks requiring shifts of attention between hemifields, those with autism have been shown to exhibit both hemispheres activating indiscriminately instead of the usual hemispheric-specific patterns of activation (Belmonte, 2000).

Physiological measures suggest that perceptual filtering in autism occurs in an all-or-nothing manner with little specificity in selecting the location of the stimulus, for the behavioral-relevance of the stimulus or even the sensory modality in which the stimulus occurs (Belmonte, 2000). It has been suggested that this tendency for hyperarousal to sensory input must result from some pervasive underlying abnormality in neural processing rather than one specific brain locus (Belmonte et al., 2004; Johnson et al., 2002; Akshoomoff et al., 2002). Some authors suggest this neuronal dysfunction to be low signal-to-noise ratio developing from abnormal neural connectivity (Bauman and Kemper, 1994; Raymond et al., 1996; Casanova and Buxhoeveden, 2002; Belmonte et al., 2004).

The result of this type of processing is that all stimuli are given equal priority by the autistic brain causing an overwhelming flood of sensory information to be handled. The typical brain is able to identify and ignore irrelevant stimuli and focus valuable attention on that which is task-relevant creating a much more efficient processing system. The autistic brain, on the other hand, takes it all in and then must actively discard irrelevant information at a later processing stage causing, in effect, a processing bottleneck (Belmonte, 2004). Functional neuroimaging studies show that the brains of those with autism tend to show increased activation in areas that rely on primary sensory processing and decreased activity in areas typically supporting higher-order processing (Ring et al., 1999; Critchley et al., 2000; Schultz et al., 2000; Pierce et al., 2001; Baron-Cohen et al., 1999; Castelii et al., 2002).

It has been proposed that this low-level processing disruption underlies the higher-level abnormalities exhibited in autism (Belmonte, 2004) and that the widely observed symptomology of autism (including issues of Theory of Mind and executive function) is an emergent property of abnormal neural growth (Akshoomoff, 2002). There is molecular evidence that this abnormality is present at birth (Nelson et al., 2001) even though obvious behavioral symptoms often do not typically arise until 18–24 months. A child born reliant on this over-aroused, underselective sensory processing is open to a flood of stimuli that is thought to overload the newly emerging higher-order cognitive processes (Belmonte and Yurgelun-Todd, 2003). When faced with this processing constraint, the developing and plastic brain is forced to re-organize to accommodate that constraint (Johnson et al., 2002). This is manifested in the abnormal organization of the autistic brain as described above and the cognitive style characteristic of autism that relies heavily on lower-order, local feature processing at the expense of higher-order, global information processing known as weak central coherence (Happe, 1999; Frith and Happe, 1994).

Central coherence describes the ability to process incoming information in context, pulling information together for higher-level meaning, often at the expense of memory for detail (Happe, 1999). Weak central coherence then is the tendency of those with autism to rely on local feature processing (the details) rather than taking in the global nature of the situation. Kanner (1943) saw, as a universal feature of autism, the "inability to experience wholes without full attention to the constituent parts." It is this cognitive style that makes people with autism superior at resisting visual illusions (Happe, 1999), have a higher occurrence of absolute pitch (Heaton et al., 1998), excel at the Embedded Figures Task (Shah and Frith, 1983; Jolliffe and Baron-Cohen, 1997) and possess the ability to copy "impossible" figures (Mottron et al., 2000).

These neurophysiological and neuroanatomical studies paint a picture of the world occupied by those with autism as chaotic, overwhelming and filled with "noise." Coupled with this is an internal environment of hyperarousal (Hirstein, 2001; Cohen and Johnson, 1977; Hutt and Hutt, 1979; Hutt et al., 1965; Kootz and Cohen, 1981; Kootz et al., 1982). This is corroborated by autobiographical reports from some people with autism (Bluestone, 2002; Williams, 1994; Gillingham, 1995; Jones et al., 2003). Considering this fragmented, chaotic and overwhelming world implies then that a child's external environment is a key and primary factor to be considered when designing a treatment program for children with autism. Physical environments with higher amounts of sensory stimulation (e.g bright visual displays, background noise, etc.) will add to the "noise" in an already overloaded sensory system, making any new learning extremely challenging. While there is acknowledgment that children with special needs do require specifically designed environments (Carbone, 2001; Reiber and McLaughlin, 2004; Schilling and Schwartz, 2004), the extent to which rooms can be tailored to meet the needs of these children is highly constrained by a typical classroom setting, mainly due to the presence of other children and the subsequent size of the room—even something as ubiquitous as fluorescent lighting has been shown to affect the behavior of children with autism (Colman et al., 1976). These environmental considerations are often overlooked and their importance underestimated.

The SRP bypasses the constraint of the classroom by employing a room (usually in the child's home) that is specifically designed to lower sensory stimulation. Only neutral colors are used and distracting patterns or highly contrasting colors are avoided. There are no distracting visual displays or noises and only incandescent or natural lighting is employed. All toys and objects are kept off the floor on wall-mounted shelves to provide a distraction-free floor area for play. Most importantly, play sessions in the playroom usually include one adult and one child. This means that the child does not have to try and filter out the noise and movement of other children but deals only with a predictable adult whom s/he trusts. The SRP holds that these simple measures aid in soothing the autistic child's over-active nervous system by making the world digestible and manageable. There is evidence for a sub-set of children with autism who do not exhibit an overactive autonomic system but instead display unusually low levels of arousal (Hirstein et al., 2001). These are the children who tend to engage in "extreme" activities (e.g., climbing very high, constantly moving, etc.) in order to "kick-start" their arousal levels. The SRP playroom provides a safe and contained environment in which to do these activities, many of which are not feasible in a typical classroom.

It can be seen that this treatment principle of SRP is supported by the current neuroanatomical and physiological data. Direct investigation of the effects on children with autism of the SRP playroom in contrast with traditional classrooms has not yet been undertaken. Children in home-based Son-Rise Programs often instigate going into the playroom, will play in there even when they are alone and talk about how much they enjoy their special room. There is much anecdotal evidence supporting this claim but to date, no study has looked at either qualitative measures of children's perceptions of their playrooms or quantitative physiological measures of nervous system activity of children with autism in these environments.

PRINCIPLE: CREATE AN OPTIMAL SOCIAL LEARNING ENVIRONMENT

This weak central coherence processing style may then impede the development of joint attention and shared affect in children with autism (Klin et al., 1992; Rogers and Pennington, 1991). These are two fundamental components of social interaction in which accurate response to stimuli depends crucially on social context. This explains why social situations are incredibly challenging for those with autism and why even high-functioning adults who score well on explicit measures of social reasoning fail to translate this to their everyday social interactions (Klin et al., 2000).

A precursor to joint attention and shared affect is social orienting—that a child will spontaneously, or upon request, direct attention to another person. Children with autism show social orienting impairments early in life by preferentially orienting to nonsocial over social stimuli. Osterling et al. (2002) found 1-year-olds, who were later diagnosed with ASD, looked at people and oriented to their own name less frequently than children without a subsequent diagnosis. Lack of interest in faces at 6 months (Maestro et al., 2002) and lack of orientation to the human voice at 24 months (Lord, 1995) have both been shown to be robust predictors of later ASD diagnosis. Dawson et al. (2004) found that autistic children tended not to respond to a variety of stimuli more often than typical or developmentally delayed children, but that the effect was more severe in response to social stimuli. Numerous studies have shown deficits in basic visual processing of faces in autism that were not paralleled by failures in developmentally equivalent nonsocial processing tasks (Langdell, 1978; Hobson et al.; 1988; Klin et al., 1999; Boucher and Lewis, 1992; Weeks and Hobson, 1987). Children with autism have been similarly shown not to respond as typical children do to the human voice (Klin, 1991, 1992; Osterling and Dawson, 1994; Werner et al., 2000).

When children and adults do orient to social stimuli they have been seen to process the information differently than their typically developing counterparts. Typically developing children show a differentiated brain event-related potential when viewing familiar and unfamiliar faces; children with autism do not show this effect (Dawson et al., 1994). Klin et al. (2003) found that autistic adults viewing a naturalistic social scene focus twice as much on the mouth region of faces than controls and 2.5 times less frequently on the eye regions than controls. Preferential looking at eyes rather than mouths has been shown in typically developing infants as young as three months (Haith et al., 1979). Typical children will show large skin conductance responses when looking at a person who looks back and much lower responses when looking at neutral objects. Children with autism have been found to show no difference in skin conductance response whether they are looking at a person or looking at a cup (Hirstein et al., 2001).

These basic processing differences then translate into higher order reasoning and attribution-making tasks. When viewing an animation of geometric shapes acting like humans, typical viewers recognize the social nature of these interactions and provide narratives describing relationships portrayed by the shapes and attributions of mental states. Viewers with autism tended to use physical explanations of the movement of the shapes (e.g., "because it's heavy") even though these individuals had all earlier passed explicit social reasoning tasks (Heider and Simmel, 1994).

It is not clear why children with autism avoid social stimuli. It may be due to a general impairment in attentional functioning (Bryson et al., 1994). Others believe that the rapid shifting in attention required to process social stimuli is to blame (Courchesne et al., 1995). An additional suggestion holds that children with autism avoid social stimuli because they are complex, variable and unpredictable and are thus difficult to process (Dawson, 1991; Dawson and Lewy, 1989; Gergely and Watson, 1999).

The autistic bias towards nonsocial stimuli is well documented in psychology and serves as illustration for the autobiographical descriptions offered by writers with autism (Williams, 1994; Grandin, 1986). This body of evidence shows how children with autism selectively attend to nonsocial aspects of their environment—seemingly to take care of their over-active perceptual systems—and in so doing, deprive themselves of learning about the social world from an early age. Klin points out that "to impose social meaning on an array of visual stimuli is an adaptive reaction displayed by typical children, from infancy onwards, at an ever increasing level of complexity. This spontaneous skill is cultivated in countless hours of recurrent social engagement." (Klin et al., 2003, p. 356). It is widely accepted that typically developing children develop through reciprocal social interactions that involve the child's active participation (Stern, 1977; Bronfenbrenner, 1979; Piaget, 1963; Vygotsky, 1978; Bandura, 1986; Brunner, 1977; Wertsch, 1985). These theories view developmental learning to be dependent upon children's *voluntary involvement in social interaction*, not upon the specific activity or information to which children are exposed (Kim and Mahoney, 2004). It is becoming more widely recognized that this principle holds true for children with autism (Greenspan and Wieder, 1998; MacDonald, 2004; Williams, 1988; Koegel et al., 2001) as theorists and therapists begin to develop treatment approaches that recognize the importance of voluntary social orienting and joint attention in the way SRP does.

It seems that due to their perceptual processing challenges, children with autism are selectively avoiding this social education which negates the learning of "pivotal developmental behaviors" (i.e., attention, persistence, interest, initiation, cooperation, joint attention and affect) (Koegel, Koegel, and Carter, 1999). This lack of development subsequently impacts all further learning. The development of the joint attention skill is considered essential to language, cognitive and social development in all children (Tomasello, 1995). The more time a child spends engaged with a significant adult, the more that child will learn. Children with autism who demonstrate greater skill with joint attention have been seen to reach greater levels of language development (Mundy et al., 1990; Sigman and Ruskin, 1997; Dawson et al., 2004). Individual differences in social orienting also predict the degree to which children with autism process nonverbal affective information (Dissanayake et al., 1996) crucial to comprehending any social situation. A 25-year follow-up of a group of 91 individuals originally showing serious social or mental challenges showed that the best predictor of outcome was social impairment—those who were socially impaired, particularly those in the aloof category, showed a poorer outcome (Beadle-Brown, Murphy, and Wing, 2005).

The implications for treatment are clear—to provide an environment that consistently and intensively favors social information and endeavors to increase the salience of the social world for children with autism. Theoretically, the SRP fulfills the treatment implications drawn from this body of work. The SRP suggests that through hours of immersion in this type of social environment, children with autism (a) increase their frequency of spontaneous social orienting, (b) maintain joint attention for longer and longer durations, and (c) intentionally initiate social interactions more frequently. Rigorous, empirical testing must be performed to substantiate these anecdotal observations.

This treatment implication then raises the question of *how* to provide an environment that consistently and intensively favors social information and endeavors to increase the salience of the social world for children with autism. The SRP proposes a unique method, some key principles of which will be outlined below in the context of current research.

A CHILD-CENTERED APPROACH MAKES SOCIAL INTERACTION MOTIVATING

Facilitators and parents employing the SRP make social interaction their primary focus when working one-on-one with a child with autism, recognizing that social avoidance is the crux of the autistic challenge. There are two ways in which a child-centered approach makes social interaction motivating.

Follow the Child: Start with the Child's Motivation

The SRP works with objects and activities for which the child is internally motivated. This play-based approach starts with the child's area of motivation (e.g., jumping on a trampoline). The adult joins in with this area of play until the child spontaneously socially orients to the adult (e.g., makes eye contact, physical contact or a vocalization attempt). This spontaneous expression of social interest from the child is then responded to by the adult in a manner designed to be motivating to the child (based on the individual child's interests and previous response patterns), for example, jumping on the trampoline while pretending to be a monkey. Any subsequent responses by the adult to the child's expressions of interest are similarly fine-tuned to be motivating to the child. Thus ensues a cycle of reciprocal social exchange within the area of the child's motivation. The SRP proposes that this approach raises the salience level of social interaction by tying the child's internal motivations to social interaction.

Autistic children can become very focused on their particular areas of motivation, often to the point of being termed "obsessional" or "perseverative." Many traditional approaches have tried to steer children away from their areas of motivation in an attempt to broaden the child's range of interest. The SRP instead recognizes these interests as doorways into that child's world, a means of forming a connection to become the foundation for more spontaneous and flexible social exchange. Support for this perspective comes from Koegel, Dyer, and Bell (1987) who found a negative correlation between social avoidance and child-preferred activities in autistic children. That is, when prompted to engage in activities the children had already demonstrated an interest in, children were much less socially avoidant than when prompted to engage in activities chosen by the adult.

Baker, Koegel, and Koegel (1998) further underlined the effectiveness of the child-centered approach with autistic children in a group setting. They took the obsessional interests of a group of children with autism (e.g., U.S. geography) and made them into common games that could be played by the autistic child and his/her peer group (e.g., tag game on a giant map of the U.S.). From very low levels of social interaction in the baseline condition, the percentage of social interactions increased dramatically during the intervention period and continued to be high at a 2-month follow-up. These increases in social play interactions continued even in the absence of the adult who had done the initial prompting. Furthermore, the autistic children began to engage more in other nonobsession-themed games after the intervention. Baker et al. (1989) conclude that "the obsessional themes of children with autism, which are typically viewed as problematic, can be transformed successfully into common games to increase positive social play interactions" (p. 306–307).

The parents of the autistic children involved in this study reported either no increase, or a decrease, in the child's engagement in the target obsessional theme at home, after the initiation of the obsessional themed games. This finding is consistent with Charlop et al. (1990) who used obsessional themes as reinforcers for children to complete other tasks and found no increase in the children's use of these particular obsessional themes. The SRP similarly maintains that using a child's obsessional theme or topics of perseveration as a platform for social interaction does not encourage further perseveration but instead helps transform perseverative, rigid play or conversation into socially appropriate, flexible, reciprocal interaction, because it makes social interaction more motivating than previously. Again, direct empirical observation is required to assess these observations.

Give Control: Be Responsive and Sensitive to the Child

The second crucial factor in facilitating the emergence of a genuine and spontaneous interest in the social world is giving control or employing a responsive style of interaction (Beckwith and Cohen, 1992). The SRP is child-centered. This means (a) the topic of play is derived from the child's individual interests, and (b) the child actively chooses when to begin and end that interaction. This is critical and the juncture at which traditional approaches to special education tend to differ. Trivette (2003) defined this responsive style of interaction as involving two important components. First, the adult responds only to the child's production of a behavior. This means that the adult responds only after the child makes a physical gesture (e.g., waves, smiles, touches), a vocal sound (e.g., a coo, a word) or an action (e.g., throws a ball, picks up toy). Second, the adult's response to this action is sensitive, that is, appropriate in its level of intensity. A sensitive response is one in which the intensity level matches the child's developmental level and mood. For example, if the child is crying, the adult may offer a soothing song; if the child is excited and laughing, the adult might offer a swing in the air (Trivette, 2003).

In a meta-analysis of 13 studies looking at the effects of this style of interaction, Trivette (2003) concluded "that a responsive caregiver style of interaction positively influences the cognitive development of children with, or at risk for, developmental disabilities" and also "has a positive influence on the social-emotional development of these children" (Trivette, 2003, p. 5). All 13 studies meeting inclusion criteria for this meta-analysis (1,336 children in total) showed the same result—that adult responsiveness substantially helped these children's cognitive and social-emotional development.

Subsequent research has continued to support this finding (Mahoney and Perales, 2003; Mahoney and Perales, 2005) and found that responsive interactive style also has positive outcomes on language development (MacDonald, 1989; Manolson et al., 1995). In a long-term study, Siller and Sigman (2002) found that the more mothers of children with autism engaged in responsive interaction with their children, the higher the levels of communication functioning their children attained at 1, 10, and 12 years of age. Mahoney et al. (1998) reported that in a large scale, multi-site early intervention research project (Infant Health and Development Program, 1990), maternal responsiveness accounted for six times more of the variance in the developmental functioning of low birth-weight children than did the children's participation in an intensive (25 hour per week) high-quality school program. Investigating responsive teaching is especially important in the light of findings that mothers of developmentally delayed children tend to be more directive (not responsive) when interacting with their children (Spiker et al., 2002).

Lewis and Goldberg (1969) suggest that this responsive style of interaction has such a positive effect on children's development because it facilitates the child's feelings of control and self-efficacy. This contributes to the child's sense of competence and so increases the likelihood of the child engaging in subsequent interactions and learning situations. Mahoney and Perales (2003) propose that a responsive style of interaction enhances social behaviors that may be the same as the pivotal response behaviors seen to enhance the efficacy of discrete trial training interventions (Koegel et al., 1999). Pivotal behaviors "are the processes children employ to learn and practice new behaviors during spontaneous interactions. Following this line of reasoning, it seems possible that as parents engage in higher levels of responsive interaction with their children, they are actually encouraging children to learn and use pivotal developmental behaviors, which are the processes enabling them to acquire untrained socioemotional competencies" (Mahoney and Percales, 2003, p. 84). This would explain why studies using interventions focusing on these pivotal developmental behaviors show children learning skills that they then generalize to other learning situations (Koegel, Koegel, and Carter, 1998; Kaiser, Carter, and Koegel, 2003).

The SRP employs, exclusively, a responsive style of interaction that they call "giving control." Under the SRP, each time a child makes spontaneous social contact, the adult responds in a "sensitive" manner as described above; additionally, when a child disengages from social contact, the adult responds by respectfully withdrawing and waiting for a social cue from the child before pursuing any further interactions. Each time this happens, the child learns that s/he has control over her/his social environment. Considerable research shows that children develop to the degree that they have control over their behavior and their effects on the environment (MacDonald, 2004). A child inhabiting the fragmented, unpredictable, chaotic perceptual world described above, who is also extremely challenged by communicating his/her wants, and whose autonomic system appears to be out of control, does not have a sense of being in control of the world or even of his/her body in the way a typically developing child does (Bluestone, 2004). Thus, the importance of providing a social environment maximizing the child's sense of control can be seen.

That children with autism do not have a sense of control in the world could explain why they seek out patterns—meaning, predictability and order in a chaotic world. Baron-Cohen (2004) found the content of rituals and topics of perseveration (of higher-functioning children and adults with autism and Asperger's Syndrome) is not random, but tends to cluster in the domain of systems (including technical, natural and abstract systems). These systems are underlain with rules and regularities more easily grasped by the autistic mind (Baron-Cohen, 2004). The social world is not an organized system regulated by fixed rules but rather a fluid, ever-changing bombardment of sensory input. If the autistic child is to feel comfortable in the social world, then the social world must be made as controllable as possible to encourage the autistic child to participate. This is exactly what is done by the SRP. So when a child in an SRP playroom disengages from the social interaction, the facilitator respects this and allows the child to disengage, does not keep pursuing the interaction as recommended in other relationship-based approaches (Greenspan and Wieder, 1998) and waits for the child to re-engage before continuing to build social interaction. When consistently immersed in a social environment of this nature, SRP proposes the child learns that he has control over the previously uncontrollable social world. This puts the child in the driver's seat and shows him that he can indeed effectively elicit a response from another when he chooses; this sense of control forms a foundation for reciprocal interaction (Dawson and Galpert, 1990). Koegel, Koegel, and McNerney (2001) review data suggesting that "when children with autism are motivated to initiate complex social interactions, it may reverse a cycle of impairment, resulting in exceptionally favorable intervention outcomes" (p. 19).

A POSITIVE ATTITUDE FACILITATES DEEPER SOCIAL CONNECTION

According to the SRP, the next vital factor in facilitating the emergence of a genuine and spontaneous interest in the social world is the use of a positive attitude. A positive attitude is one of acceptance of the child, appreciation and enjoyment of the child and the animated expression of such. The SRP stands alone in its assertion of the critical importance of a positive attitude. There are two fundamental reasons for this emphasis.

Acceptance Promotes Responsiveness

The SRP suggests that only an attitude of acceptance and appreciation of a child will allow parents to maintain consistently a responsive style of interaction. Acceptance is defined as nonjudgment, i.e., not labeling the child, or his/her condition, with any value-judgments (good/bad, right/wrong). The SRP does not view this type of acceptance as a passive resignation to the child's condition but instead as the first step to actively encouraging the child to develop. Professionals teaching the SRP consistently observe that when a parent lacks acceptance (as defined here), they instead label the child as "wrong" in some way ("needs fixing," "abnormal," "defective," etc.). The SRP holds that a parent with that perspective will find it very challenging to be responsive, that is, not to be directive, not to "teach" something to his/her child, even when the parent cognitively understands the importance of being responsive and giving the child control. The cognitive architecture behind a responsive style of interaction has yet to be addressed in the literature and points to another avenue of research crucial for training parents to run home-based interventions.

This importance of a positive attitude is empirically supported by the work of Gerald Mahoney and colleges using the Maternal Behavior Rating Scale (MBRS; Mahoney, 1992). The MBRS has been used in a variety of studies to assess the link between parents' interactional styles and the development of their children. It has 12 items assessing four dimensions of interactive style: responsiveness, affect, achievement orientation and directiveness. Use of the MBRS has been instrumental in highlighting the importance of caregiver responsiveness in children's development. These studies additionally show the "affect" dimension is similarly correlated with increases in various developmental performance outcomes.

In the MBRS, the affect dimension is composed of five measures: Acceptance, Enjoyment, Expressiveness, Inventiveness and Warmth. Mahoney and Perales (2005) found both responsiveness and affect to be significantly related to increases in children's levels of language development, social competence, joint attention and self-regulation. Kim and Mahoney (2004) again found maternal responsiveness and affect to be significantly correlated with the child's level of engagement, with maternal responsiveness accounting for 33 percent of the variance and affect accounting for 30 percent of the variance. This research still requires replication with larger and more diverse samples; nonetheless, the emerging direction of this new field of research is in line with the observations of the SRP—a positive attitude goes hand in hand with responsiveness in facilitating development in children with developmental disabilities.

Appreciation Encourages Engagement.

The other key component of a positive attitude in the SRP is a genuine appreciation and enjoyment of the child; this builds on the foundation of acceptance. The SRP advocates the use of animated expressions of appreciation, enjoyment and delight in the child. The SRP proposes that this will encourage a greater frequency of social orientation, extend periods of joint attention and increase child affect and motivation level within a social interaction. This, it is suggested, leads to more and longer periods of social interaction that result in the child learning more new behaviors and skills.

Typically developing children who naturally orient to social stimuli and engage in joint attention with adults experience the displays of positive affect that typically accompany these periods of joint attention (Kasari et al., 1990). Shared affective experience serves to motivate the typically developing child to attend to and engage in joint attention with adults (Dawson et al., 2004; Trevarthan and Aitken, 2001). These experiences then facilitate the child's development into a social "expert" as s/he attends to more and more initiations from adults and remains engaged in these interactions for longer and longer. Typical development revolves around mutual affective exchanges that both the child and adult find rewarding (Mundy et al., 1992). This process goes awry in children with autism for two reasons that interact to create a negative feedback loop. First, the child with autism engages in joint attention less frequently and for shorter periods than the typically developing child (Dawson et al., 2004), so has less opportunity to experience the positive affect associated with this social engagement. Dawson and Lewy (1989) suggest that this is because the affect-laden social interaction may be too over-stimulating for the autistic child due to the unpredictable and complex nature of these stimuli. Second, it appears that children with autism are less likely to display positive affect when engaged in joint attention (e.g., smile while making eye contact) (Kasari et al., 1999) and are much less likely to smile in response to their mother's smile than typical children (Dawson et al., 1990). The result is that mothers of autistic children are less likely to respond to their children's smiles than mothers of typical children (Dawson et al., 2004), probably because the children's smiles were not viewed as communicative as they were not accompanied by eye contact. Thus, from an early age, children with autism seem not to experience the delight and joy typical children are bathed in from birth that motivates them to keep moving towards deeper and deeper connections with other people. When this process is disrupted in otherwise typically developing children, for example when the mother suffers post-natal depression and does not engage as much in these affective exchanges, there can be serious effects for that child's development (Goldsmith and Rogoff, 1997).

The implication for treatment from this research again is clear: to redress this imbalance—to link joint attention to positive affect and motivate children to move towards more frequent and longer periods of joint attention in the way a typical child does. This is what the SRP claims to do. Whenever a child in an SRP playroom makes social contact (eye contact, language attempts or physical communication), he is greeted with a celebration: a visual and auditory display of positive affect and an expression of joy and delight from the adult to the child's initiation of joint attention. This is fine-tuned to the individual child's particular sensory requirement to maintain its function as a motivator and not allow it to become over-stimulating for the child.

The affect dimension of the MBRS (Mahoney, 1992) has five items, four of which—acceptance, enjoyment, expressiveness and warmth—involve directly, animatedly expressing positive affect and attitude to the child. It is this dimension (along with responsiveness) that has been closely linked to promoting child engagement and cognitive and language development. The fifth item on the MBRS affect dimension is inventiveness—the number of different approaches the adult uses, his/her ability to find different games and activities to interest the child, different ways of using toys and inventing games with and without toys. This is also an important part of the SRP. Once a child is engaged in a social interaction, the adult's intention is then to maintain that interaction for as long as the child will allow. Expressing positive affect is one way that those trained in the SRP maintain interactions; the second is through inventiveness or creativity. Decades of training people to use the SRP leads their trainers to assert that a positive attitude underlies the ability to be creative in the ways described on the MBRS. The logic is that when one is truly enjoying an interaction, one is more inclined to think of ways to add to the interaction to maintain it, whereas when one is not enjoying an interaction, one tends to be thinking of ways to end it. Again, the cognitive architecture underlying "inventiveness" warrants empirical investigation as an avenue for increasing the efficacy of professional and parental training.

The SRP suggests that the principles of taking a child-centered approach and having a positive attitude, when used in an optimally designed physical environment, have the effect of encouraging children with autism and other developmental delays to engage more in social interaction. This has the effect of helping these children be more motivated to initiate and engage in social interaction and grow stronger in pivotal developmental behaviors which pave the way for learning new skills and information. Longitudinal studies involving children actively engaged in home-based SRP*s* are needed to investigate these observations more fully.

The SRP asserts (as do other proponents of home-based programs; e.g., Lovaas, 1973) that this approach must be applied intensively and consistently over time for maximum efficacy. A 30-minute session twice a week will not retrain a brain that for years has skewed itself away from the social world. Children in the SRP typically spend from 15 to 50 hours a week in the playroom being responded to in this way. Facilitators and parents are trained to be exceptionally observant and attentive to the child to maximize the number of spontaneous social orienting events that are responded to in this way.

JOINING EXCLUSIVE AND REPETITIVE BEHAVIORS PROMOTES SOCIAL INTERACTION

This core principle of the SRP extends the principles of child-centeredness and responsiveness and takes them from a position radically different from that of any other treatment approach known by this author. A key behavioral symptom of autism, not yet addressed by this paper, is the engagement in stereotypical, repetitive movements or activities. Traditionally, the approach to these behaviors has been to attempt to eliminate them, the rationale behind this being the more "normal" the child looks, the more likely s/he is to be accepted by peers, and thus increase the likelihood of successful social experience. This perspective, however, seems to have negated attempts to understand the function of these behaviors, and this aspect of autism has received much less scientific scrutiny than any other (Turner, 1999). This perspective goes against the principle of acceptance and enjoyment of the child that has proved to be so fruitful.

The research that does exist in the domain of stereotypical and repetitive behaviors suggests that these repetitious behaviors are helpful to the child and are not, in fact, random byproducts of the disorder that serve no function (as has been suggested; e.g., Lewis et al., 1987). Repetition is a natural part of any child's development; Piaget (1952) noted that typically developing infants will repeat activities that affect the environment in ways that inspire their interest. Thelen (1979) found that typically developing infants show a variety of rhythmic and pronounced stereotypic behaviors, each with a characteristic age of onset, peak performance and decline. These behaviors appear to mark unmistakable phases in the stages of neuromuscular development. Children seem to move through these behaviors until they have gained a full sense of mastery over their muscles and, presumably, until they can predict the effects of their own movements on the environment. Militerni et al. (2002) looked at repetitive behaviors in two age groups of children with autism. They found that the younger children (age 2–4 years) exhibited motor and sensory repetitive behaviors while those in the higher age group (7–11 years) had more complex repetitive behaviors. Similarly, those children with estimated higher IQs also showed more complex repetitive behaviors. Militerni et al. (2002) suggest that these repetitive behaviors may be equivalent to the motor and cognitive behaviors seen in typical development.

Needless to say, in children with autism and related disorders, these behaviors are much more pronounced, more intense and engage more of the child's attention than in typically developing children. Hirstein et al. (2001) suggest that children with autism may employ repetitive behaviors in an attempt to control an autonomic system that fails to govern itself. Hirstein et al. (2001) measured skin conductance responses (SCR) in normal and autistic children in a variety of situations. They found that the SCRs of children with autism started rising at the beginning of the experiment and continued to rise, whereas the typically developing children's SCR returned to normal baseline level with the progression of the experiment. It appeared that the children with autism were not able to bring their SCR levels down once they had started to rise. Attempts at interaction with people exacerbated SCR levels. The researchers found, however, that the children with autism could bring down the SCR levels by plunging their hands into a container of dry beans. Similarly, sucking sweets, being wrapped in a heavy blanket and receiving deep pressure helped the children with autism lower their SCR levels. They also discovered that a subset of children with autism was characterized by a flat level of SCR that was only increased by extreme behaviors (e.g., self-injury, climbing, etc.).

Hirstein et al. (2001) additionally found that interruption of these self-stimulatory and calming activities by other people "often produced extremely large responses with agitated behavior following immediately"

(p. 1885). They go on to suggest that "the resistance to change one sees in autistic children may be caused by or exacerbated by bursts of sympathetic activity, which the child actively tries to avoid or dampen down" (Hirstein et al., 2001, p.1886). Hirstein et al. (2001) suggest that the autonomic nervous system of the autistic child is on constant alert; every incoming stimulus is tagged as relevant and so the child acts to shut the system down (conversely in the subset of children with low autonomic activity, it seems that nothing is tagged as relevant and extreme behaviors are engaged in to produce a sense of relevance). This is consistent with the research on perceptual filtering challenges in those with autism cited above. It has been suggested that the amygdala-limbic system may be involved, as this system typically is responsible for attaching a sense of value to incoming perceptual stimuli and is found to be abnormal in those with autism (Schultz, 2005; Critchley et al., 2000; Pelphrey et al., 2004; Akshoomoff et al., 2002; Baron-Cohen et al., 2000).

This work indicates that the repetitive, self-stimulatory behaviors of children with autism are not random or functionless but actually help the child to regulate his own autonomic system in a quest for homeostasis (Nijhof et al., 1998). Autobiographical reports from adults with autism again support the idea that repetitive behaviors serve to calm and soothe (Bluestone, 2004). Judith Bluestone likens these activities to meditation—turning off parts of the mind or body by intensely focusing on one thing—and points out that meditation has been accepted by the Western medical establishment for over 30 years as one of the best ways to reduce stress and increase mental organization (Bluestone, 2004). Willemsen-Swinkels et al. (1998) found that autistic children who were negatively excited showed a slower heart rate after they began engaging in a repetitive activity. Hirstein et al. (2001) predict that if children are prevented from engaging in these calming activities, one would expect to see signs of chronically high sympathetic activity. The biochemical consequences of this are elevated levels of cortisol and adrenaline. These hormones interfere with the ability to concentrate, learn and remember and increase vulnerability to viruses, over-reactivity to medications, and heightened sensitivities to certain foods or food additives (Bluestone, 2004), all of which are commonly observed in children with autism.

From a treatment standpoint, this research points to the need for a new perspective on repetitive behaviors. Rather than seeing these behaviors as something holding the child back from social acceptance and thus to be eliminated, this new perspective sees repetitive behaviors as useful to the child—something to be worked with rather than fought against. The SRP sees repetitive behaviors as functional and an avenue for building rapport which will form the basis of more expansive social interaction. Rather than trying to eliminate repetitive behaviors from the autistic child's repertoire to make the child more socially acceptable, the SRP facilitator starts with acceptance of the child—a deep, genuine appreciation for that child and holding the perspective that all his/her behaviors are attempts to take care of him-/herself. This attitude allows the SRP facilitator to a) not attempt to stop the child when he is engaging in repetitive, self-stimulatory behaviors, but wait for the child to spontaneously engage in social interaction and b) physically demonstrate this acceptance by joining in with the repetitive activity. This, the SRP suggests, is a more powerful way of communicating to the child that s/he is accepted and appreciated than a solely verbal communication and of demonstrating to the child that s/he has control over the interaction. This is a radical departure from more traditional approaches to autism, but is one that has been shown to be effective in helping children with autism to engage in social interaction more and, seemingly paradoxically, to spend less and less time engaging in repetitive, self-stimulatory behaviors.

Numerous studies have found that imitative play facilitates social responsiveness in children with autism; that is, joining in with their self-stimulatory, repetitious behaviors encourages children to engage more in social interaction. Dawson and Adams (1984) found that autistic children who had a low level of imitative ability were more socially responsive, showed more eye contact and played with toys in a less perseverative manner when the experimenter imitated the child instead of modeling other either familiar or unfamiliar actions. A similar study found that children with autism would look at the experimenter more frequently and for longer periods when the experimenter imitated the child's play (Tiegerman and Primavera, 1984). Dawson and Galpert (1990) took this line of investigation even further. They asked mothers to imitate their child's play for 20 minutes each day for two weeks. At the pre-intervention assessment, they found, as predicted by the earlier research, that autistic children's gaze at their mother's face was longer, and their toy play more creative, during imitative play sessions as compared to free play sessions. After only two weeks of this intervention (20 minutes a day), the post-intervention assessment found significant cumulative increases in duration of gaze at the mother's face and of creative toy play. Parents of children using the SRP are instructed to engage in imitative play ("joining") whenever their child is playing in an exclusive or repetitive way.

Another study experimenting with imitating autistic children split children into two groups; those of one group spent time with an adult who imitated their play, while members of the other group spent time with an adult who simply tried to play with the child on three separate occasions. In the second session, children in the imitation group spent a greater proportion of time than the other children showing distal social behaviors towards the adult—looking, vocalizing, smiling and engaging in reciprocal play. In the third session, children in the imitation group spent a greater proportion of time than the other children showing proximal social behaviors towards the adult—being close to the adult, sitting next to the adult and touching the adult (Field et al., 2001).

These results, that imitative play increases social responsiveness and joint attention, should not be surprising to those who study the development of typical infants and children. Parents of typically developing infants commonly imitate their infants' expressions, often in an exaggerated way (Malatesta and Izard, 1984; Papousek and Papousek, 1977; Trevarthen and Aitken, 2001). In fact, infants of 3 and 5 months old have been seen to prefer interaction with people who have been responsive to them in the past and avoid interaction with those who were unresponsive or whose responses were not congruent with the infant (Bigelow and Birch, 1999). This imitation forms the basis of communication and further growth by promoting a sense of shared mutuality, an experience of congruence by both partners that is mutually motivating (Nadel et al., 1999; Uzgiris, 1981; Panksepp et al., 1994). This normal interplay of nonverbal imitation between mother and infant is widely documented to be essential to promoting the child's neurological, cognitive, social and emotional growth (see Trevarthen and Aitken, 2001). Studies with typically developing (Rollins and Snow, 1998) and autistic children (Mundy et al., 1990; Rollins, 1999) suggest that emotional engagement and joint attention are more critical to language development than is instrumental use of language. Emotional engagement and joint attention are increased by imitative play. Trevarthen and Aitken state, "Imitative responses are found to be attractive to autistic children and can act as a bridge to collaborative play or communication, and improve the child's access to language (Dawson and Galpert,1990; Nadel, 1992; Nadel and Peze, 1993; Tiegerman and Primavera, 1982, 1984)" (Trevarthen and Aitken, 2001, p. 32). Siegel (2001) states simply that "Children need such joining experiences because they provide the emotional nourishment that developing minds require" (p. 78).

Studies with typical adults indicate that this intuitive use of imitation continues into adulthood, maintaining its function of building rapport between two people. Chartrand and Bargh (1999) found that participants mimicked, nonverbally, by a confederate in a variety of situations reported liking that confederate more than confederates who did not mimic them. Those who were mimicked also described the interaction as more smooth and harmonious. Similarly, Bernieri (1988) found a strong relationship between reported rapport and degree of reported movement synchrony. When looking at nonconscious mimicry, Larkin and Chartrand (2003) found that in situations where participants had either a conscious or nonconscious desire to affiliate with their experimental partner, they were more likely to nonverbally mimic that person than when they had no desire to affiliate with that person. It seems that mimicry can build rapport between adults. It has been suggested that this behavior evolved from initially having survival value (learning new skills) into a form of social glue that holds relationships together and allows access to a particular group (Larkin et al., 2003).

Imitation helps build rapport between typical adults, typical infants or children and their caregivers and between adults and autistic children. Dawson and Galpert (1990) postulate that imitative play works so well for autistic children because it puts the child in control (one of the fundamental principles of the SRP). This gives the child a predictable and salient response to his actions. "This strategy maximizes the possibility that the child will learn to expect and effectively elicit a response from another person, in this way providing a foundation for reciprocal social interaction" (Dawson and Galpert, 1990, p. 152). Additionally, imitative play is sensitive to the child's optimal range of sensory stimulation; the child can adjust the amount of sensory stimulation by adjusting his or her own actions creating an easy, controllable and predictable form of social interaction that is more digestible for the autistic child. Field (1977, 1979; cited in Dawson and Galpert, 1990) studied the effects of maternal imitation with pre-term infants who showed high levels of gaze aversion, negative affect and elevated tonic heart rates. When mothers imitated their infants' behavior, the infants became more attentive than when mothers spontaneously interacted with their infants. Decreases in tonic heart rate were recorded during imitative play. Applying this research to the autistic population by examining physiological measures during imitative play has yet to be done.

Dawson and Galpert (1990) conclude that "imitative play may be used to provide a foundation for establishing social interest and interactive play. This foundation can then be built upon by using other, more sophisticated, interactive strategies and games" (p. 161). This is exactly how imitative play, or "joining," is used by the SRP. Children are "joined" or imitated while they are playing in a self-stimulatory and exclusive way because the SRP recognizes the curative, calming and organizing nature of this self-stimulatory play. Through joining the child rapport is created and a social bridge is built. A relationship of trust is formed as the child learns that s/he is in control of the interaction and can initiate and end it at will, without the need for language. It follows then that children will start to initiate social contact more and more when immersed in this environment. This will open up increasing opportunities to build on this connection in a manner motivating to that child (as described above) and thus increase the frequency and duration of joint attention that leads to the child's neurological, cognitive, social and emotional development. Observational analysis of parents and SRP facilitators working with autistic children is required to fully understand the subtle variables involved in this type of interaction.

The technique of joining builds on the principle of being responsive. In Trivette's (2003) definition of the responsive style of interaction, an appropriate response is one that matches the child's developmental level and mood. The SRP adds a further requirement—that the adult's response be sensitive to the child's level of exclusivity, exclusivity indicating the child's *level of motivation for social interaction*. The SRP maintains that all children, regardless of diagnosis, have the capacity to move along an exclusive-interactive continuum. At the exclusive end of this continuum the child is not motivated for social interaction, and is absorbed in his own world; this state is usually accompanied by repetitive behaviors and activities or perseveration on repetitive topics. At the interactive end of the continuum, the child is motivated for interaction with another person and shows interest by maintaining joint attention, displaying positive affect and participating in an interactive and fluid activity or conversation. Observing the child's level of motivation for interaction, or degree of exclusivity, is the first vital step in the SRP to responding in a manner that will facilitate (a) the maximum amount of responsiveness from the child and (b) the maximal degree of new learning.

When the child is exclusive (not motivated for social interaction), the SRP holds that the most effective response is to join with the child's behavior. This type of response allows the child to use their repetitive activity to gain control of their autonomic system and facilitates more spontaneous social orienting from the child. As the child's level of motivation for social interaction increases, s/he will start to spontaneously orient to the adult more (e.g., by making eye contact, attempting verbal or nonverbal communications or making physical contact). The SRP-trained facilitator will begin to respond to these behaviors in the manner described by Trivette (2003)—by offering an activity they believe the child will find enjoyable. As the child's level of motivation for social interaction increases, the frequency and duration of the child's spontaneous social orientations will increase, as will their displayed positive affect. Once the child has reached a level of motivation for social interaction characterized by frequent or sustained eye contact, positive affect and nonverbal or verbal attempts to re-initiate the activity, the SRP-trained facilitator will move into a style of interaction that combines responding to the child to maintain the level of motivation, and requesting the child to participate in new ways (e.g., use more or clearer language, use more eye contact, be more flexible, use academic or friendship skills, etc.). The Son-Rise Program Social Developmental Model (Hogan and Hogan, 2004) provides guidelines indicating which skill to focus on depending on the child's developmental level. Once the child is motivated for social interaction and for the particular activity on offer, s/he will make attempts at the new skill in order to maintain the interaction. When the child's level of motivation changes, the facilitator will be responsive to this, observe where the child is on the exclusivity-interactive continuum, and respond accordingly.

It is through this subtle dance between maintaining a responsive interactive style, giving control, and excitedly requesting new skill use that the SRP claims to be able to facilitate extraordinary development in children with severe developmental disorders, as documented in the case studies by the founders (Kaufman, 1981, 1994). To the knowledge of this author, there is no research to date investigating the efficacy of changing one's responsive style based on the child's level of motivation for social interaction or an empirical investigation of the concept of an interactive-exclusive continuum. This is a gap in the literature that demands attention and could create a deeper understanding of children with autism and the most effective way to facilitate social interaction with this population.

CONCLUSION

A wealth of research spanning half a century has painted a clearer picture of the disorder first outlined by Kanner in 1943. This has helped us gain a deeper understanding of the physiology, neurology and cognitive psychology of those with autism and allows us to see some clear implications for treatment. The SRP developed over the past thirty years via a different route—from two parents' desire to reach their autistic child. Through their intensive experimentation, observation and deep longing to connect with their son, they developed a treatment approach that can now be seen to be supported by the more recent scientific literature. These two pathways—to essentially the same solution—have remained separate as the SRP has not been subjected to rigorous scientific study by independent researchers until very recently. The current work shows that the principles of SRP are solidly grounded in accepted theories of child development and supported by empirical study of the individual principles, although no study has yet addressed SRP in its entirety. The sheer number of families who have chosen to use SRP (over 8,000 to date) is testament to the fact that parents are looking for something other than what is offered by traditional approaches to autism. Approaches such as the SRP thus warrant more empirical investigation.

The SRP is parent-led; that is, parents are empowered to act as facilitators, trainers and managers of their home-based programs. In the eyes of the SRP, training parents to implement therapy with their children is more effective than relying on schools or specific professionals to implement therapies because, as discussed above, the intensity of the approach is essential. A parent trained in the SRP is able to implement the principles and techniques inside and outside of the playroom, intensifying the child's immersion in a responsive, socially enhancing environment. Again, the literature supports the efficacy of home-based programs. One study assessing the relative efficacy of behavioral programs with autistic children compared residential, out-patient and home-based programs. They found that only the home-based group showed significant improvements on the behavioral observation measures (Sherman et al., 1987). Another study matched children receiving home-based behavioral treatments with those receiving conventional school-based and brief one-on-one interventions. Children receiving home-based treatments had significantly higher post-intervention IQs than their school-based counterparts; significant reductions in symptom severity were also found (Sheinkopf and Siegel, 1998).

More recent research has looked at changing the conventional discrete-trial format of traditional behaviorist approaches, to make them more adaptable to the home environment and thus more in line with the responsive nature of the SRP. Delprato (2001) reviewed eight studies looking at normalized behavioral language interventions, defined as consisting of loosely structured sessions of indirect teaching with everyday situations, child initiation, natural reinforcers and liberal criteria for reinforcer presentation. In all eight studies with children with autism, this method of language training was found to be significantly more effective than discrete-trial training. Kaiser and Hancock (2003) similarly found that teaching parents to implement naturalistic language intervention strategies at home can be highly effective. Furthermore, in the two studies in the Delprato (2001) review looking at parental affect, the normalized treatment yielded more positive affect than the discrete-trial training. In a study of families using The Son-Rise Program in their homes, Williams (2004) found that the families felt generally more positive since implementing the SRP and reported that interaction among the whole family had also improved.

The current literature supports an intervention for children with autism that emphasizes a specifically designed physical environment, with a focus on enhancing social relationships, having a positive attitude and joining a child's repetitive behaviors. The SRP focuses on precisely these principles.

REFERENCES

Akshoomoff, N., Pierce, K., and Courchesne, E. (2002). The neurobiological basis of autism from a developmental perspective. *Developmental Psychopathology*, 14, 613–634.

Alegria, J., and Noirot, E. (1978). Neonate orientation behavior towards human voice. *International Journal of Behavioral Development*, 1(4), 291–312.

American Psychiatric Association (1994). *Diagnostic and Statistical Manual of Mental Disorders* (*DSM*-IV). 4th ed. Washington, DC: APA.

Baker, M. J., Koegel, R. L., and Koegel, L. K. (1998). Increasing the social behavior of young children with autism using their obsessive behaviors. *Journal of the Association of Peoples with Severe Handicaps,* 23(4), 300–308.

Bandura, A. (1986) *Social Foundations of Thought and Action*. Englewood Cliffs, NJ: Prentice Hall.

Baron-Cohen, S. (2004.) The cognitive neuroscience of autism. *Journal of Neurology, Neurosurgery and Psychiatry,* 75, 945–948.

Baron-Cohen, S., Ring, H. A., Bullmore, E. T., Wheelwright, S., Ashwin, C., and Williams, S. C. R. (2000) The amygdala theory of autism. *Neuroscience and Biobehavioral Reviews*, 24, 355–364.

Baron-Cohen, S., Ring, H. A., Wheelwright, S., Bullmore, E. T., Brammer, M. J., Simmons A. et al. (1999). Social intelligence in the normal and autistic brain: An fMRI study. *European Journal of Neuroscience*, 11(6), 1891–1898.

Bauman, M. L., and Kemper, T. L. (1994). Neuroanatomic observations of the brain in autism. In M. L. Bauman and T. L. Kemper (Eds.), *The Neurobiology of Autism*. Baltimore: Johns Hopkins University Press.

Beadle-Brown, J., Murphy, G., and Wing, L. (2005). Long-term outcome for people with severe intellectual disabilities: Impact of social impairment. *American Journal of Mental Retardation*, 110(1), 1–12.

Beckwith, L., and Cohen, S. E. (1992). Maternal responsiveness with preterm infants and later competency. In M. H. Bornstein (Ed.), *Maternal Responsiveness: Characteristics and Consequences. New Directions for Child Development*, 43, 75–87.

Belmonte, M. K., (2000.) Abnormal attention in autism shown by steady-state visual evoked potentials. *Autism*, 4, 269–285.

Belmonte, M. K., Cook, E. H., Anderson, G. M., Rubenstein, J. L. R., Greenough, W. T., Beckel-Mitchener, A. et al. (2004). Autism as a disorder of neural information processing: directions for research and targets for therapy. *Molecular Psychiatry*, 9(7), 646–663.

Belmonte, M. K., and Yurgelan-Todd, D. K. (2003). Functional anatomy of impaired selective attention and compensatory processing in autism. *Cognitive Brain Research*, 17, 651–664.

Bernieri, F. J. (1988). Coordinated movement and rapport in teacher-student interactions. *Journal of Nonverbal Behavior*; 12(2), 120–138.

Bigelow, A. E., and Birch, S. A. J. (1999). The effects of contingency in previous interactions on infants' preference for social partners. *Infant Behavior and Development*, 22(3), 367–382.

Bluestone, J. (2004) *The Fabric of Autism: Weaving the Threads into a Cogent Theory*. Seattle: The Handle Institute.

Boucher, J., and Lewis, V. (1992). Unfamiliar face recognition in relatively able autistic children. *Journal of Child Psychology and Psychiatry*, 33, 843–859.

Bronfenbrenner, U. (1979). *The Ecology of Human Development*. Cambridge, MA: Harvard University Press.

Brunner, J. (1977). Early social interaction and language acquisition. In: H. R. Schaffer (Ed.), *Studies in Mother-Infant Interaction*. New York: Academic Press.

Bryson, S. E., Wainwright-Sharp, J. A., and Smith, I. M. (1990). Autism: A developmental spatial neglect syndrome. In: J. Enns (Ed.), *The Development of Attention: Research and Theory* (pp. 405–427). North Holland: Elsevier.

Casanova, M. F., and Buxhoeveden, D. P. (2002). Minicolumnar pathology in autism. *Neurology*, 58, 428–432.

Carbone, E. (2001). Arranging the classroom with an eye (and ear) to students with ADHA. *Teaching Exceptional Children*, 34(2), 72–81.

Castelii, F., Frith, C., Happe, F., and Frith, U. (2002). Autism, Asperger syndrome and brain mechanisms for the attribution of mental states to animated figures. *Brain*, 125, 1839–1849.

Charlop, M .H., Kurtz, P. F., and Casey, F. G. (1990). Using aberrant behaviors as reinforcers for autistic children. *Journal of Applied Behavior Analysis*, 23, 163–181.

Chartrand, T. L., and Bargh, J. A. (1999). The chameleon effect: The perception-behavior link and social interaction. *Journal of Personality and Social Psychology*, 76, 893–910.

Cohen, D. J., and Johnson, W. T. (1977). Cardiovascular correlates of attention in normal and psychiatrically disturbed children. *Archives of General Psychiatry*, 34, 561–567.

Colman, R. S., Frankel, F., Rivito, E., and Freeman, B. J. (1976). The effects of fluorescent and incandescent illumination upon repetitive behaviors in autistic children. *Journal of Autism and Developmental Disorders*, 6(2), 157–162.

Courchesne, E., Chisum, H., and Townsend, J. (1995). Neural activity-dependent brain changes in development: Implications for psychopathology. *Development and Psychopathology*, 6, 697–722.

Critchley, H. D., Daly, E. M., Bullmore, E. T., Williams, S. C. R., van Amelsvoort, T., Robertson, D. M. et al. (2000). The functional neuroanatomy of social behavior: changes in cerebral blood flow when people with autistic disorder process facial expressions. *Brain*, 123, 2203–2212.

Dawson G. (1991). A psychobiological perspective on the early socio-emotional development of children with autism. In: S. Toth and D. Cicchetti (Eds.), *Rochester Symposium on Developmental Psychopathology* (Vol. 3, pp. 207–234). Mahwah, NJ: Erlbaum.

Dawson, G., and Adams, A. (1984). Imitation and social responsiveness in autistic children. *Journal of Abnormal Child Psychology*, 12(2), 209–226.

Dawson, G., and Galpert, L. (1990). Mothers' use of imitative play for facilitating social responsiveness and toy play in young autistic children. *Development and Psychopathology*, 2, 151–162.

Dawson, G., and Lewy, A. (1989), Arousal, attention and the socio-emotional impairments of individuals with autism. In: G. Dawson (Ed.), *Autism, Nature, Diagnosis and Treatment* (pp. 49–74). New York: Guilford.

Dawson, G., Toth, K., Abbott, R., Osterling, J., Munson, J., Estes, A. et al. (2004). Early social attention impairments in autism: Social orienting, joint attention, and attention to distress. *Developmental Psychology*, 40(2), 271–283.

Dawson, G., Webb, S. J., Carver, L., Panagiotides, H., and McPartland, J. (2004). Young children with autism show atypical brain responses to fearful versus neutral expressions of emotion. *Developmental Science*, 7(3), 340–359.

Delprato, D. J. (2001). Comparisons of discrete-trial and normalized behavioral language interventions for young children. *Journal of Autism and Developmental Disorders*, 31(3), 315–325.

Dissanayake, C., Sigman, M., and Kasari, C. (1996). Long-term stability of individual differences in the emotional responsiveness of children with autism. *Journal of Child Psychology and Psychiatry*, 36, 1–8.

Eimas, P., Siqueland, E., Jusczyk, P., and Vigorito, J. (1971). Speech perception in infants. *Science*, 171, 303–306.

Field, T., Field, T., Sanders, C., and Nadel, J. (2001). Children with autism display more social behaviors after repeated imitation sessions. *Autism*, 5(3), 317–323.

Frith, U., and Happe, F. (1994). Language and communication in autistic disorders. *Philosophical Transactions: Biological Sciences*, 346(1315), 97–104.

Gerland, G. (1997). *A Real Person: Life on the Outside* (trans. J. Tate), London: Souvenir Press.

Gergely, G., and Watson, J. S. (1999). Early socio-emotional development: Contingency perception and the social bio-feedback model In: P. Rochat (Ed.), *Early Social Cognition: Understanding Others in the First Months of Life* (pp. 1001–1136). Mahwah, NJ: Erlbaum.

Gillingham, G. (1995) *Autism: Handle with Care*. London: Future Horizons.

Goren, C. C., Sarty, M., and Wu, P. Y. (1975). Visual following and pattern discrimination of face-like stimuli by newborn infants. *Pediatrics*, 56(4), 544–549.

Goldsmith, D. F., and Rogoff, B. (1997). Mothers' and toddlers' coordinated joint focus of attention: Variations with maternal dysphoric symptoms. *Developmental Psychology*, 33, 113–119.

Grandin, T. (1986). *Emergence: Labeled autistic*. Novato, CA: Arena Press.

Greenspan, S. I., and Wieder, S. (1998). *The Child with Special Needs: Encouraging Intellectual and Emotional Growth*. Cambridge, MA: Perseus Publishing.

Haith, M. M., Bergman, T., and Moore, M. J. (1979). Eye contact and face scanning in early infancy. *Science*, 198, 853–855.

Happe, F. (1999). Autism: cognitive deficit or cognitive style? *Trends in Cognitive Neurosciences*, 3(6), 216–222.

Heider, F., and Simmel, M. (1994). An experimental study of apparent behavior. *American Journal of Psychology*, 57, 243–259.

Hirstein, W., Iverson, P., and Ramachandran, V. S. (2001). Autonomic responses of autistic children in response to people and objects. *Proceedings of the Royal Society of London B*, 268, 1883–1888.

Hobson, R. P., Ouston, J., and Lee, A. (1988) What's in a face? The case of autism. *British Journal of Psychology*, 79, 441–453.

Hogan, B., and Hogan, W. (2004). *The Son-Rise Program Social Developmental Model*. Sheffield, MA: Autism Treatment Center of America (available from the authors).

Hutt, C., and Hutt, S. J. (1970.) Stereotypies and their relation to arousal: A study of autistic children. In: C. Hutt and Hutt S. J. (Eds.), *Behavior Studies in Psychiatry* (pp. 175–204). New York: Pergammon Press.

Hutt, C., Hutt, S. J., Lee, D., and Ounsted, C. (1964). Arousal and childhood autism. *Nature*, 28(204), 908–909.

Infant Health and Development Program (1990), Enhancing the outcomes of low birthweight, premature infants: A multi-site randomized trial. *Journal of the American Medical Association*, 263, 3035–3042.

Johnson, M. H., Halit, H., Grice, S. J., and Karmiloff-Smith, A. (2002). Neuroimaging of typical and atypical development: A perspective from multiple levels of analysis. *Developmental Psychopathology*, 41, 521–536.

Jolliffe, T., and Baron-Cohen, S. (1997). Are people with autism and Asperger syndrome faster than normal on the Embedded Figures Test? *Journal of Child Psychology and Psychiatry*, 38, 527–534.

Jones, R. S. P., Quigney, C., and Huws, J. C. (2003). First-hand accounts of sensory perceptual experiences in autism: A qualitative analysis. *Journal of Intellectual and Developmental Disability*, 28(2), 112–121.

Kaiser, A. P., and Hancock, T. B. (2003). Teaching parents new skills to support their young children's development. *Infants and Young Children*, 16(1), 9–21.

Kaiser, L. K., Carter, C. M., and Koegel, R. L. (2003). Teaching children with autism self-initiations as a pivotal response. *Topics in Language Disorders*, 23(2), 134–145.

Kanner, L. (1943). Autistic disturbances of affective content. *Nervous Child*, 2, 217–225.

Kasari, C., Sigman, M., Mundy, P., and Yirmiya, N. (1990). Affective sharing in the context of joint attention interactions of normal, autistic and mentally retarded children. *Journal of Autism and Developmental Disorders*, 20, 87–100.

Kaufman, B. N. (1976). *Son-Rise*. New York: Harper-Collins.

Kaufman, B. N. (1981). *A Miracle to Believe In*. New York: Ballantine Books.

Kaufman, B. N. (1994). *Son-Rise: The Miracle Continues*. Tiburon, CA: H. J. Kramer Inc.

Kemner, C., Verbaten, M. N., Cuperus, J. M., et al. (1995). Auditory event-related brain potentials in autistic children and three different control groups. *Biological Psychiatry*, 38, 150–65.

Kemner, C., Verbaten, M. N., Cuperus, J. M., Camfferman, G., and van Engeland, H. (1994). Visual and somatosensory event-related brain potentials in autistic children and three different control groups. *EEG Clinical Neurophysiology*, 4, 269–285.

Kim, J., and Mahoney, G. (2004). The effects of mother's style of interaction on children's engagement: Implications for using responsive interventions with parents. *Topics in Early Childhood Special Education*, 24(1), 31–38.

Klin, A. (1991). Young autistic children's listening preferences in regard to speech: A possible characterization of the symptom of social withdrawal. *Journal of Autism and Developmental Disorders*, 21, 29–42.

Klin A. (1992). Listening preferences in regard to speech in four children with developmental disabilities. *Journal of Child Psychology and Psychiatry*, 33, 763–769.

Klin, A., Jones, W., Schultz, R., and Volkmar, F. (2003). The enactive mind, or from actions to cognition: lessons from Autism. *Phil. Trans. R. Soc. Lond. B*, 358, 345–360.

Klin, A., Sparrow, S. S., de Bildt, A., Cicchetti, D. V. Cohen, D. J., and Volkmar, F. R. (1999). A normed study of face recognition in autism and related disorders. *Journal of Autism and Developmental Disorders*, 29, 497–507.

Klin A., Volkmar F. R., and Sparrow, S. S. (1992). Autistic social dysfunction: some limitations of the theory of mind hypothesis. *Journal of Child Psychology and Psychiatry*, 33, 861–876.

Koegel, R. L., Dyer, K., and Bell, L. K. (1987) The influence of child-preferred activities on autistic children's social behavior. *Journal of Applied Behavior Analysis*; 20(3): 243–252.

Koegel, R. L., Koegel, L. K., and Carter, C. M. (1998). Pivotal responses and the natural language teaching paradigm. *Seminars in Speech and Language*, 19(4), 355–371.

Koegel, R. L., Koegel, L. K., and Carter, C. M. (1999.) Pivotal teaching interactions for children with autism. *School Psychology Review*, 28, 576–594.

Koegel, R. L., Koegel, L. K., and McNerney, E. K. (2001). Pivotal areas in intervention for autism. *Journal of Clinical Child Psychology*, 30(1), 19–32.

Koegel, L. K., Koegel, R. L., Shosan, Y., and McNerny, E. (1999). Pivotal Response Intervention II: Preliminary long-term outcome data. *Journal of the Associations for Persons with Severe Handicaps*, 24(3), 186–198.

Kootz, J. P., and Cohen, D. J. (1981). Modulation of sensory intake in autistic children: cardiovascular and behavioral indices. *Journal of the American Academy of Child Psychiatry*, 20(4), 692–701.

Kootz, J. P., Marinelli, B., and Cohen, D. J. (1982). Modulation of response to environmental stimulation in autistic children. *Journal of Autism and Developmental Disorders*, 12(2), 185–193.

Langdell, T. (1978) Recognition of faces: An approach to the study of autism. *Journal of Child Psychology and Psychiatry*, 19(3), 255–268.

Larkin, J. L., and Chartrand, T. L. (2003). Using nonconscious behavioral mimicry to create affiliation and rapport. *Psychological Science*, 14(4), 334–339.

Larkin, J. L., Jefferis, V. E., Cheng, C. M., and Chartrand, T. L. (2003). The chameleon effect as social glue: Evidence for the evolutionary significance of nonconscious mimicry. *Journal of Nonverbal Behavior*, 27(3), 145–162.

Lewis, M. H., Baumeister, A. A., and Mailman, R. B. (1987). A neurobiological alternative to the perceptual reinforcement hypothesis of stereotyped behavior: A commentary on "Self-stimulatory behavior and perceptual reinforcement." *Journal of Applied Behavioral Analysis*, 20(3), 253–258.

Lewis, M., and Goldberg, S. (1969). Perceptual-cognitive development in infancy: A generalized expectancy model as a function of the mother-infant interaction. *Merrill-Palmer Quarterly*, 15, 81–100.

Lord, C. (1995) Follow-up of two-year-olds referred for possible autism. *Journal of Child Psychology and Psychiatry*, 36(8): 1365–1382.

Lovaas, O. I., Koegal, R. L., Simmons, J. Q., and Long, J. S. (1973). Some generalizations and follow-up measures on autistic children in behavior therapy. *Journal of Applied Behavior Analysis*, 6, 131–166.

MacDonald, J. D. (1989.) *Becoming partners with children: From play to conversation*. San Antonio, TX: Special Press.

MacDonald, J. (2004). *Communicating Partners*. London: Jessica Kingsley Publishers.

Maestro, S., Muratori, F., Cavallaro, M. C., Pei, F., Stern, D., Golse, B., and Palacio Espas, F. (2002). Attentional skills during the first 6 months of age in autism spectrum disorder. *Journal of the American Academy of Child and Adolescent Psychiatry*, 41(10), 1239–1245.

Mahoney, G. (1992). *The Maternal Behavior Rating Scale—Revised*. Cleveland. OH: Case Western Reserve University (available from the author).

Mahoney, G., Boyce, G., Fewell, R., Spiker, D., and Wheeden, C. A. (1998). The relationship of parent-child interaction to the effectiveness of early intervention services for at-risk children and children with disabilities. *Topics in Early Childhood Special Education*, 18, 5–17.

Mahoney, G., and Perales, F. (2003). Using relationship-focused intervention to enhance the socio-emotional functioning of young children with autism spectrum disorders. *Topics in Early Childhood Special Education*, 23, 74–86.

Mahoney, G., and Perales, F. (2005). Relationship-focused early intervention with children with pervasive developmental disorders and other disabilities: A comparative study. *Developmental and Behavioral Pediatrics*; 26(2), 77–85.

Malatesta, C., and Izard, C. (1984). The ontogenesis of human social signals: From biological imperative to symbol utilization. In: N. Fox and R. Davidson (Eds.), *The Psychobiology of Affective Disturbance* (pp.106–216). Hillsdale, NJ: Erlbaum.

Manolson, A. (1995). *You Make a Difference in Helping Your Child Learn*. Toronto: Hanen Centre.

Militerni, R., Bravaccio, C., Falco, C., Fico, C., and Palerno, M. T. (2002). Repetitive behaviors in autistic disorder. *European Child and Adolescent Psychiatry*, 11(5), 210–218.

Mills, M., and Melhuish, E. (1974). Recognition of mother's voice in early infancy. *Nature*, 252, 123–124.

Mottron, L., Belleville, S., and Menard, E. (2000). Local bias in autistic subjects as evidenced by graphic tasks: Perceptual hierarchization or working memory deficit? *Journal of Child Psychology and Psychiatry*, 40(5), 743–755.

Mundy, P., Sigman, M., and Kasari, C. (1990). A longitudinal study of joint attention and language development in autistic children. *Journal of Autism and Developmental Disorders*, 20, 115–128.

Mundy, P., Sigman, M., Kasari, C. (1992). Joint attention, affective sharing and infant intersubjectivity. *Infant Behavior and Development*, 15, 377–381.

Nadel, J. (1992). Imitation et communication chez l'enfant autiste et le jeune enfant prélangagier. In: J. Hochman and P. Ferrari (Eds.), *Imitation et Identification chez l'Enfant Autiste* (pp. 1–5). Paris: Bayard.

Nadel, J., Guerini, C., Peze, A., and Rivet, C. (1999). The evolving nature of imitation as a format for communication. In: Nadel, J., and Butterworth, G. (Eds), *Imitation in Infancy* (pp. 209–234). Cambridge: Cambridge University Press.

Nadel, J., and Peze, A. (1993). Immediate imitation as a basis for primary communication in toddlers and autistic children. In: J. Nadel and L. Camiono (Eds.), *New Perspectives in Early Communicative Development* (pp. 139–156). London: Routledge.

Nelson, K. B., Grether, J. K., Croen, L. A., Dambrosia, J. M., Dickens, B. F., Jelliffe, I. L. et al. (2001). Neuropeptides and neurotrophins in neonatal blood of children with autism or mental retardation. *Annals of Neurology*, 46, 597–606.

Nijhof, G., Joha, D., and Pekelharing, H. (1998). Aspects of stereotypic behavior among autistic persons: A study of the literature. *British Journal of Developmental Disorders*, 44(1), 3–13.

Osterling, J., and Dawson, G. (1994). Early recognition of children with autism: A study of first birthday party home videotapes. *Journal of Autism and Developmental Disorders*, 24, 247–257.

Osterling, J., Dawson, G., and Munson, J. (2002). Early recognition of one year old infants with autism spectrum disorders versus mental retardation: A study of first birthday party home videotapes. *Development of Psychopathology*, 14, 239–252.

Panksepp, J., Nelson, E., and Siviy, S. (1994). Brain opioids and mother-infant social motivation. *Acta Paediatrica Suppliment*, 397, 40–46.

Papousek, H., and Papousek, M. (1977). Mothering and cognitive head-start: Psychobiological considerations. In: H. R. Schaffer (Ed.), *Studies in Mother-Infant Interaction: The Loch Lomand Symposium* (pp. 63–85). London: Academic Press.

Pelphrey, K. A., Sasson, N., Reznick, S., Paul, G., Goldman, B. D., and Piven, J, (2004). Visual scanning of faces in autism. *Journal of Autism and Developmental Disorders*, 32 (4), 249–261.

Piaget, J. (1952). *The Origins of Intelligence in Children*. New York: International Universities Press.

Piaget, J. (1963). *The Psychology of Intelligence*. Totowa, NJ: Littlefield, Adams.

Pierce, K., Muller, R-A., Ambrose, J., Allen, G., and Courchesne, E. (2001). Face processing occurs outside the fusiform "face area" in autism: Evidence from functional MRI. *Brain*, 124, 2059–2073.

Raymond, G. V., Vauman, M. L., and Kemper, T. L. (1996), Hippocampus in autism: A Golgi analysis. *Acta Neuropathologica*, 91, 117–119.

Reiber, C., and McLaughlin, T. F. (2004), Classroom interventions: Methods to improve academic performance and classroom behavior for students with attention-deficit/hyperactivity disorder. *International Journal of Special Education*, 19(1), 1–13.

Ring, H., Baron-Cohen, S., Wheelwright, S., Williams, S., Brammer, M., Andrew, C. et al. (1999). Cerebral correlates of preserved cognitive skills in autism: A functional MRI study of Embedded Figures Task performance. *Brain*, 122, 1305–1315.

Rogers, S. J., and Pennington, B. F. (1991). A theoretical approach to the deficits in infantile autism. *Developmental Psychopathology*, 3, 137–162.

Rollins, P. R. (1999). Early pragmatic accomplishments and vocabulary development in preschool children with autism. *American Journal of Speech Language Pathology*, 8, 181–190.

Rollins, P. R., and Snow, C. E. (1998), Shared attention and grammatical development in typical children and children with autism. *Journal of Child Language*, 25, 653–673.

Schilling, D. L., and Schwartz, I. S. (2004). Alternative seating for young children with autism spectrum disorder: Effects on classroom behavior. *Journal of Autism and Developmental Disorders*, 34(4), 423–432.

Schultz, R. T. (2005). Developmental deficits in social perception in autism: The role of the amygdala and fusiform face area. *International Journal of Developmental Neuroscience*, 23, 125–141.

Schultz, R. T., Romanski, L., and Tsatsanis, K. (2000). Neurofunctional models of autistic disorder and Asperger's syndrome: clues from neuroimaging. In: A. Klin, F. R. Volkmar, and Sparrow, S. S. (Eds.), *Asperger's Syndrome* (pp. 179–209). Plenum Press: New York.

Shah, A., and Frith, U. (1983). An islet of ability in autism: A research note. *Journal of Child Psychology and Psychiatry*, 24, 613–20.

Sheinkopf, S. J., and Siegel, B. (1998), Home-base behavioral treatment of young children with autism. *Journal of Autism and Developmental Disorders*, 28(1), 15–23.

Sherman, J., Barker, P., Lorimer, P., Swinson, R., and Factor, D. C. (1987). Treatment of autistic children: Relative effectiveness of residential, out-patient and home-based interventions. *Child Psychiatry and Human Development*, 19(2), 109–125.

Siegel, D. J. (2001). Toward an interpersonal neurobiology of the developing mind: Attachment relationships, "mindsight" and neural integration. *Infant Mental Health*, 22 (1–2), 67–94.

Sigman, M., and Ruskin, E. (1997). Joint attention in relation to language acquisition and social skills in children with autism. Paper presented at the Society for Research in Child Development. Washington, DC. Cited in: Mundy, P., and Markus, J. (1997). On the nature of communication and language impairment in autism. *Mental Retardation and Developmental Disabilities Research Reviews*, 3(4), 343–349.

Siller, M., and Sigman, M. (2002). The behaviors of parents of children with autism predict the subsequent development of their children's communication. *Journal of Autism and Developmental Disorders*, 32 (2), 77–89.

Simion, F., Valenza, E., Umilta, C., and Dalla Barba, B. (1998). Preferential orienting to faces in newborns: A temporal-nasal asymmetry. *Journal of Experimental Psychology Human Perception and Performance*, 24(5), 1399–1405.

Spiker, D., Boyce, G. C., and Boyce, L. K. (2002). Parent-child interactions when young children have disabilities. *International Review of Research in Mental Retardation*, 25, 35–70.

Stern, D. N. (1977). *The first relationship: Infant and mother.* Cambridge MA: Harvard University Press.

Thelen, E. (1979). Rhythmical stereotypies in normal human infants. *Animal Behavior*, 27, 699–715.

Tiegerman, E., and Primavera, L. H. (1982). Object manipulation: An interactional strategy with autistic children. *Journal of Autism and Developmental Disorders*, 11(4), 427–438.

Tiegerman, E., and Primavera, L. H. (1984). Imitating the autistic child: Facilitating communicative gaze behavior. *Journal of Autism and Developmental Disorders*, 14(1): 27–38.

Tomasello, M. (1995). Joint attention as social cognition. In: C. Moore and P. Dunham (Eds.), *Joint Attention: Its Origins and Role in Development* (pp. 103–130). NJ: Hillsdale, Erlbaum.

Tordjman, S., Anderson, G. M., McBride, P. A., Hertzig, M. E., Snow, M. E., Hall, L. M. et al. (1997). Plasma beta-endorphin, adrenocorticotropin hormone, and cortisol in autism. *Journal of Child Psychology and Psychiatry*, 38(6), 705–15.

Townsend, J., and Courchesne, E. (1994). Parietal damage and narrow "spot-light" spatial attention. *Journal of Cognitive Neuroscience*, 6, 220–232.

Trevarthan, C., and Aitken, K. (2001). Infant intersubjectivity: Research, theory and clinical applications. *Journal of Child Psychology*, 42(1), 3–48.

Trivette, C. M. (2003). Influence of caregiver responsiveness on the development of young children with or at risk for developmental disabilities. *Bridges*, 1(3), 1–13.

Turner, M. (1999). Repetitive behavior in autism: A review of psychological research. *Journal of Child Psychology and Psychiatry and Allied Disciplines*, 40, 839–849.

Uzgiris, I .C. (1981). Two functions of imitation during infancy. *International Journal of Behavioral Development*, 4, 1–12.

Vygotsky, L. S. (1978). *Mind in Society: The Development of Higher Psychological Processes* (Trans. and Eds. M. Cole, V. John-Steiner, S. Scribner, and E. Soubourne). Cambridge, MA: Harvard University Press.

Weeks, S., and Hobson, R. (1987). The salience of facial expressions for autistic children. *Journal of Child Psychology and Psychiatry*, 28, 137–151.

Werner, E., Dawson, G., Osterling, J., and Dinno, H. (2000). Recognition of autism spectrum disorder before one year of age: A retrospective study based on home videotapes. *Journal of Autism and Developmental Disorders*, 30, 157–162.

Wertsch, J. (1985). *Culture, Communication and Cognition: Vygotskian Perspectives*. Cambridge: Cambridge University Press.

Willemsen-Swinkels, S., Buitelaar, J. K., Dekker, M., and van Engeland, H. (1998). Subtyping stereotypic behavior in children: The association between stereotypic behavior, mood and heart rate. *Journal of Autism and Developmental Disorders*, 28(6), 547–557.

Williams, D. (1988). *Autism and Sensing*. London: Jessica Kingsley Publishers.

Williams, D. (1994). *Nobody Nowhere*. New York: Perennial.

Williams, K. (2004). The Son-Rise Program Intervention for Autism: An Investigation into Prerequisites for Evaluation and Family Experiences. PhD Summary, University of Edinburgh, UK.

APPENDIX 2

COMPARISON OF APPLIED BEHAVIOR ANALYSIS AND THE SON-RISE PROGRAM

This appendix is designed to provide you with a summary of the differences between The Son-Rise Program (SRP) and applied behavioral analysis (ABA). The two methodologies fall on opposite ends of the autism treatment spectrum, with ABA at the behavioral end and SRP all the way at the social-relational end.

The appendix includes:

- A table listing some key differences
- A more in-depth discussion of these differences
- Links to ten "commercials" that playfully and humorously pinpoint these key differences—filmed in the style of the famous Mac versus PC television commercials
- A link to a ninety-minute webcast where I discuss these differences in detail

I understand that some of these items may be controversial. An ABA practitioner may see the distinctions between the two methodologies differently than I do. And not all ABA practitioners—or versions of ABA—are the same. However, all versions of applied behavior analysis (the middle word is "behavior," after all) rest upon the same fundamental concept (changing behavior through reinforcers) and question (how to eliminate behaviors we don't want and promote behaviors we do want). As well, we at the Autism Treatment Center of America—and I personally—have received many glowing written responses from ABA practitioners expressing excitement, delight, and great respect for the principles and techniques of The Son-Rise Program. Many have said that their exposure to these principles has permanently and completely altered their way of seeing and treating children on the autism spectrum.

Wherever you stand, I hope that you find the items useful and thought-provoking.

APPLIED BEHAVIOR ANALYSIS VS. THE SON-RISE PROGRAM

Applied Behavior Analysis	Son-Rise Program
Understanding of Autism	
Sees autism as a **behavioral disorder**, with behaviors to be either extinguished or reinforced	Sees autism as a **social interactivity disorder**, where the central deficit is relating to other people
The child needs **structure** and must learn to sit appropriately, follow a schedule, and comply with requests	Helping the child to be **flexible and spontaneous** enables him/her to handle change and enjoy human interaction
Area of Focus	
Changing the behavior of the child	**Creating a relationship** with the child
Seeks to **"extinguish"** the child's repetitive "stimming" **behavior**	Uses **"joining"** technique to participate in the child's repetitive **behavior**
Method of Teaching New Skills	
Repetition: Uses discrete trials or similar method to prompt the child to perform a behavior (followed by a reward) over and over again until the child has demonstrated mastery	**Motivation:** Builds the child's own interests into every game or activity so that the child is excited, "comes back for more," generalizes skills, and relates naturally rather than robotically
Areas of Learning	
Often focuses on **academic skills**	Always teaches **socialization** first
Sees academic areas such as math as an excellent way to help the child **compensate** for lack of social skills	Seeks to help the child **overcome** social skills deficits

Role of the Parents	
Professionals are the major players, with parents having a more observational role	**Parents are given the most central role** because their love, dedication, and experience with their child is unmatched

Facilitator's Attitude	
Sees attitude as largely irrelevant, with effective application of behavior-shaping techniques being what matters	**Sees attitude as vitally important**, since having a nonjudgmental and welcoming attitude determines whether the child feels safe and relaxed enough to interact and learn

UNDERSTANDING OF AUTISM

ABA treats autism as a behavioral disorder, with behaviors to be either extinguished or promoted. This means that repetitive, exclusive "stimming" behaviors common to children with autism are not permitted during learning sessions, "correct" behaviors are rewarded, sometimes with food, and new skills and behaviors are taught through structured repetition sometimes referred to as "discreet trials."

The Son-Rise Program sees autism as a social relational disorder. The central deficit of children on the autism spectrum is that they have difficulty connecting with and relating to other people. Almost all other difficulties spring from this primary challenge. Therefore, we do not seek to "correct" so-called inappropriate behaviors in the absence of a deeply bonded relationship. Rather, we endeavor to build a relationship with each child—a relationship that is the platform for all future education and development. We then help our children learn to connect and build relationships with others and to genuinely enjoy such interaction. All skills we teach are addressed within the context of our focus on human interaction.

We also believe that each child has a reason for every behavior they perform. Rather than forcing children to conform to a world they do not yet understand, we enter their world first. We seek to understand so that we can be most effective in helping the child. In The Son-Rise Program, the children show us the way in, and then we show them the way out.

Area of Focus

The focal points of each program are based upon how we see autism. In simple terms, ABA focuses on changing behavior; The Son-Rise Program focuses on creating a relationship.

An ABA facilitator might punish, reprimand, or attempt to discourage or redirect a repetitive or aggressive behavior. Compliance is seen as very important. Of course, there are a range of ABA-type programs and facilitators out there. Some using strong punishments of behaviors and others using much gentler forms of discouragement, but the overall focus is the same: behavior change and compliance with the requests of the facilitator. New behaviors and skills are often taught using a system based upon repetition and rewards sometimes called discreet trials, which will be discussed in more detail below.

In The Son-Rise Program, we consistently seek to built rapport and relationships with our children. One critical way in which we do this is called *joining*. Instead of prohibiting or discouraging repetitive, "autistic" behavior, we actually *participate* in these activities with the child. Far from reinforcing "autistic" behaviors (a concern voiced by some), we have seen, with thousands of children from around the world, the exact opposite. When children are joined, they tend to look at us more, pay more attention to us, and include us more in their activity. We see such children "stimming" less and interacting more. After all, we are building a stronger and stronger bond with the child, and at the same time, by showing genuine interest and participation in what is important to the child, we are actually teaching the very interpersonal skills that many of our children lack. When we have the child's willing engagement, we then use a variety of motivational and educational techniques to promote learning and skill acquisition.

Repetition vs. Motivation

With ABA, when attempting to teach a particular behavior or skill (such as getting dressed, to use a simple example), discreet trials are often used. With this methodology, a child might be told (or made) to sit in a chair. The facilitator would then say "coat on" and endeavor to train the child to put his coat on, doing this over and over again until the child has "mastered" the skill. Each time the child gets it right, he would get praise, a piece of food, or some other reward. While this approach can definitely succeed at getting some children to perform particular activities or skills, a common complaint we hear from parents is that, although their children perform the prescribed activity, they tend to do so in a manner that appears robotic and preprogrammed, rather than displaying any kind of spontaneity or enthusiasm. A second difficulty that we see is that many children, after participating in this program over a period of time, learn to loathe what they are being trained to do and can become aggressive and rebellious. A third drawback is that children get much of their training free of context (learning, for instance, to put their coats on when told rather than when it is cold out), often resulting in them learning compliance rather than the real skill (thus lacking the ability to generalize the skill).

In The Son-Rise Program, we want each child to "come back for more." This means that we want the child's willing engagement over time, so that we can teach them all that they need to learn and so that they value and enjoy interaction. We also see the importance of children being able to generalize learned skills to other areas, so that they don't need prompts, rewards, or our presence to act on what they've learned. Therefore, we do not want to continually repeat commands when the child, in all likelihood, does not understand *why* she is being asked to do this.

Consistently, we have found that motivation works faster and more powerfully and promotes greater generalization than repetition does. If a child likes a particular toy or physical movement or numbers, then we use this motivation as a teaching tool by combining it with an educational goal. For instance, if a child likes Thomas the Tank Engine and one of our educational goals is toilet training, we would construct a game that centered around Thomas and involved using the toilet. In this way, we create a desire to learn and use a skill (going to the toilet), and we keep the interaction with the child alive and well (and fun). An additional benefit of this approach is that it does not tend to produce a robotic, preprogrammed response because children get genuinely excited about the learning process. For this reason (as well as because of joining and the attitudinal component, described below), we also do not see children becoming aggressive or rebellious from participating in The Son-Rise Program.

Structure vs. Spontaneity

In ABA, a high premium is placed upon structure. It is important for children to sit still in a seat and perform activities in a prescribed, regulated fashion. The thought behind this is that children on the autism spectrum need this kind of structure. Also, if they are to ever participate in school, they must learn to sit appropriately, obey a schedule, and comply with requests from the teacher.

In The Son-Rise Program, we see it differently. If children are to be successful in school and in life, what is most important for them to learn is to interact with others, make their own decisions, and be *flexible* (something which many children with autism have difficulty with). Because of this, we spend our time engaging in interactive games (when we aren't joining). In addition to teaching interaction and socialization, these games challenge children to be more flexible (rather than needing things to go a particular way) and to use their imagination to come up with different ideas and directions on the fly. We also keep the games fun, so that our children see that participating in our world (versus staying in their own) is both enjoyable and useful, rather than rigid and demanding.

Academic vs. Social Development

ABA practitioners tend to focus heavily on academic skills such as reading, writing, and math (in addition to verbal communication and basic "appropriate" behavior). We in The Son-Rise Program would certainly agree that such skills are important. However, if choosing between helping a child to be great at math and or to be great at making friends, we choose the latter every time. In actual fact, academic and social skills are not mutually exclusive, and there are many instances where we do teach reading, writing, and math. When we do, though, it is always in the context of an activity that teaches socialization first. If our children can learn to enjoy people, make friends, laugh at a funny joke, socialize, etc. (which many of our children do), then they have achieved what, for most of us, makes life most meaningful.

The Role of the Parents

ABA has many dedicated practitioners who often work with children in their own homes. The way the programs generally work, though, is that parents tend to be in a more observational role in their programs. The professionals are seen, in most cases, as the major players in the program, with parents watching on the side so that the practitioners can do their jobs.

We in The Son-Rise Program have seen nothing that matches the motivation, love, dedication, and lifelong commitment possessed by parents for their special children. Furthermore, no one has the kind of long-term, day-to-day experience *with their own particular child* that parents possess. Without question, professionals and other family members can be critically important. At the same time, because of their unique position in their child's world, parents can positively affect their child's life in a way no one else can. Therefore, not only do we acknowledge parents as the child's most important resource, but we seek to empower them to the child's advantage. This is why we teach them how to design, implement, and take a central role in their children's programs.

The Facilitator's Attitude

ABA focuses heavily on *what* the facilitator does. The Son-Rise Program not only focuses on what the facilitator does, but also on *how* the facilitator does it. We address and provide training in an area that we see as the most overlooked factor of autism treatment: the attitude of the facilitator. We see a nonjudgmental and optimistic attitude as crucial to effective child facilitation. What does this mean? First, it means that we don't label our children's repetitive and ritualistic behaviors as inappropriate, wrong, or bad. This principle is every bit as practical as it is idealistic. We see time and again that children with autism tend to move away from people they perceive as uncomfortable or judging and toward people they see as comfortable, easy, fun, safe, and nonjudgmental. Thus, we can use our attitude to become an interaction magnet.

As well, having a sincere sense of optimism—really believing in the child with which one is working—is key to helping that child to break through barriers that previously seemed insurmountable. We do not put limits on any child ahead of time, we do not believe that hope can ever be "false," and we believe in the potential of every child, regardless of age or diagnosis.

Moreover, we believe in the parents who work tirelessly to reach their children. That is why we spend a significant percentage of our time and effort providing parents with attitudinal training. We help them to create and sustain a nonjudgmental, optimistic, and hopeful attitude with their children. In this way, they can maximize their children's progress while finding peace with their children's diagnosis.

TEN HUMOROUS ABA VERSUS THE SON-RISE PROGRAM "COMMERCIALS"

On my Web site, at www.autismbreakthrough.com/appendix2, are links to ten sixty-second videos that playfully pinpoint the key differences between ABA and The Son-Rise Program. (That's me playing The Son-Rise Program!) These "commercials," which pay homage to the famous Mac versus PC ads, created quite stir when they were first released. I hope you enjoy them.

WEBCAST DISCUSSING DIFFERENCES BETWEEN ABA AND THE SON-RISE PROGRAM

At www.autismbreakthrough.com/appendix2 readers will find a 90-minute webcast, in which I discuss, in great detail, what The Son-Rise Program does differently than ABA and why.

APPENDIX 3

TEN HOLIDAY HICCUPS AND HOW TO AVOID THEM

Ah, the holidays. Special meals. Special family gatherings. And, of course, our special children! Oftentimes, we just barrel through the holidays, hoping for the best but not taking the time and focus to make sure this celebratory time really feels like a celebration for us and for our children on the autism spectrum. Most of us find ourselves unwitting participants in at least one of the ten holiday hiccups.

We know we're in a hiccup when our special child is having more meltdowns . . . when our extended family members appear at a loss . . . or when we, ourselves, feel stressed out or burned out.

We may blame the hectic holidays, but, in reality, it's not the holidays causing the difficulty; it's the pitfalls we accidentally step into. This is great news because it means that our challenges are preventable!

Take a look below at the ten holiday hiccups and how to prevent them. You'll be thanking yourself from now till New Year's!

1. **Stopping your child from isming ("stimming")**
Given the commotion and changes in routine of the holidays, this is the most important time for our children to be allowed to self-regulate and cope with their environment. We know that isming is crucially important to our children and their nervous systems. Ideally, of course, we would join our children in their isms. But even during the times over the holidays when we aren't able to do this, we can still let our children do their thing. When we do this, everybody wins!

2. **Feeding your child "crash and burn" foods**
Yes, it's the holidays. Sugary, wheat-filled, dairy-crazy foods abound. It can be tempting to allow our children to partake in this glorious cornucopia. We might think it will be easier to just let them have it this once. Let me assure you: it will not be easier! There are a host of foods that we *know* are not going to be processed well by our children. Yes, the first few minutes of allowing them to eat whatever is around might seem easier. But a few minutes later . . . it's crash-and-burn time. The meltdowns, overeating, challenging behavior, and diarrhea that will result are truly not worth it. Taking the forethought to either keep these foods away from our children or, better yet, not have them around at all will make the whole holiday experience a million times easier.

3. Surprising your child

Sometimes, we can be so busy planning and getting ready for a holiday outing (e.g., going to Grandma's) or project (e.g., putting up the Christmas tree) that we forget to notify a crucial participant: our special child. Although our intention is not to surprise our children, this is often what happens when we depart on an outing or embark on a project without explaining everything that will happen to our children in advance. Even for our nonverbal children, explaining ahead of time what will happen and why it will be fun for them will go a long way toward minimizing tantrums and maximizing cooperation.

4. Leaving no way out

It is very common to go to someone else's house for a holiday celebration. Usually, we just take our child and hope for the best, thinking that we don't have a lot of control over the matter. But we do! We can designate, in advance, a calm room or space where our child can go to decompress once they begin to be overwhelmed by all the commotion and sensory input that comprise most celebrations. Every so often, it can really help to take our child to this room and spend some time alone with her.

5. Focusing on stopping challenging behaviors

Most of us dread our children behaving in a challenging way. We worry about it, we look for it, and we try to stop it as soon as it happens. Ironically, this puts all the focus on what we *don't* want from our children. If we don't want our children to hit, for instance, focusing on "not hitting" can actually create more hitting. Instead, we can celebrate our children every time they do something we do want. If we have a child who sometimes hits, it can make a huge difference to actively look for any time our child is at all gentle—and then cheer wildly!

6. Giving an over-stimulating present

Sure, we derive great joy from the experience of giving presents for our children. But when it comes to our special children, we want to be especially cognizant of what type of present we give. If we give a present with flashing lights and loud beeps, we're asking for challenging behavior later. Let's take some time to sincerely consider whether the gift we are about to give is going to contribute to the overstimulation of our children with sensitive sensory systems.

7. Leaving our children out of the giving process

We always consider our special child when purchasing gifts. But do we think of our special child as a potential *giver* of gifts? Thinking of other people—what they want, what we could do for them—is an essential element of the socialization that we want our children to learn. The holidays provide the perfect opportunity for this! We can schedule sessions with our special child in advance where we help them create something for one or more of the people in his or her life. (These gifts and activities can range from very simple to more complex, depending on our particular child's level of development.) Then, on the day of gift-giving, we can invite our special child to present (as best he can) any gifts that he has made.

8. Expecting your family to "get it"

Many of us may, at times, feel frustrated with members of our extended family for not being more understanding and responsive when it comes to our special child. But remember, if our extended family members don't live with our child, they won't "get it." When taking our special children on visits to extended family for holiday visits, we can send e-mails to them explaining what they can do to make the visit comfortable for us and our child. We can take this opportunity to explain why sudden loud noises might be problematic, or tell everyone the answer our child likes to hear when she asks the same question over and over. This way, we stack the deck in our child's favor.

9. Thinking that activities need to happen outside your home

We know that children on the autism spectrum will always do better when they are not overstimulated by the many sights, sounds, smells, and unpredictable events of the outside world. So we can create experiences in our homes that we would normally go out for. For instance, instead of going to an evening parade with a festival of lights, we can put Christmas or Hanukkah lights around the house, turn off all the lights, and play holiday music at a gentle volume. Some of us might be concerned about depriving our children of fun holiday experiences, but keep in mind that when our children can't digest the experience, they're not having the fun experience we want for them, anyway. That's why, if we can create a digestible version of the outing at home, our children can really take in and enjoy the experience. Thus, we are actually giving our children *more*, not less.

10. Seeing the wrapping instead of the gift

So often, we get caught up in the trappings of the holidays—the tree, the presents, the outings that have to go exactly as planned. It's okay to arrange fun things, but remember that these are only trimmings. They aren't the gift, they're just the wrapping. The gift is our special child. The gift is sharing sweetness with the people we love. Instead of using the holidays as a planning fest, we can use it to see the beauty in our child's uniqueness, to celebrate what our child can do, and to feel and encourage compassion for our child's very different way of experiencing the world.

HELPFUL ORGANIZATIONS

Autism Hope Alliance (AHA): www.autismhopealliance.org

United States Autism & Asperger's Association (USAAA): www.usautism.org

Alert Program®: www.alertprogram.com

American Medical Autism Board (AMAB): www.americanmedicalautismboard.com

The Listening Program®/Advanced Brain Technologies: www.thelisteningprogram.com

NAA (National Autism Association): www.nationalautismassociation.org

Talk About Curing Autism (TACA): www.tacanow.org

Medical Academy of Pediatric Special Needs (MAPS): www.medmaps.org

Autism One: www.autismone.org

Generation Rescue: www.generationrescue.org

ACKNOWLEDGMENTS

So many people helped me with this book, and I am so grateful!

For giving me integral, astute, and crucial feedback on ways to make the book better, I thank my sister Bryn, my brother-in-law William, my mom, and, most especially, my dad, who put an enormous amount of time, love, and thought into his detailed thoughts on each and every chapter. And a huge thanks to Bryn again for being my first Son-Rise Program teacher professionally and to my dad for teaching me the ins and outs of facilitating groups, which is now a huge part of my life. And, once again, a deep and abiding gratitude to both of my parents, who not only recovered me from severe autism but have been there for me in a thousand different ways big and small, supporting me and believing in me for my entire life.

A thanks and a cheer for all of the families—talked about and not talked about in the book—who are as much my teachers as my students, allowing me to be part of their wondrous journeys and showing me, in countless ways, what real love looks like.

A jumping-up-and-down thanks to the dedicated, creative, passionate, playful, totally sincere staff of the Autism Treatment Center of America, who love and care for our families like no one else in the world and are the most incredible people to work with!

My most sincere and warm appreciation to Stephanie Tade, the most awesome agent in the universe! With boundless thanks for loving, believing in, and truly "getting" the book from the very beginning—and working tirelessly to get it out to the world.

Gargantuan thanks to Nichole Argyres, my editor from heaven at St. Martin's Press, a very sharp, thoughtful, intelligent, caring, *very* patient, and wonderfully kind woman who made the book better and worked with me in such a sweet way. And a shout-out to Laura Chasen for her gracious help as well!

For publishing, supporting, and championing this book—and for backing it with a spectacular team—I give my heartfelt thanks to St. Martin's Press.

And how could I leave out Mr. Steve Small, my sixth grade English teacher and all-around terrific guy, who first stoked my huge love of writing (and has been a fantastic and caring teacher to my niece!) through kindness, excitement, smarts, support (giving me my first writing award!), and absolute fun. This book started with you!

INDEX

About the Author

As the former CEO of the Autism Treatment Center of America, Raun K. Kaufman conducts lectures and seminars worldwide. In addition to his work with families and professionals over the past fifteen years, Kaufman brings a distinctive qualification to the realm of autism treatment—his own personal history. As a child, he was diagnosed with severe autism and recommended for lifelong institutionalization. Instead, his parents developed The Son-Rise Program, which enabled their son to completely recover from his autism with no trace of his former condition. His story was recounted in the best-selling book *Son-Rise: The Miracle Continues* and the award-winning NBC-TV movie, *Son-Rise: A Miracle of Love*. Now an international speaker, author, teacher, and graduate of Brown University with a degree in Biomedical Ethics, Kaufman has completed lecture tours in the United States, the United Kingdom, Ireland, the Netherlands, Sweden, Norway, Poland, Spain, and Portugal. He has written articles featured in journals such as *Good Autism Practice* and *The Autism File* and books such as *Silver Linings* and *Cutting-Edge Therapies for Autism 2010–2011*, and he has been interviewed by media such as National Public Radio, BBC Television, Fox News Channel, the London Telegraph, and *People* magazine. Kaufman was the recipient of the Best Presenter award at the national Autism One conference, given to the winner of their nationwide survey. He is currently the Director of Global Education for the Autism Treatment Center of America and serves on the advisory boards of the United States Autism and Asperger's Association (USAAA) and the Autism Hope Alliance (AHA). He cohosts the radio show *Raun and Kristin: Bringing Hope into Your Home* on Autism Approved Radio.

Contact Information
www.autismbreakthrough.com
www.raunkkaufman.com
Autism Treatment Center of America
2080 South Undermountain Road
Sheffield, MA 01257
www.autismtreatment.org
sonrise@autismtreatment.org
1-800-714-2779
1-413-229-2100